"Joey Coleman reminds us that the **true, lasting path to profitability** is building customer relationships for life—and in this book, he shows you **exactly how to do it.**"

—Dorie Clark, author of *Stand Out* and *Entrepreneurial You*;
adjunct professor, Duke University Fuqua School of Business

"Joey's work and expertise in the customer space are **bleeding edge.** *Never Lose a Customer Again* is a **must-read** for anyone growing a company, or wanting to grow in their role inside a company."

—Cameron Herold, founder of COO Alliance;
author of *Double Double* and *Meetings Suck*

"Whether you're a solo entrepreneur or a Fortune 100 enterprise, this book is the **ultimate road map for making your brand stand out.** It's **guaranteed to become a classic**—not only in the genre of customer experience, but among business books in general. Implementing these revolutionary techniques is the best gift you can give your customers, your business, and yourself!"

—John Ruhlin, founder of Ruhlin Group; author of *Giftology*

"The techniques outlined in this book are **the absolute best way I know to keep your customers.** *Never Lose a Customer Again* is **directly applicable, funny to read, and filled with great examples.** By learning how to better care for your customers you will dramatically improve your bottom line. Read this book!"

—UJ Ramdas, cofounder of Intelligent Change

"If you believe as I do that customer experience is the last true brand differentiator, and you're wondering how you can differentiate your business in a sustainable, competitor-proof way, then you have picked up the perfect book. There is **no one on Earth more passionate about the customer experience than Joey** Coleman (trust me, I've tried to match his passion!), and he translates that passion into an **actionable guide** to treating your customers right and taking your business to the next level. So many companies make the mistake of focusing all of their resources on acquiring new customers; instead, Joey's approach is to focus on keeping the customers you already have. And when you treat your customers and clients with the respect and consideration they deserve, they will pay you back with loyalty and a willingness to share their great experience with the world."

—Dan Gingiss, senior director of global social media, McDonald's Corporation;
author of *Winning at Social Customer Care*

"Joey's **step-by-step guide** will show you how to wow your customers so that you'll never lose one again."   —Vanessa Van Edwards, author of *Captivate*

"*Never Lose a Customer Again* provides a **gold mine of ideas, examples, and ready-to-implement action steps** designed to hook your customers early in the relationship and turn them into lifelong fans!"

—Nir Eyal, author of *Hooked*

"I was in the audience at the conference where Joey first tried out his First 100 Days® philosophy and watched it ripple through the crowd of seasoned entrepreneurs and business executives. He received a **standing ovation**. Since then, Joey has become an **incredibly in-demand speaker and writer**. *Never Lose a Customer Again* is the next step in that journey."

—Ryan Holiday, Wall Street Journal bestselling author
of *The Obstacle Is the Way* and *Ego Is the Enemy*

"*Never Lose a Customer Again* is a roadmap for the most practical marketing strategy you can employ: creating an exceptional customer experience."

—John Jantsch, author of *Duct Tape Marketing* and *The Referral Engine*

"Joey is **top of the field** when it comes to customer experience design. I have called on his counsel through most of my career. When he showed me his model in this book, **my jaw dropped** because I realized—**it usually takes years to develop world-class customer service**. But **this process can get a company there in weeks**."

—Robert Richman, former culture strategist at Zappos and
author of *The Culture Blueprint*

NEVER LOSE A CUSTOMER AGAIN

NEVER LOSE A CUSTOMER AGAIN

Turn Any Sale into
Lifelong Loyalty in 100 Days

JOEY COLEMAN

PORTFOLIO / PENGUIN

Portfolio/Penguin
An imprint of Penguin Random House LLC
375 Hudson Street
New York, New York 10014

Most Portfolio books are available at a discount when purchased in quantity for sales promotions or corporate use. Special editions, which include personalized covers, excerpts, and corporate imprints, can be created when purchased in large quantities. For more information, please call (212) 572-2232 or e-mail specialmarkets@penguinrandomhouse.com. Your local bookstore can also assist with discounted bulk purchases using the Penguin Random House corporate Business-to-Business program. For assistance in locating a participating retailer, e-mail B2B@penguinrandomhouse.com.

Library of Congress Cataloging-in-Publication Data

Names: Coleman, Joey (C. Joseph), author.
Title: Never lose a customer again : turn any sale into lifelong loyalty in 100 days /
    Joey Coleman.
Description: New York : Portfolio/Penguin, [2017] | Includes bibliographical references.
Identifiers: LCCN 2017052226 | ISBN 9780735220034 (hardcover) | ISBN 9780735220041 (epub)
Subjects: LCSH: Customer relations. | Customer loyalty. | Marketing.
Classification: LCC HF5415.5 .C6144 2017 | DDC 658.8/12—dc23
LC record available at https://lccn.loc.gov/2017052226

Printed in the United States of America
10 9 8 7 6 5 4 3 2 1

To Berit, with whom every day is a remarkable experience
(some 5,588 days and counting)

CONTENTS

NEVER LOSE A CUSTOMER AGAIN

Since this book is all about creating remarkable experiences through-out the customer journey, I want to give you the chance to have an unprecedented experience when reading *Never Lose a Customer Again*. Go to: *www.JoeyColeman.com/ExperienceTheBook* to register (for free) for what promises to be a unique (and hopefully fun) way to enhance your book-reading experience. To get the full experience, make sure to sign up now—before you read any further. I don't want you to miss out on any of the cool things that are about to happen to you as you read the book!

CHAPTER ONE

A Letter from the Author:
The Future of Business Is H2H

Dear Reader:

Thanks so much for purchasing *Never Lose a Customer Again*! Or picking it up at the bookstore and reading this first chapter—trust me, you should save time and go buy this now as I offer a 100 percent refund guarantee at the end of this letter, so no need to worry!

It's time to stop thinking B2B or B2C—the future of business is H2H™.*

There is a natural human tendency to learn about a new way of doing business and immediately jump to excuses about why it won't work for you.

"I could never do that in my business, because [insert reason here]."

"That sounds good in theory, but it would never actually work in practice."

"Maybe they can do that, but real people can't. It's unrealistic."

Please do me a favor. . . . Do not approach this book with that mindset!

---

*My friend Bryan Kramer wrote a great book on this—*Human to Human: H2H*—which you should definitely check out.

The philosophy, methodology, and processes I describe in this book have radically changed both B2B and B2C businesses. The examples highlighted in this book run the gamut of size, scope, and industry. This approach has succeeded in small, medium, and large businesses. Nearly every type of product and/or service offering you can imagine has implemented this process: international and domestic-based operations; small, medium, and large customer bases; high- to low-dollar items.

The ideas in this book are not my *theories*. They come from real-world *experiences*—both my own and those of companies I have worked with over the last twenty-plus years. These companies range from internationally renowned brands like Zappos, Deloitte, Hyatt Hotels, NASA, and the World Bank to small, local, mom-and-pop businesses.

You might be concerned about the size of your company and whether you can implement these ideas. Don't worry—you can. You may wonder, "What if my business has only two employees?" The techniques in this book will still work for you. "What if my business has more than five hundred employees?" These approches still apply.

Case Study Examples—Categorized by Number of Employees

Phase	Less than 10	10–30	31–50	51–99	100+
Assess chapter 8	Notes from the Universe	Wealth Factory			Corporate Executive Board
Admit chapter 9	Maverick1000, Notre Dame Glee Club	Zogics			Build a Bear, Ridemakerz, Anthony Robbins Companies
Affirm chapter 10	CADRE		Total Debt Freedom, Book in a Box		CD Baby, Casper Beds, Zappos, CarMax, Lands' End
Activate chapter 11		Cornerstone Retirement			Apple, Tech 4 Kids, 23andMe, World Bank
Acclimate chapter 12		San Francisco CrossFit	PolicyMedical	Acceleration Partners	Domino's Pizza, Delta Airlines
Accomplish chapter 13	Online Trainer Academy	Yoko Co	Ongoing Operations		Audible, Baro
Adopt chapter 14		Lady Gaga			Sephora, Apple, Harley-Davidson, dōTERRA, Starwood Hotels, Chicago Cubs, Taylor Swift
Advocate chapter 15	4Knines, Maverick1000, MastermindTalks				Viacord, Dropbox, American Express, Delta

In fact, I've included case studies of companies that range in size from one employee to more than 340,000 employees!

You may worry about whether you can afford to implement the strategies and techniques discussed in this book. Again, you needn't fear, because you can. If your business has less than $100,000 in revenue, you can afford the techniques described in this book. If your business is making billions of dollars, you're more than covered. I've included case studies of companies where the annual revenue ranges from $50,000 to more than $220 billion.

Whether you sell products, services, or some combination of both, this book has examples for you. Whether you operate within the domestic United States or around the world, this book has examples for you. Whether you consider yourself an online business, a brick-and-mortar business, or some combination of both, this book has examples for you.

My point is very simple: *Yes, this works, and yes, it applies to YOUR business.*

Case Study Examples—Categorized by Revenue

Phase	Less than $1M	$1M–$5M	$5M–$10M	More than $10M	More than $50M
Assess chapter 8		Notes from the Universe	Wealth Factory		Corporate Executive Board
Admit chapter 9	Notre Dame Glee Club	Maverick1000	Ridemakerz	Zogics	Build a Bear, Anthony Robbins Companies
Affirm chapter 10	CADRE		Total Debt Freedom	Book in a Box	CD Baby, Casper Beds, Zappos, CarMax, Lands' End
Activate chapter 11			Cornerstone Retirement	23andMe	Apple, Tech 4 Kids, World Bank
Acclimate chapter 12		San Francisco CrossFit	PolicyMedical	Acceleration Partners	Domino's Pizza, Delta Airlines
Accomplish chapter 13		Online Trainer Academy, Yoko Co		Ongoing Operations, Baro	Audible
Adopt chapter 14					Sephora, Apple, Harley-Davidson, Lady Gaga, dōTERRA, Starwood Hotels, Chicago Cubs, Taylor Swift
Advocate chapter 15		4Knines, Maverick1000, MastermindTalks			ViaCord, Dropbox, American Express, Delta

One of the biggest myths in business is the supposed difference between B2B and B2C. I get comments like this all the time:

"Joey, I loved your example, but it was a B2C business. Do you have an example that is B2B?" or *"Joey, you talked about a large B2B operation. We're a small, B2C company—what should we do?"*

These questions are based on the premise that there is a huge difference between the two types of customers (businesses and consumers).

There is not.

While there are certainly differences between B2C and B2B operations, they are less significant than most people imagine. *All* business is ultimately the same, because all business boils down to humans dealing with humans. I like to focus on a human-to-human (H2H) equation, because that is what matters most.

When we think about the typical B2C environment, we know we're selling to a single buyer and our focus is on that individual. Without an H2H approach, we fail to think about the other people who will interact with the purchased item. Imagine a male customer who purchases a new shirt. We forget to consider the girlfriend who appreciates the way he looks in the shirt, the roommate who borrows the shirt, the parents who think he "looks sharp" in the shirt, etc.

In contrast, when we think about an H2H interaction in a B2B setting, we have to recognize that every business is an organization comprised of people, and therefore your product or service is interacting with humans—and many of them. The person who made the purchasing decision probably isn't going to be the only person using the product. In fact, they may not be the person using it at all. With an H2H approach, we must think of all the people who aren't involved in the sales conversation but will be using the service, and about the constraints operating on the person who is making the purchasing decision.

With H2H thinking, we consider *all* of the people who interact with and experience the product.

When you shift to H2H thinking, you find more commonalities between yourself and your customer or client.* You can then take what you know about human nature and infuse it into your business operations.

To never lose a customer again, you must meet your customers (whoever they are) where they are in their emotional journey.

If you can meet your customers where they are, you can avoid missing the opportunity to take them out of the sterile B2B environment or single-minded B2C environment and into the more emotionally resonant H2H environment.

The next time you find yourself thinking in terms of B2B or B2C, remind yourself that you are selling something *to* people that will be *used by* people. If you always keep that in mind, you will move your customer through the phases of the ideal journey, and you will make every customer a customer for life, regardless of your business or industry.

In essence, you'll never lose a customer again.

Some consider this idea—that all business is about human-to-human interaction—controversial. Not everyone agrees with this approach to business. That's fine.

---

*Regardless of whether you serve customers, clients, patients, members, students, users, or some other category of people—they are all humans. Throughout this book, I most often refer to customers, but don't let that serve as a barrier to your understanding or your feelings about the applicability of the message. If you sell to or serve human beings, this methodology will work for you.

If you find yourself disagreeing with this mentality, *I encourage you to put the book down and if you purchased it, to email me directly so I can give you a full refund of the price you paid for the book.*

The entire philosophy I describe in this book is based on this human-to-human concept, and if you disagree with it, I don't want you to waste your time reading any further.

I am very serious about the refund offer. Email me at *RefundFrom Joey@JoeyColeman.com*, and I will arrange for you to receive a full refund.*

That's how serious I am about this philosophy and approach to life. I wrote this book because I genuinely believe that business is ultimately about solving problems to help human beings. You don't have to agree with me, but if you don't, this book probably won't help you, and I would rather reimburse you than bear your disappointment.

Let's get started!

Joey

P.S. If you have any questions, want to make any comments, or just want to share how you're going to implement these systems to never lose a customer again, send me an email at *JoeyC@JoeyColeman.com*. I'd love to hear from you!

---

*The lawyers want me to note that you'll need to provide proof of purchase prior to a refund being issued.

CHAPTER TWO

If a Dentist Can Do It, Why Can't You?

As I bit into the purple SweeTART®, my mouth exploded in pain.

The taste I expected from the sweet and sour candy was replaced by the crunching, painful realization that my back molar had shattered. Tooth fragments filled my mouth and pain shot through my gums, taking me back instantly to previous dental disasters.

But as intense as the pain was, my first thought was not actually about the pain. It was about one of my greatest fears. The thing I dread the most in life: I was going to the dentist.

Then it dawned on me. I didn't even have a dentist.

When I moved from Washington, D.C., to Denver a few months earlier, I didn't take the time to seek out and establish a relationship with a new dentist. This should come as no surprise because, like most people:

I DESPISE GOING TO THE DENTIST!

Thankfully, a good friend recommended that I go see Dr. Katie McCann at Aurora Modern Dentistry—promising that she would take great care of me.

Dreading the impending dentist visit, I reluctantly called Aurora Modern Dentistry. I was surprised when a warm, caring, concerned receptionist answered on the first ring. I did my best to explain the problem, and she said, "Joey, we need to get you in as quickly as possible. It sounds like you're in a great deal of pain and we want to resolve that right away." The receptionist adjusted Dr. McCann's schedule to get me an appointment two hours later.

This considerate and fast-acting reaction set the tone for the level of care I was going to receive from Dr. McCann and her office. The fact that a receptionist would make space available immediately for a brand-new patient was a good sign.

Yet despite this initial positive experience, I was still skeptical.

I did not have a good history with dental procedures. Years prior, I underwent a root canal where, despite the fact that I was under anesthesia, I swear the dentist climbed up onto a stepladder and jumped into my mouth with a sledgehammer, wreaking havoc as he went. The pain from that procedure lasted for days.

As past experiences with other dental care providers rushed into my mind (root canals, wisdom teeth extractions, cavity fillings, etc.), I tried to mentally and emotionally prepare myself for the upcoming appointment with Dr. McCann.

The receptionist asked me if I would have access to email and the Internet between our call and the time of my appointment. I told her I would and she said, "If you're willing and able, you can complete the intake forms online, which will make your appointment go that much faster." Almost instantly a message appeared in my email inbox.

Not only did the message welcome me to the practice, but it included a link to a website where I could answer all the necessary questions to detail my entire dental history. I didn't need to print PDFs and fill them out by hand. I didn't need to navigate poorly formatted Microsoft Word attachments and try to insert my personal data.

Moving quickly through the various intake prompts gave me a sense of relief that I was able to complete my "paperwork" on my own time, as opposed to while I waited in the dentist's office. The ratty clipboard and chewed-cap ballpoint pen approach to filling out yet another insurance form, medical history, and HIPAA release was replaced with a customer experience befitting the twenty-first century. I quickly navigated through a website that asked for my information only once, didn't require me to repeat myself from form to form, and allowed for the capture of my electronic signature.

I completed all of the forms in less than six minutes. It was simple. It was easy. It was refreshing. I hit Submit with a sense of accomplishment, but I was still curious whether this online form truly covered everything the dentist would need. Surely it couldn't be this easy?

I arrived at the dentist's office two hours later for my scheduled appointment, walked in the front door, and the moment my foot crossed the threshold, the receptionist stood up to greet me.

"Hello, Joey. How are you feeling?"

How did she recognize me? We'd never met before!

She immediately guided me back to the examination room where Dr. McCann was waiting. After a quick but thorough examination—not only of the broken molar, but of the area around it—Dr. McCann informed me that I needed a crown to repair the damage.

Fantastic (can you feel the "biting" sarcasm?). I'd never had a crown before, but it sounded like an awful experience. My mind flooded with questions: How long will this take? How painful is the procedure? How much will it cost?

Dr. McCann answered all of my unarticulated questions thoroughly, patiently and gently anticipating my cares and concerns in the process.

She explained that her office had the newest in dental technology and that they would be able to mill the crown in the office while I waited.

"From beginning to end, you'll be here about an hour and a half, but you'll never have to come back for us to check the fit again. We'll take a digital impression of the area. We'll construct a new tooth. We will 3D mill it, and then we'll insert it and check for a proper fit. We'll make sure that everything is working well and is fully seated prior to you leaving our office."

I couldn't believe it.

Getting a crown was once a complicated medical procedure that took weeks to complete. Now this new dentist was telling me that everything could be accomplished in an hour and a half? It felt too good to be true. But Dr. McCann didn't stop with the explanation of the crown creation/installation procedure. She went further.

She offered me payment plans (crowns aren't cheap), described her in-house insurance option (which was so much better than any dental insurance I had ever heard of), and shared other ways to reduce the cost of this dental emergency. When I agreed to the procedure, Dr. Mc-Cann said, "That's great. We'll get started right away. Prior to that, I just need you to sign this consent form for us to do the work."

Suddenly, the screen attached to the examination chair, which up until now had shown X-rays of my mouth and the damaged tooth, displayed a simple, straightforward consent form. She presented an electronic signature pad and stylus, which I hadn't noticed attached to the dental chair, and I signed the consent form electronically.

When I was finished, Dr. McCann turned the screen back around, once again brought up the image of the area that she would be repairing, and set to work. Dr. McCann offered me the opportunity to listen to music during the procedure, but I decided to stay "in the moment" and be present. I thought this would help me react faster if something went awry. As the old adage observes, this wasn't my first rodeo.

Throughout the procedure, Dr. McCann made pleasant conversation—a difficult task when I had a series of tools in my mouth and was struggling to talk. Her ability to artfully navigate asking easy yes/no questions to advance the conversation left me feeling that I was in the hands of a trained professional.

An hour and a half later, I left Dr. McCann's office with a new crown and a newfound appreciation for the fact that an industry notorious for creating horrible patient experiences could easily upend those beliefs.

This dental office anticipated my needs, made the interactions seamless, and at every step of the way managed my emotional state. I entered the office with a broken tooth and left a lifelong client and a huge fan. My first visit to Dr. McCann and Aurora Modern Dentistry completely changed my experience with the entire industry of dental medicine.

Two hours after I returned home, I received a call from Dr. McCann's office. The receptionist greeted me like an old friend and said, "We just wanted to call because by now the numbing agents are surely wearing off and we wanted to assess your pain level."

Wow. Dr. McCann knew that how I was "feeling" after the procedure would worsen as time went by, and she wanted to make sure I was managing the pain. I told her I was feeling good, and the receptionist said, "That's fantastic news. Did you pick up your painkiller prescription?"

The receptionist asked every necessary follow-up question to make sure I would continue to feel good going forward. She then shared Dr. McCann's personal cellphone number and told me to call Dr. McCann directly anytime in the coming days if I felt pain, experienced more bleeding, or wanted to check in about anything I was experiencing or anxious about.

Have you ever had a medical professional offer a personal cell-phone number after a procedure and invite you to call if you needed anything? Neither had I. And I had just met Dr. McCann for the first time a few hours before!

Interaction	TYPICAL DENTIST	DR. McCANN
Scheduling	next available appointment	prioritizes emergencies/returning patients
Paperwork	poorly photocopied on a wooden clipboard with a chewed pen	mobile-friendly online form (only answer questions once)
Duration	late start, rushed exam, multiple visits across three weeks	on time, as long as you wish, everything done in a single visit
Follow-up	"call if there is a problem"	check-in call two hours after procedure, follow-up 24 hr. (email) and 7 days (phone)
Overall Experience	frustrating	remarkable

Since the crown-repair procedure, I have been a loyal and faithful patient of Dr. McCann's. Regular cleanings, annual checkups, and the occasional dental repair work have left me singing the praises of my dentist and her office time and time again. Despite the fact that I know very few people who live in my newly adopted state of Colorado, I've already referred five new patients to her office and will continue to send friends and colleagues her way whenever I can.

A recent exchange on Facebook illustrated how quickly word of mouth spreads and how far ahead of the curve your company will be if you follow the advice in this book. Who absolutely loves their dentist? Not just me. Other people love Dr. McCann as well:

Dr. McCann's commitment to creating a remarkable customer experience is without compare in the dental industry (at least in my personal experience). If there is someone better in this industry, I will probably never find out because Dr. McCann has earned my business forever. After an initial experience like this, why would I even think about trying any other dentist?

Not only did Dr. McCann create an effortless experience, but she anticipated and served my emotional needs with nearly telepathic accuracy, made me feel like part of a tribe by giving me her phone number, and used other techniques that I'll teach you in this book so that once you earn a customer's business, you never lose that customer again.

If a dentist can create a remarkable customer experience and earn lifelong loyalty, every business in every industry in the world can do the same.

CHAPTER THREE

The Cost of Losing a Customer

How much time do you spend wining, dining, and courting prospective customers?

How much money do you spend trying to acquire new customers for your business?

How many people in your company focus on marketing and sales?

Now let me ask you a much more important question:

How much time, money, and energy do you spend trying to keep your customers?

Nearly every business spends a huge amount of time, money, and energy trying to land new clients. Customer acquisition is usually the highest single cost center in a business, and many executives can detail their customer acquisition cost down to the dollar, if not the penny.

And yet in almost all of these businesses, where so much effort is spent trying to persuade people to become customers, virtually no effort is spent trying to *keep the customers once they have them*.

So what happens? Customers leave.

MOST BUSINESSES ARE HEMORRHAGING CUSTOMERS AND DON'T EVEN REALIZE IT

I first became aware of the customer retention epidemic that plagues almost every industry in the late 1990s. While reading a report about how banks market and advertise to gain new customers (I know, I'm that cool), I learned something startling.

Historically, banks spend a significant sum of money on acquiring new customers—approximately $300 per account.[1] This was justified as making economic sense because the relationship between a consumer and a bank was supposed to follow a regular pattern:

1. the consumer opens a bank account
2. the account remains open for a long time

The longer an individual or business stayed with the bank, the more fees were paid for banking services. The more customers the bank acquired, the more money the bank made.

In reading the Corporate Executive Board report "New Customer Onboarding Programs in Service Industries," I discovered a dirty little secret about the world of banking that diminished the acquisition strategy employed by banks: *32 percent of new customers who join a bank will leave that bank before their one-year anniversary!*[2]

I was shocked. Consider the basic math. On average, it costs $300 to acquire a banking customer. That customer pays a monthly account maintenance fee of approximately $12.[3] Looking only to the guaranteed income from maintenance fees, it takes twenty-five months (more than two years) before the bank earns back the initial investment in acquiring that customer. If 32 percent leave before reaching the twelve-month mark, that means the bank has the potential to lose money on 32 percent of its newly acquired customers!

Which raises the urgent question of *why*. Why are customers leaving at such great personal cost? While the financial cost to the bank is staggering at scale, the personal inconvenience to customers who go through the enrollment process and then decide to leave is even worse.

Think back to the last time you opened a new bank account. Let's be honest, it's a pain in the . . . neck.

To open the typical bank account, you go into a local bank branch, present your government-issued ID, fill out reams of paperwork, and make an initial deposit to fund the account. After that, you order checks, request an ATM card, set an ATM code, and re-enroll for online bill paying and direct deposit. You then wait while things continue to process in your old bank account (many people keep both the new and old bank accounts open for several months of overlap) before finally shutting down the old bank account and transferring any remaining money into the new account.

It is mind-boggling that a customer would ever leave after going through all of these steps and investing this much time, effort, and patience. *And yet 32 percent do just that!*

In fact, 20 percent of the customers who leave in the first year do so without ever having conducted a *single* transaction.[4] Not one ATM withdrawal, not one check clearing, and not one payment of an online bill.

A shocking 50 percent of the customers who leave in the first year quit doing business with the bank in the first 100 days![5] The relationship has barely started, the customer may not even have closed their prior bank account, and already they are leaving.

This revelation about banks losing customers left me with one burning question: If customer defection is an epidemic in the world of banking, where paying close attention to the bottom line, the cost of acquisition, and the rate of retention is part of "banker DNA," *what must it be like in other industries?*

I started researching all kinds of businesses and marketplaces around the world and what I found was staggering.

Despite the fact that cellphone contracts are notoriously draconian and require you to give up your firstborn child to break them, 21 percent of cellphone customers break the contract within the first 100 days.[6]

While no one likes it when their car breaks down, even fewer people like their car repair experience. Between 60 and 70 percent of car owners go to an auto repair shop once and will never visit that shop again because the first experience is so poor.[7]

Restaurants live or die based on their ability to keep customers in the seats—and yet 46 percent of new customers to a Chuck E. Cheese's pizza restaurant will never visit a Chuck E. Cheese's again after their initial visit.[8] Almost *half* of the new customers the restaurant worked so hard to acquire appear to dislike the experience so much that they *never* return.

This defection turns into a downpour in the ever-expanding software as a service (SaaS)/cloud industry. Twenty percent of newly acquired customers don't make the 100-day anniversary before leaving.[9]

The combination of Internet, phone, and cable television services offered by integrated telecom providers sees staggering rates of customer defection in the first 100 days. While most companies are unwilling to share these rates publicly, defection rates of greater than 30 percent during these first few months are not uncommon.[10]

Regardless of where your business operates, what industry you work in, or the size of your operation, you are likely losing approximately 20 to 70 percent of your newly acquired customers in the first 100 days of the relationship. Companies spend incredible amounts of time, money, and energy to obtain new customers, but are hemorrhaging customers *after* the sale.

Why don't businesses focus on retaining the customers they worked so hard to earn?

WHY YOU LOSE CUSTOMERS

While there are a number of specific reasons why you may lose a customer, when viewed more holistically, they boil down to a single fact:

You lose customers because they feel neglected after the sale is made.

Think back to the last time you quit doing business with someone. . . .

You may have said it was the price, when in reality you could have paid for it. You may have said you were going in a different direction, when you didn't really need to do that. You may have said you weren't getting value anymore, but really you still were. You may have just stopped doing business with them—without saying why—and your decision was affirmed when the company didn't seem to care that you were leaving.

The typical business does a great job of getting the attention of the customer and persuading them to buy, but then does *very little* to create a meaningful or remarkable experience for them *after* the sale.*

---

*Every writer faces a problem when writing in the English language because it lacks a gender-neutral, singular pronoun. Because *The Associated Press Stylebook* (arguably one of the foremost arbiters of grammar) recently added an entry for "they" as a singular, gender-neutral pronoun, I have made the decision to use this convention throughout the book. While I was concerned about using the grammatically improper "they," I do think it works better than the alternative options of a "he or she" reference that would be annoying to readers over the

There are many reasons why customers leave, but the main reason is that businesses systematically ignore the emotional journey of the customer. It's not that they don't care. It's that the way they do business and the way their incentives and structures are set up creates a blind spot around customer experience, and that blind spot is the problem.

EMOTIONS AND EXPERIENCE ARE AN AFTERTHOUGHT

Over the years, companies have evolved into larger enterprises with more moving parts, more people, more rules, and more regulations. Humanity has slowly but surely been removed from the majority of interactions and discussions. In the modern business, one often hears phrases like "It's not personal, it's business"; and "Work is work, and personal is personal, and the two aren't meant to mix." There is a strong belief that personal relationships, conversations about feelings, and displays of emotion should be kept at home, out of the business arena.

As businesses have grown colder and more structured around policy—without taking into consideration the people the policies impact and affect—consumers increasingly feel uncared for and not considered. Customers no longer feel special because more and more the operations and structures are designed to keep the "personal" out of the "business."

In most organizations, new customer onboarding and experience is not consciously designed, logically structured, or consistently executed in a way that meaningfully contributes to the customer's emotional journey.

For example, it is assumed that the customer read the fine print in

---

course of an entire book. Using "they" is also a way to recognize the need for a pronoun for people who don't identify as a he or a she. Since most businesses serve a variety of customers, I find that using "they" subtly encourages readers to constantly consider the specific needs of their customers—regardless of gender. I hope you can view my usage of "they" as an attempt to be as inclusive as possible.

the proposal/contract and know what comes next in the process—
even though the people making these assumptions don't usually read
the contracts/proposals they themselves are asked to sign!

This failure to be "on the same page" causes problems when the
fine print comes back to harm the customer later in the relationship.
These situations arise when an individual rents a car, enrolls with a
cellphone provider, selects a health insurance plan, etc.—only to find
out that the customer's understanding at the time of purchase doesn't
align with the way the company handles things when conflicts arise.
Customers are surprised to learn that they are responsible for the cost
of repairing common door dings on a rental car. Customers are infuri-
ated to learn about the huge financial penalties for switching to another mobile phone service provider before the end of the contract
term. Customers are crushed to learn that a necessary health procedure isn't covered by their insurance.

Finally, the steps in the new customer process are done in an order
and sequence that aligns with the company's operations, with little
care or concern for the customer's experience or needs. Most customer
experience is haphazard at best, with no clear road map or milestones
for the customer or the company to follow.

BRAIN SCIENCE AND FUNDAMENTAL HUMAN
BEHAVIOR ARE IGNORED

Brain science teaches that even if a prospect knows, loves, and believes
in a company's offerings, after they become a customer, fear, doubt,
and uncertainty will plague their thoughts.

Having the customer's brain stacked against the company from
the outset, combined with the lack of guidance from the organization
at this point in the customer life cycle, puts new customers into a state

of heightened negative emotions. This state is exacerbated by the stark difference between the new customer's feelings of fear, doubt, and uncertainty and the company's joy, euphoria, and excitement about acquiring a new customer.

THEY'RE LEAVING FASTER THAN YOU KNOW

Current business trends glamorize growth, incentivize acquisition, fail to consider the emotional journey of the customer, undervalue retention, and underpay and underequip customer-facing employees. Not to mention the fact that they completely ignore their customers' basic biology and human behavior.

It's no surprise that customers are leaving so quickly after they sign up. But how can you stop the hemorrhaging? You need to focus on what your new customers *experience* when they start working with you.

CHAPTER FOUR

Customer Defection: A Structural and Cultural Problem

BUSINESSES ARE STRUCTURED AROUND CUSTOMER ACQUISITION, NOT CUSTOMER EXPERIENCE

I've worked in and researched customer experience and retention for almost twenty years, and in the process have found that regardless of business size, scope, location, revenue, or offerings, there are three key reasons organizations struggle with customer retention:

1. Businesses Don't Catch as Well as They Chase

An old adage posits that the excitement is in the chase, not the catch. This seems particularly true for most companies. Businesses wine and dine prospects on the front end, taking potential customers to sporting events, celebrity-filled outings, and amazing meals. But once the "target" transitions from prospect to customer, the sales team and their limitless budgets usually disappear.

Much like the advice in dating how-to books, most businesses put their focus and attention toward persuading someone to date them.

There isn't much effort or emphasis on what to do *after* the date ends and the relationship begins.

You can see this clearly in how the average organization treats a customer as soon as they make a purchase. When the sale is made, the customer is handed off to an account manager or service representative (who never attended any of the "dates"). Aside from a dinner or phone call when it comes time for the annual review/renewal, there isn't much courting by the salesperson anymore.

Can you imagine if dating were like this? If you did the exciting stuff with one person, and then, once you committed to the relationship, you were "assigned" to a totally different person?

The chase is now over. The drama and the intrigue that kept both the prospect and the sales team excited and engaged evaporates. Newly minted customers are left feeling like a number in a vast enterprise (which is no surprise, as almost every business assigns new customers an impossible-to-remember customer number as one of their first internal actions).

The customer no longer feels wanted, let alone special.

But if you're feeling guilty about how you treat your customers right now, don't beat yourself up too much. . . .

This is *the blind spot* in business today. You're not alone.

Even some of the most successful companies—those that are sophisticated and savvy in every other way—fail miserably when it comes to keeping their customers.

The rude and jarring experience as an individual transitions from prospect to customer is exacerbated by the complete lack of a handoff. The information shared with a salesperson is rarely transferred to the account manager—leaving the new customer feeling unheard, unappreciated, and insignificant (not to mention irritated that they will need to explain everything again to the next customer representative they speak with about the issue).

2. Companies Reward Acquisition over Retention

The very structure of most businesses is set up to reward the acquisition of new customers. In most businesses, the "stars" are the employees who bring in new clients, not the employees who keep clients happy after the sale.

As if this didn't stack the deck enough, the leaders of most companies usually came up through the ranks of marketing or sales.[1] Because they understand sales and marketing, they are quick to look there for guidance and advice, as well as focus and interest. It's what they know.

This creates a propensity within the typical organization to reward, acknowledge, and promote those who are outward facing and focused on new business development, rather than recognize individuals who are internal facing and focused on keeping current customers happy.

The number of resources devoted to marketing and sales are enormous compared to those directed toward customer retention. The 2017 edition of the annual CMO Survey (conducted by the Fuqua School of Business at Duke University, Deloitte LLP, and the American Marketing Association) found that the average business spends 6.9 percent of total company revenue on marketing—and yet less than one fifth of that total spending is dedicated to customer retention activities.[2]

As if the actual dollar spend didn't prove this devotion to marketing and sales above everything else, consider the insight that comes from a simple search of books available on Amazon. A query conducted the week this book was sent to print showed 311,257 books listed in a search of the word "marketing," 1,013,313 books listed in a search of the word "sales," and just 30,198 books listed in the *combined* search results for: customer service, customer experience, and customer care.

These results break down into a ratio of 43:1 when it comes to focusing on presale versus postsale activities. To make this even more obvious, consider the following illustration of the customer life cycle:

The Customer Life Cycle

Awareness · Knowledge · Consideration · Selection Trial · Satisfaction · Loyalty · Advocacy

Prepurchase   **Purchase**   **Post Purchase**

Most businesses spend all of their time on the *left side* of the graphic. They try to increase the prospect's *awareness* and *knowledge* of their business or brand, and then move the prospect to *consider* the offerings before the customer finally *tries* or *selects/purchases* the product or service. This is the focus on marketing and sales efforts that is commonplace in business today.

Despite the fact that the customer life cycle graphic is balanced with three elements on each side of the "purchase," very few businesses devote any attention to the *right side* of the graphic—ensuring *satisfaction*, garnering *loyalty*, and driving *advocacy*. In the typical business today, what happens *after* the sale gets little to no attention.

3. Customer Service/Experience Employees Are Marginalized

Most business hierarchies place account management and customer service employees at the bottom.

Generally, employees in these roles are paid hourly. In most organizations there are no financial incentives, trips to Hawaii, or award ceremonies for good performance in "account management" roles. Those perks go to the marketing and sales teams.

Individuals working in customer service/experience usually report to another department (marketing, sales, operations, etc.), and that department head reports directly to the CEO. The customer service/experience voices go unheard for lack of a seat at the executive table. As a result, the work they do is often seen as a commodity or ignored altogether.

In many companies, these customer-facing employees are actually incentivized to spend *less time* with each customer, with bonuses paid for how quickly they process inbound customer calls.[3]

This is a big deal. Multiple factors contribute to rampant customer defection and, in the process, destroy your bottom line.

THE FINANCIAL IMPACT OF A BAD CUSTOMER EXPERIENCE

Losing a customer costs a business in far more ways than direct revenue.

First, there are the sunk costs spent on acquisition that will never be recovered. Second, for every lost customer, overall profits decrease. Third, without solid customer retention, sustaining a business is nearly impossible. Fourth, every time a customer leaves, team morale suffers. Finally, the emotions associated with losing a customer are often felt in the moment, yet seem to be forgotten before any changes are made to stop the losses from happening in the future.

Each of these costs is significant on its own, but when combined, their impact can be substantial.

Across a wide range of industries, a 5 percent improvement in customer retention rates will yield a 25 to 100 percent increase in profits.

Or so says Frederick Reichheld in his book *The Loyalty Effect.*[4]

If you are like me and not that good at math, you are probably skeptical about this claim. How can 5 percent equate to 25 to 100 percent?

You may not know who Reichheld is, but you've certainly been exposed to his work. Reichheld is a *New York Times* best-selling author and business strategist best known for his work in the area of loyalty business models and loyalty marketing. You're probably more familiar with his Net Promoter System of management.

Here's the way Reichheld says that it works: The typical business is running at some semblance of a profit. Each retained customer increases the overall profit of the business because:

1. the carrying cost of keeping a new customer is not nearly as high as the cost of bringing on a new customer, and
2. when sales and marketing costs go to zero, all money being spent on customer acquisition stays in the business and flows directly to the bottom line.

In most businesses, the cost of customer acquisition falls in the top three most expensive line items in the budget.[5] Depending on the business, it may even be the number one expense.

By keeping more customers, and reducing the money spent on customer acquisition, the marketing and sales people might not be too happy, but *actual profits* will increase by 25 to 100 percent. This has been proven time and time again, in a variety of industries.[6]

Now ask yourself the following questions:

How big would your company be if you still did business with every customer you ever worked with in the past?

If you never lost a customer, how much more money would you save?

How much more money would you keep as profit?

How much faster would your company grow?

THE MANY BENEFITS OF KEEPING YOUR CUSTOMERS

Putting the focus on creating amazing customer experiences for your existing customers is more efficient, more effective, and more profitable than spending that effort on getting new customers.

When an organization prioritizes customer experience, it sparks creativity as employees rally to enhance specific touchpoints and customer interactions. Morale improves as employees begin to see a greater purpose in their jobs and find new reasons to come to work every day. Profitability and revenue rise as customers find additional reasons to do business with this "new and improved" organization that values their business. The entire ecosystem flourishes as the customer experience improves, which leads to enhancements in the employee experience, which in turn boosts customer experience, and the cycle continues on and on.

But don't just believe me.

According to Marketing Metrics, when selling to a new prospect there is a 5 to 20 percent chance of making the sale. When selling to an existing customer, that probability skyrockets to 60 to 70 percent.[7] Focusing on existing customers makes it easier to sell and grow the business.

The lifetime value of a loyal customer can be greater than ten times the value of their first purchase.[8] Like money left in the bank account, investments in customer loyalty compound over time.

It is six to seven times more expensive to acquire a new customer than it is to keep a current customer.[9] Keeping a focus on current customers keeps costs low.

When asked about their spending habits, seven out of ten Americans said they were willing to spend more with companies they believe provide *excellent* customer service and nine out of ten would pay more to ensure a *superior* customer experience.[10] Working with existing customers is not only easier, but it results in a greater "share of wallet." While many businesses may feel they are providing superior service, the techniques and tactics covered in this book are designed to leave *customers* feeling a superior level of customer experience—a significant distinction given that most companies' "good" just isn't "good enough." Using dozens of case studies, we'll explore hidden opportunities for customer experience enhancements and detail specific implementation plans for delivering a superior experience.

Study after study shows customers across all industries are *interested in doing business with the company they already know.* If you're providing a remarkable customer experience, customers will continue doing business with you. And they will bring their friends along as well (we'll discuss that more in the chapters to come).

IN THE FUTURE, RETENTION WILL MATTER MOST

Trends are often easiest to spot by observing the behaviors of start-ups in Silicon Valley. In the last two years, venture capitalists have attached significantly higher valuations to companies with low customer churn rates (VC speak for losing customers). In an example offered by Gainsight, two companies with different churn rates have a very similar valuation in year one.[11]

The valuations are dramatically different when the difference in churn rates (5 percent vs. 20 percent) is extrapolated across a five-year time line:

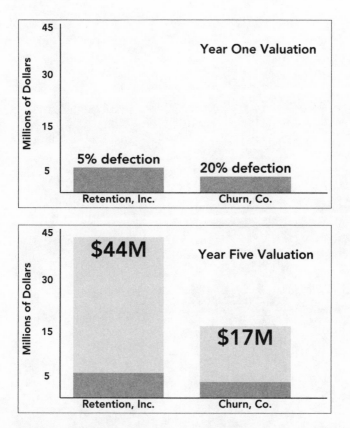

The improved retention represents a 280 percent difference in the company valuation just five years later. Keeping more customers really pays off with the compounding effect that occurs as a business continues to mature.

Given the significant costs associated with losing a customer, it's understandable why so many businesses want to keep their customers. But before we can focus on keeping customers, we must first clearly understand why they leave in the first place.

CHAPTER FIVE

What Is Customer Experience?

This question is not as ridiculous as it sounds. In my experience, most business leaders think they know what customer experience is—and yet the same leaders run businesses losing 20 percent or more of their customers every year.

Before I teach you how to fix this problem, let me give a very quick explanation of how we got to where we are, and what it means.

A (VERY BRIEF) HISTORY OF CUSTOMER EXPERIENCE (DID I MENTION IT'D BE BRIEF?)

In the 1960s and '70s, when you went to a store and purchased a new product, there was a pretty good chance it would be broken when you opened the package at home.

These days it's hard to believe this type of business behavior was ever accepted. Many customers reached the point where they would open the product *in the store* (before they took it home) to ensure that it worked (I am old enough to remember watching my parents do this). It is not a stretch to say that customers used to feel satisfied by simply getting what they paid for, regardless of whether it led to the desired results. In fact, if they got only what they paid for, they often seemed thrilled.

In the 1980s, the business practice of *kaizen* (Japanese for "improve") put the spotlight on striving for zero defects in manufacturing. The *kaizen* movement focused on total quality management and the standardization of programs and processes with the goal of eliminating defects and waste.[1]

This approach was first practiced in the automotive manufacturing industry (e.g., "The Toyota Way") and quickly spread across all aspects of manufacturing. As the philosophy and practice were adopted by other industries, customer expectations around the globe began to shift.

In 1986, Motorola engineer Bill Smith developed the concept of "Six Sigma"—a specific set of techniques and tools for process improvement. When Jack Welch made it central to his business strategy at General Electric, this approach quickly took over American big business.[2] It was no longer acceptable to sell a broken product. Companies that failed to adopt these improved operational practices and limit their defects didn't survive.

In the 1990s, Dell Computer Corporation popularized "just-in-time" manufacturing.[3] Prospective customers would call Dell, discuss their computing needs with a "technical specialist"—who also functioned as a salesperson—and a new computer was built to the customer's personal specifications. Consumers were no longer forced to buy things "as is." This desire to customize products quickly spread to other products. Consumers wanted everything in their life to be customized, from their cars to their golf clubs to their stove-top ranges.

Companies quickly learned that, in order to stay competitive, they needed to offer at least some level of customization. Organizations that allowed uniqueness and personality to permeate their brand excelled while companies that "played it safe" became beige boxes about which nobody cared.

In the 2000s, as manufacturing costs declined and global shipping and logistics management improved, the average cost of products in all categories dropped.[4] Walmart, with its motto "Always Low Prices," expanded dramatically, bringing low-cost goods to every corner of the world.[5]

The 2000s saw a major shift in business as the cost to manufacture and distribute goods on a global scale plummeted and customers began to expect many services and products to be available twenty-four hours a day, seven days a week, 365 days a year.[6]

By 2010, the Internet was available on cellphones and tablets, and consumers became accustomed to interacting with any product or service they wanted, at any time, from anywhere in the world, at a moment's notice.

So to sum up:

In the 1970s and 1980s, a business could differentiate itself by having zero defects.

In the 1990s, differentiation was attainable via customization.

In the 2000s and 2010s, the ability to differentiate on price reached its apex and then waned.

In the 2000s and 2010s, being accessible 24/7/365 was a way to differentiate, but that quickly went away as every business came "online."

So what now?

With zero product defects, customized offerings, bargain basement pricing, and ubiquitous availability becoming the norm across all industries, the only thing left for a business to differentiate itself from the competition is the *customer's experience*.

CUSTOMER SERVICE IS NOT CUSTOMER EXPERIENCE

Many people mistakenly interchange the terms "customer service" and "customer experience." I believe they describe very different situations. *Customer service is reactive, while customer experience is proactive.*

To make sure we're on the same page, customer service is defined as:

> "The assistance and advice provided by a company to those people who buy or use its products or services."[7]

Compare this with customer experience, which is defined as:

> "How customers perceive their interactions with your company."[8]

Trust me, you may want to memorize these definitions so you can explain them to someone else one day!

Customer experience encompasses the emotions a customer feels when they interact with a product or service. When that experience goes beyond what the product or service is supposed to deliver, the consumer feels like they have a great experience and becomes emotionally involved with the brand.

Customer service is how a business responds when things go wrong or a customer expresses a need. Customer experience, on the other hand, comes on the front end. It anticipates what might go wrong and structures the interactions to avoid this from ever happening. Customer experience is proactive. It's the environment, the feeling, and the scenario a business creates for the customer to trigger a series of desired emotions.

CUSTOMER EXPERIENCE IS MORE THAN RAVING FANS

In the early 1990s, the book *Raving Fans* by Ken Blanchard and Sheldon Bowles offered a new take on the relationship between a business and its customers. The book's premise was that if a company did a great job creating a remarkable experience for its customers, not only was it good for business (because the company had fewer complaints, customer service queries, and overall drains on resources), but it would also create raving fans in the process.

These raving fans would then go and tell everyone they knew about the product or service the business offered. Because of these fans, there was less need to put effort into marketing because the customers were already doing that. In many ways, *Raving Fans* is the book that popularized the benefits of "word of mouth."

This concept has been around for years. In fact, many of you probably read the Blanchard and Bowles book and are thinking you already know the importance of creating raving fans. Your business might already be working toward getting more of them.

That's great. We have indeed come quite far and we can all agree that both treating our customers well and inspiring word of mouth are important. Here's the problem, though: Most companies draw generalized, vague conclusions about customer satisfaction rather than examining hard data. If they're honest and do a true assessment, they find a much smaller percentage of raving fans than they think. But most don't even assess their actions.

The work they're doing is not working. And most don't even know it.

According to research by Bain & Company, when asked, 80 percent of companies say they deliver "superior" customer service.[9] The customers' perception of the service level was very different. Only 8 percent of customers felt the companies delivered "superior" customer service.[10]

These companies don't track customer emotions, or experiences, nor do they have regular reporting, or even a clear read on the pulse of their customer. Many companies want to create better experiences but feel like their resources are already 100 percent expended.

We all want raving fans, but we haven't been taught how to create them.

Raving Fans was a good start to the movement, but it was more inspirational than prescriptive. *Never Lose a Customer Again* is the next logical step. It builds on what came before and provides a road map for where to go next: building a *remarkable customer experience*, delivered consistently to all of your customers, starting the moment they transition from prospect to customer.

Unlike product features, design elements, functionalities, and materials, it is very difficult (if not impossible) to "copy" another business's customer experience, making it the ultimate differentiator between you and your competitors.

I've been giving speeches about this topic for over a decade, and I've asked approximately 100,000 audience members—almost all of whom worked in business—why they don't provide a great customer experience for their customers. The answer almost always boils down to this:

"We know customer experience is important, but we don't know what to do or how to start."

I'm going to show you.

CHAPTER SIX

You Only Have 100 Days (If That Long) to Get It Right

When I say customer experience is important, I mean that a memorable experience *must* take place during a certain window of time. It's not just that any experience a customer has with you should be pleasant; *when* the customer has that experience is crucial.

In his book *Duct Tape Selling*, my good friend and fellow speaker John Jantsch notes that "a sale is not a 'finished' sale until the customer receives a result."[1]

A customer usually needs to use a service or product for a fair amount of time before they consider the purchase "worth it." The customer must get their desired result before they can become a true fan of your company. You can't do a good job once and have an advocate for life. It doesn't work that way.

One of the reasons it takes time is because very few businesses are like Altoids. You purchase a tin of Altoids, pop a few in your mouth, and boom, your breath is fresher! The result happens fast and the Altoids live up to their "curiously strong" tagline. But with almost every other product and service, the "result" is not immediate. There is a lag between an item being purchased and the customer experiencing the fruits of the purchase.

Despite the fact that it may be some time before a customer achieves their desired result, their feelings about working with you start to accumulate the moment the purchase is made. From the very outset of the relationship, a clock starts ticking and every interaction, touchpoint, exchange, and communication contributes to their overall perception of your organization. Each of these interactions matters and as they compile, their importance increases, as does the weight of their impact on the overall experience. It doesn't work to plan on making good impressions once the customer is proven loyal six months down the road. You'll never reach that stage in the relationship if the early interactions aren't remarkable.

I like to emphasize the First 100 Days® after the sale as a critical window for securing customer loyalty—not because it is an exact time limit, but because it is easy to remember, short enough to maintain focus, and long enough to deliver value. This hundred-day time period gives you the opportunity to form a relationship, impress the customer several times, and deliver consistently so they trust and like you.

These initial impressions, the first few interactions, the early progress, and the rapport-building moments contribute to the customer's long-term opinion of you and your business. That being said, if you get these First 100 Days of the relationship right, you can keep a customer for life.

The specific applicability of a hundred-day time line varies depending on the industry. In some businesses, by the time a customer reaches the hundred-day anniversary, they may still be waiting for the desired result. If the product is a highway, the land may not even be surveyed in one hundred days. In other businesses, by the time the customer reaches one hundred days, they might be actively giving referrals, as they achieved their desired result and more.

While the time period for someone to transition from new customer to raving fan *can* be less than one hundred days, it is rarely the case. More often than not it takes several months for the organization to develop a track record, establish a foundation of trust, and prove it can deliver on its promises. This groundwork must be in place before the average customer will put their reputation on the line and refer friends or family to you.

Regardless of where a business falls on this spectrum, the point is the same: a hundred-day time frame is long enough that it requires thoughtful consideration, yet short enough to feel manageable.

To be clear, the start day (Day 1) can vary within a company based on its procedures/offerings. For example, when you buy something online, Day 1 is when you hit Purchase after entering in your payment information. In a service business, Day 1 is the day a new customer signs a contract with you. In a retail establishment, Day 1 is when the customer signs the credit card receipt and the merchant hands over the merchandise. In short, if money is being exchanged, or contracts are being signed, the hundred-day clock has started.

Customers won't wait 101 days to make up their minds about you. The brain is moving way too fast and is designed to determine your status as a "friend or foe" much earlier in the relationship. As the world has shifted from agriculture to industry, and the volume of information, associated time pressures, and variety of choices have increased, humans are actually forced to make more decisions—and these decisions happen faster and faster.[2]

From whether or not to "like" a Facebook status update, to what kind of salad dressing to order, to which shirt to wear, to which brand of butter to buy, customers are constantly making decisions. Research shows we make on average 219 decisions per day related to food alone.[3] The number of decisions humans face daily is only increasing. If you want to influence customers' perceptions about your business in this ever-accelerating world, you must become more nimble and responsive with each passing year.

Given the overstimulated nature of the modern world, a consistent, systematic approach to customer experience, sustained for one hundred days, is *necessary* to build a rock-solid foundation of trust and rapport.

THE JOURNEY OF 100 DAYS CONSISTS OF EIGHT PHASES

All customers have the potential to transition through a series of eight phases over approximately one hundred days. That realization came to me when I started a marketing and design business in January 2002 called Design Symphony.

My first service offering was logo design. I believed at that time (and still believe today) that the goal of a logo is to get the person who sees it to have both a mental and emotional reaction. The mental reaction is that they understand what your product, service, or brand does. The emotional reaction is how they feel about your product, service, or brand based on their initial interactions with the logo.

My objective in designing logos was to pair what the company did with the warm feelings of how they did it. I worked with my clients to create this feeling of connection in their logo, and then quickly expanded to helping them build mental and emotional connections and reactions into their advertisements, websites, marketing materials, and even their internal operations.

As my business evolved, I discovered that when a company could pair what it did with the feelings of how it did it, the company would experience greater success—and on a faster schedule.

"Designing" businesses in this way is not unlike creating movies. If a movie has made you cry, laugh, or feel fear, it almost certainly wasn't an accident. The director and the producer knew you were going to have that specific emotional reaction and they designed and structured the movie to create the experience for you.

Applying this Hollywood technique in business, the customer's emotional journey becomes the primary focus. If businesses approached their customer interactions in the same way movies approach their audience interactions—figuring out the emotions a customer should have every step of the way—the entire world of business would change.

This is why the First 100 Days of a new customer relationship are so critical. During this period, the customer embarks on their own emotional journey. If it's a remarkable one, they will stay. If it isn't emotionally satisfying, they will leave.

As I built my business, and then helped other people build their businesses, I realized there was a clear and systematic way to create a customer experience. In fact, it came as a shock to me to realize that every single business went through the same process of customer experience—whether it was the smallest retailer selling trinkets on Etsy, eBay, or Amazon, or the largest company selling huge airplanes or complex highways.

The customer experiences eight phases, and they are the same no matter what the customer is buying, how they are buying it, or how long it takes to deliver a result.

Now that you understand the ticking clock that is the First 100 Days of the customer life cycle, it's time to explore the eight phases of the customer journey.

The Eight Phases
of the Customer Experience

The eight phase model takes customers from the first interaction to the point where they are raving fans. Every customer has the *potential* to travel through all eight phases, yet most businesses fail to guide the customer all the way through to the end. In fact, most stall out somewhere between phases 4 and 6, missing out entirely on the benefit of loyal customers and raving fans.

Each subsequent chapter of this book will dive deep into each individual phase, showcasing companies that are creating remarkable customer experiences and outlining a series of steps you can take to make your customer interactions incredible in each potential phase of the customer journey. Before that, allow me to offer an overview of the eight phases.

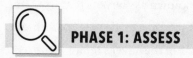 **PHASE 1: ASSESS**

In the Assess phase, the customer is deciding if they want to do business with you. They are learning what to expect from your organization and sharing (explicitly and implicitly) their expectations for the relationship. The customer is hopeful that you'll be able to help, but it's cautious optimism at best. If you don't position yourself as fulfilling their needs while wrapping them in a great customer experience, they won't choose to work with you. If you can convince them that you are the best choice, they will move forward with the purchase. This dance between the customer and the organization is what most people would refer to as "sales and marketing." The potential customer is *assessing* their options.

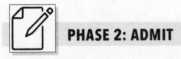 **PHASE 2: ADMIT**

The Admit phase begins when the customer admits they have a problem or a need and believe you—the company or organization—can solve it. As a result, they buy your product or sign up for your service. This is often referred to as "the sale," and sadly, in most businesses, this is where any customer-focused initiatives end. At this point, the customer is feeling joy, euphoria, and excitement that the search is over. If you fail to acknowledge this, you miss the chance to strongly associate this emotional high with your product or service. If you meet the customer's emotional state in this moment, you can prolong these positive feelings. This person transitions from prospect to customer when they *admit* that they need your product or service.

PHASE 3: AFFIRM

The Affirm phase is more commonly known as "buyer's remorse." The customer begins to doubt the decision they just made to work with you. Almost every businessperson has heard of the buyer's remorse concept, yet few businesses do anything to counter their customer's feelings of fear, doubt, and uncertainty. If you don't address these feelings, you will need to work overtime to get back to the state of joy, euphoria, and excitement the customer felt in the Admit phase. If you focus on these temporary feelings (before they become permanent), you can quickly shift the customer back to positive feelings. You must quickly *affirm* the new customer's decision to do business with you.

 ## PHASE 4: ACTIVATE

The Activate phase begins with the first major postsale interaction, when the relationship between customer and organization first materializes in a meaningful way and the business begins to deliver on the promises made during the Assess phase. The Activate phase can be marked by the receipt of a purchased product, the start of a service, or an initial kickoff meeting to get things rolling. The customer is excited to get started but somewhat anxious about whether everything will go as promised. If you don't start things off on the right foot, it will be hard to overcome that first impression. If you do start things off strongly, you can build momentum to carry you deep into the relationship. This phase's title and associated icon should prompt you to energize the relationship and propel it forward. You need to *activate* the new relationship in a significant and meaningful way.

 ## PHASE 5: ACCLIMATE

In the Acclimate phase, the customer learns about (and hopefully grows comfortable with) an organization's way of doing business. Too many businesses that have delivered their product or service dozens, hundreds, thousands, or millions of times assume that everyone in the world knows their particular process. For the customer, this is most likely the first time they've ever experienced this particular way of doing things. They are at best unsure and at worst frustrated by the lack of familiarity. If you don't properly onboard the customer and get them bought in to your approach, they will never become a long-standing, loyal customer. If you do hold their hand along the way, you can ensure a smooth transition as they embrace your approach. You must *acclimate* customers to your way of doing business.

 ## PHASE 6: ACCOMPLISH

The Accomplish phase of the customer experience occurs when the customer achieves the result they were seeking when they decided to do business with you in the first place. This may be the time they use the product and achieve the desired impact, or the time when your service delivers on the hopes they had at the beginning of the relationship. If you don't deliver, the customer's emotions can range from unsatisfied to angry. If you do deliver (and the customer agrees), they will vacillate between happy and ecstatic that everything went as planned. In order for the relationship to advance, the customer must *accomplish* their original goal.

 ## PHASE 7: ADOPT

In the Adopt phase, the customer takes ownership of the relationship, leading the charge on deepening and strengthening the bond. In this phase they proudly show their support and affinity for your brand and are thrilled to be associated with your reputation. If you don't make them feel like they're part of an exclusive tribe, receiving unique rewards and participating in a special, shared language, you will never have their complete loyalty. If they do feel compelled to embrace you, you will have a customer for life. You want the customer to *adopt* your way of operating and take an ownership stake in the relationship.

 ## PHASE 8: ADVOCATE

In the Advocate phase, the customer becomes a raving fan, zealous promoter, and eager referral engine all in one. In this phase, they develop into a built-in, unpaid, uncommissioned marketing representative, singing your praises far and wide to other potential customers who might benefit from your product or service. If you don't persuade them to promote you by making it worth their while, they will likely continue as a customer but will never help you grow the business. If they are motivated to promote you, your business will grow in unimaginable ways. The ultimate customer is one who becomes an *advocate* for your business or brand.

YES, ALL EIGHT PHASES APPLY TO YOU

All eight of these phases are the same for *every* business. They show up in the same order, regardless of the type of customer you serve, the industry you operate within, or your product or service offerings.

All customers go through the initial phases. If you help them along the way, they will continue through the process, eventually arriving at the final phase where they become advocates for you and your business.

If you don't guide them along the way, customers can get stuck in a phase, revert backward, or in the worst case, exit the journey altogether.

Depending on the type of business, the amount of time a customer stays in each specific phase differs. But the goal is always the same—keep moving your customer through the phases to *stop losing customers and make every customer a customer for life.*

THE SIX WAYS TO COMMUNICATE IN EACH PHASE

When interacting with your customers, there are six key mediums of communication that, when used together, create a comprehensive and remarkable experience: in-person, email, mail, phone, video, and presents. Each medium creates a different emotional experience. The impact on customer engagement depends on which phase the customer is in and how the medium is applied. I am not suggesting you must use each medium in each phase—only that it's possible. At the end of each subsequent chapter, I'll share suggestions and examples for incorporating each medium into that specific phase.

IN-PERSON

In-person interactions are the oldest medium of human communication. Sitting across the table from a customer, speaking to them directly, and looking them in the eyes is the most effective way to create and build rapport in a relationship. In-person interactions allow you to show your level of commitment to the customer and their importance to your business. These interactions also eliminate any of the misunderstandings that can arise in other forms of communication.

In addition, the ability to read the customer's body language in the moment lets you know whether the points you make are heard and understood. It also gives the customer the opportunity to read your body language and see your sincerity.

EMAIL

In a world where communication is 24/7, email has become the primary medium businesses use to interact with customers. Email is inexpensive and easy to track. With current technology tools, you can see when the customer reads the email, how many times they read it, and at some point in the hopefully not-too-distant future, whether they understood the content and intention behind the email.

Because email is so inexpensive as a medium, nearly every business uses it as their primary method of customer communication. Because it's so prevalent in business communications, email overwhelm is increasingly common.

Very few people are sitting in front of their computers or their phones right now, saying, "I wish I were receiving more email!" But email can still be a valuable way to interact with your customers, provided it feels personalized and purposeful.

 MAIL

With the proliferation of email, physical or direct mail (sometimes referred to as "snail mail") has almost disappeared from the scene.

As a result, the empty mailbox is now an even better place for reaching customers. Because there isn't nearly as much competition in the physical mailbox as there is in the electronic inbox, interacting with customers using this medium cuts through the noise quickly.

In an increasingly digital world, physical communication is more valuable today than ever before.[1] We've all experienced the emotional difference between receiving a handwritten thank-you note in our mailbox versus a form-filled thank-you note delivered to our inbox (or more likely, captured by a spam filter).

PHONE

The phrase "Reach out and touch someone" was coined in reference to the use of a phone as a medium of communication that was as close to "in person" as possible.

Today, not only is the average customer personally accessible via a phone, but most likely you can reach them at any given time of the day, in any location. Morning, noon, or night, 91 percent of people keep their phone less than three feet away from their body (within arm's reach) at all times.[2]

Picking up the phone and having a conversation with your customer, or sending a personalized text message, allows you to communicate in a tailored way that almost guarantees you will reach the customer immediately. Consider the impact of Dr. McCann's phone call to me the day after I had my new crown installed (discussed in chapter 2). The communication reached me immediately and allowed for a meaningful and thoughtful connection. In terms of speed of response, text messages are replied to faster than email. According to the trade association CTIA (which represents the wireless communications industry in the United States), it takes ninety minutes for the average person to respond to an email—but only ninety *seconds* for the average person to respond to a text message.[3]

VIDEO

Attached to your cellphone is a video camera that is more powerful and capable than the best video cameras on the market just twenty years ago.[4]

Customers are increasingly consuming information via video on

YouTube, Facebook Live, and other online video platforms.[5] Most businesses haven't even begun to take advantage of using video as a medium to communicate with their customers, despite the fact that Facebook CEO Mark Zuckerberg believes "[w]e're entering this new golden age of video. I wouldn't be surprised if you fast-forward five years and most of the content that people see on Facebook and are sharing on a day-to-day basis is video."[6]

Creating personalized, customized messages for customers is an opportunity most businesses overlook. The average business or business owner assumes they must first set up a video studio in the office, prepare a green screen, get the lighting just right, write a script, film the video, have it edited, add in sound and animations, and then send or post the video to a specific customer. This belief around the use of video couldn't be further from the truth.

Research shows that a handheld video, shot using the video camera on your mobile phone, with little to no script, and without much concern for the background or the setting, has a higher likelihood of not only getting through to your customer, but converting them to take the action you desire. In short, the informal video often works better than the more polished version.

PRESENT

The final communication medium, sending or giving your customer a present or gift, seems obvious, and yet it is one of the most overlooked ways to trigger positive customer emotions.

While some companies worry about rules and regulations, and considerations around gifting (which, depending on your industry and compliance rules, may be legitimate concerns), those that find creative ways to acknowledge their customers with presents build relationships and emotional connections with their customers that the other mediums don't allow.

The best presents are meaningful and personalized. They exhibit a level of care and consideration commensurate with the relationship. In fact, it's better not to send a gift if you're planning to give a standardized, "bulk" gift that feels sterile and common.

Worse yet, sometimes companies give "gifts" that aren't really gifts at all. Giving a customer a coupon for 20 percent off a future purchase is not a present *for the customer*; it's a present *for your company* that you hope will be used to increase your overall sales numbers. Giving a customer a mug with the logo of your business on the side of it is not a present for the customer; it's a free marketing tool you're hoping other people will see.

You don't have to put on a cape and become "Super Creative" to come up with gift ideas, nor do you need to break the bank. Just ask yourself what you'd get your favorite sibling or your best friend if they were your customer. If you like to call your customers "family" in your marketing materials, you should give gifts that treat them like family, instead of like cogs in your marketing machine.

Sending a personalized gift isn't nearly as hard as most people believe. For example, if you know a customer is a regular reader of business books, getting a book signed and personalized by a top author is a great way to give a thoughtful and meaningful gift that (1) costs less than $30 and (2) fosters the customer's growth and learning.

PHASES, TOOLS, AND CUSTOMERS, OH MY!

At this point, considering the various phases your customers go through and the tools you can use to enhance their experience might feel a bit daunting.

Instead, consider being open to the fact that you may not have considered these phases in the past—and now you can. You may only be using two or three of the communication tools available to you (this is the average number in use whenever I poll my audiences about their current customer experience journey) and now you have more options for interacting with your customers.

Phase	In-Person	Email	Mail	Phone	Video	Present
Assess *chapter 8*	Wealth Factory (p. 66)	Notes from the Universe (p. 71)	Corporate Executive Board (p. 57)			
Admit *chapter 9*	Build-a-Bear (p. 87) Rldemakerz (p. 92) Tony Robbins Cos. (p. 93) Maverick 1000 (p. 104) Notre Dame Glee Club (p. 100)	Tony Robbins (p. 95)	Zogics (p. 97)		Zogics (p.98)	Tony Robbins (p.94) Zogics (p.99)
Affirm *chapter 10*	CarMax (p. 126)	Book in a Box (p. 119) CD Baby (p.123) Casper Beds (p.126) Zappos (p.126) Lands' End (p.127)	Book in a Box (p. 133) CADRE (p. 120)	Book in a Box (p.120) CADRE (p.128)	Total Debt Freedom (p.114)	Book in a Box (p.121) CADRE (p.130)
Activate *chapter 11*	World Bank (p. 148)		Apple (p.141) Tech 4 Kids (p.143) 23andMe (p.145) Cornerstone Wealth (p.147)		Tech 4 Kids (p.143)	Apple (p.141) Cornerstone Wealth (p.147)
Acclimate *chapter 12*	PolicyMedical (p. 168) San Francisco CrossFit (p. 169)	PolicyMedical (p.146) San Francisco CrossFit (p.170) Acceleration Partners (p.174)	PolicyMedical (p.166)	Domino's Pizza (p.161) Delta Airlines (p.173)		PolicyMedical (p.182)
Accomplish *chapter 13*	Yoko Co (p. 198)	Online Trainer Acad. (p.191) Audible (p.195) Yoko Co (p.199)	Ongoing Operations (p.186) Online Trainer Acad. (p.190)	Baro (p. 205)		Ongoing Operations (p.186) Online Trainer Acad. (p.190)
Adopt *chapter 14*	Apple (p. 220) Harley-Davidson (p. 221) Starwood Hotels (p. 226)		Sephora (p. 216) Chicago Cubs (p. 228) Taylor Swift (p. 234)	Lady Gaga (p. 224)	Lady Gaga (p. 224)	Sephora (p. 216) dōTERRA (p. 225) Starwood Hotels (p. 225) Chicago Cubs (p. 228) Taylor Swift (p. 231)
Advocate *chapter 15*	Maverick1000 (p. 257) MastermindTalks (p. 260)	ViaCord (p. 240) 4Knines (p. 244) Dropbox (p. 251) Delta/AMEX (p. 254)	anonymous suitcase (p. 258)			Dropbox (p. 265) Delta/AMEX (p. 265) Maverick1000 (p. 265) MastermindTalks (p. 260)

Rest assured that in the remaining sections of the book I'll be presenting a step-by-step process for assessing the phase your customer is in, mapping their current experience, and enhancing their journey with a variety of tools and techniques.

Let's consider the beginning of the customer life cycle—Phase 1: Assess.

CHAPTER EIGHT

Phase 1: Assess

Overview of the Assess Phase

In the Assess phase, the customer is deciding if they want to do business with you. They learn about your organization and they share their expectations for the relationship. Most people refer to this as "sales and marketing."

THE $35,000 GOLF BALL

Before starting my company, I worked for an organization called the Corporate Executive Board that is best described as a "for-profit think tank." We researched the secrets of great organizations around the world and shared our findings and recommendations with clients (C-suite leadership) in the form of written reports, keynote presentations, and on-site workshops.

While it may not be obvious based on my title of associate director, member services, my job was really a sales position. I met with senior executives at Fortune 1000 firms and did my best to entice them to sign up for a membership in our organization. I would fly to a company's headquarters, meet with their senior executive(s) for one hour, and in that short time frame try to persuade them to spend (on average) $35,000 on an annual membership so they could have access to our findings and recommendations.

One day, I found myself meeting with a senior executive at an energy company in the southern United States. I walked into his office and was stunned by both the size and the decor. The office was huge. If I had to guess, I would say it was forty feet long and about twenty feet wide. What was even crazier was the fact that everything in the office was about . . . golf.

This senior executive did not have a little practice green in his office where he could put golf balls into coffee cups like a scene from a 1980s business movie. He had a *four-hole, mini golf course in his office*! It had everything but a windmill.

The office walls were covered in polished wood paneling and adorned with photographs from the world's top golf courses. Images from St. Andrews, Augusta, Pine Valley, Shinnecock Hills, and Royal County Down added a plush green hue to the scene, and there was a polished wood rack along the wall that housed a half dozen golf bags filled with clubs of all shapes and sizes.

When golfers die and go to heaven, but still have to work a desk job every day, they go somewhere like this office.

The executive ushered me to a seat right in front of his enormous, carved-wood desk. As we sat down, I found myself compelled to acknowledge the elephant in the room.

"So, Bobby, it seems to me you might be a fan of golf?"

The executive laughed and said, "What was your first clue?"

For the next fifty-seven minutes, we talked about nothing but golf. I am by no means a good golfer, but I've spent enough time on the links that I could ask interesting questions and show that I had a better-than-working-knowledge of the topic.

I was also lucky. The week after this meeting, I was going to be on vacation with my family (my dad and my brothers are all avid golfers), and we were headed out to California to play Pebble Beach (if you're not familiar with the game, Pebble Beach is basically nirvana for golfers). I shared the details of this trip with the executive and, to my surprise, he whispered, "Joey, I've never had the chance to play at Pebble Beach."

"Well, I'll make sure to let you know how it goes," I promised.

This shift in the conversation brought the "golf" portion of our discussion to a close. Realizing we had only three minutes left in the meeting, the executive said, "I'm sorry we spent all this time talking about golf, but I do have to end the meeting on time as I have another commitment."

I reached into my bag, removed a sample research report I'd brought along to share, and said, "No problem. What I can tell you is that when you are with us, you will be part of an exclusive club that will feel like Augusta. We will take care of you in ways you can't even begin to imagine. You will be surrounded by peers who you look up to, and admire, and can learn from. Like a pro caddy for your business, we will present you with the best research and the best knowledge to keep you in the fairway and avoid hazards now and in the future. This research is a sample of our work for you to consider—and I thank you so much for your time." I handed him the report and I left the room.

A week later, as I was walking through the Pebble Beach Lodge Gift Shop, I noticed a golf ball that not only had the logo of Pebble Beach, but also the logo of the U.S. Open. As luck would have it, that year marked the one hundredth anniversary of the famous tournament and it was going to be played at Pebble Beach in a few months.

I bought one of the golf balls, went to the hotel concierge for a piece of paper, and wrote:

Dear Bobby,

We had a glorious day playing Pebble Beach. When I saw this golf ball celebrating the 100th anniversary of the U.S. Open, I thought of you. I hope this memento is a welcomed addition to the fantastic golf paradise in your office!

Maybe someday we'll get the chance to play here together. . . .

Sincerely,

Joey

I put the folded letter and the golf ball into a FedEx Pak and had it shipped out for delivery the next day. Two days later, I was back on the golf course when my cellphone rang (a horrible display of golf etiquette, I know). I answered the phone and heard my prim and proper assistant ask in her lovely southern drawl, "What the heck did you do to Bobby?"

"Excuse me?" I replied.

"I just got a call from his assistant asking for our fax number and a contract because he wants to sign up and join our membership today!"

Quick Takeaway

It's not all about the sale. Connect with the customer and meet them where they are. Then follow through (sorry, I couldn't resist the golf reference). Going above and beyond takes only a little extra effort and creates a huge return.

THE ASSESS PHASE: CAN YOU SOLVE MY PROBLEM?

The first phase your customer experiences is *Assess*. This phase occurs *before someone becomes a customer*. In this phase, the potential customer *assesses* whether your company will be able to solve their problem or provide the product or service they desire. Sometimes the assessing happens on a gut level—customers often don't know what they want, but they feel they want *something*. The story you tell through your marketing either resonates emotionally with them or it doesn't.

What many sales and marketing teams don't realize is that prospective customers are trying to feel out how they'll be treated postsale (that is, once they surrender their money and all their leverage is gone). They know that sales teams can "talk the talk"—and they worry that the account reps down the line won't "walk the walk." Oftentimes this worry is subconscious.

My experience with the $35,000 golf ball taught me a valuable lesson about this phase:

How you make people feel about what it's going to be like to do business with you is even more important than your actual product or service.

Bobby later told me he hadn't even read the report I gave him. Because I had given him a taste of what it would be like to participate in our membership and be treated in a remarkable way, I made the sale.

The impact of the golf ball on my sales efforts is an example of the power of this stage. The prospect gets a taste of the continued experience of doing business with you, and if the taste is compelling enough, the prospect can't help but want more.

The best companies in the world take the customer experience offered *after* the sale and infuse it into marketing and sales, so the customer gets a flavor of the good things to come. This not only incentivizes prospects to sign on the dotted line, but it properly sets the expectations for what will happen after the sale.

WHETHER LONG OR SHORT, THE ASSESS PHASE ALWAYS HAPPENS

How much time a prospect spends in the Assess stage varies greatly. It can be a long, medium, or short process depending on the customer, the company, and the product or service being offered. This phase can last for days, weeks, or months—or even mere seconds.

Consider a senior-level executive who wants to hire an executive coach to learn how to get better at employee interaction. The executive has many options. They will likely research and review several top executive coaches, interview them, possibly read their books, and then decide which one they want to work with. This assessment will take weeks and possibly months.

On the other hand, what if you need peanut butter? You go to the peanut butter aisle at the grocery store, look at the dozens of brands of peanut butter, spot-check the prices, consider the jar size, review the ingredients, look at the packaging . . . and decide within a matter of seconds which one to add to your shopping cart.

The length of the Assess phase varies based not only on the size and significance of the purchase, but on the amount of thought and consideration the prospect is willing to invest. For an action the prospect considers to be low impact/low risk, the decision is usually made quickly. For an action that has ramifications on job security, impacts family stability, or involves high-dollar investment, the decision usually takes much longer.

MARKETING AND SALES OFTEN FAIL TO CONSIDER THE ASSESS PHASE *EXPERIENCE*

In a typical business, the activities associated with the Assess phase usually fall under the responsibility of the marketing and sales departments. Whether these efforts include running ads, distributing promotional materials, optimizing a website for search, or participating in a trade show, they are all a part of the customer acquisition effort that attempts to drive prospects to the ultimate decision—and in the process, make a sale.

The problem is that what happens *after* the sale is rarely addressed in any of these sales or marketing conversations.

Traditionally, the marketing department has seen its job as being twofold:

1. convince the customer there is a problem, and

2. present the company or product as the solution to that problem.

More advanced marketing departments present their service or product as the way customers can achieve their goals and desires. The sales department then takes those aspirational goals and aligns them with the product or service in an effort to persuade customers to invest their time and money to make a purchase.*

Yet there is rarely, if ever, a meaningful discussion about what kind of experience the customer can expect *after* the sale.

At best, salespeople say things like "We'll take care of you," or "We love our clients," or "You're important to us." These generic statements focus on the benefits of doing business with the company but don't address any of the aspects of *how* the organization is going to help prospects achieve their desired results. The customer is told that they are going to be taken care of, but they are never told how that will happen.

To bring the customer experience forward into discussions with a prospect, it's important to both *share* and *show*. *Share* your customer experience philosophy and detail the mechanisms you have in place to make sure you deliver a consistent, remarkable experience throughout

---

*This focus on marketing and sales is, in and of itself, not bad. It works. I don't think we need to demonize marketing and sales to elevate the importance of the customer service/customer experience roles. As a marketer and salesperson myself, I understand the importance of these two responsibilities.

the customer journey. *Show* the prospect what this looks like by treating them as if they are already a customer. Unexpected presents, extra little touches, and thoughtful gestures during the Assess phase offer an emotional preview of the experience to come.

THE SALESPERSON ISN'T THE PROBLEM—IT'S THE STRUCTURE

In most organizations, the person responsible for getting the sale is not the person responsible for delivering on the experience afterward.

The salesperson's job is to convince the prospect that doing business with the company is going to be an incredible experience, well worth the investment of dollars and time. Salespeople usually have no incentive to paint a proper picture of what life is like after the sale. The salesperson is not concerned about getting the right prospect—a person who will be a good fit and stay with the company for a long time—because they are typically incentivized by the total number of *new* accounts, not retained accounts.

This typical organizational structure creates a functional disconnect between what drives and motivates the salesperson and what makes for a successful customer experience. The salesperson has no reason to build a long-term relationship with the prospect. Once the goal (making the sale) is achieved, they pass the relationship to someone else. The salesperson usually doesn't care about whether the handoff goes smoothly.

The problem with this mentality is that the prospect believes that the information they share with the salesperson—the problems, the needs, the expectations, the requirements—is going to be seamlessly transferred to the account manager (or some similarly titled individual) after the sale is completed.

This is rarely the case.

Anyone who's ever been in sales—or purchased something in this scenario—knows the handoff is anything but smooth. The proverbial "baton" is dropped more often than not—so much so that the typical salesperson should be "disqualified" on nearly every deal!

Salespeople usually focus too much on the early stages of the process, glossing over the specific steps that come after the handoff, once the salesperson isn't leading the conversation. "You'll sign the contract, pay the initial invoice, and then be transitioned to your new account representative. After that, the representative will work with you to make sure the project runs smoothly. . . ."

This glib discussion of the process post handoff leaves most customers feeling uncertain about the relationship with the new account representative. The information captured from the prospect is seldom relayed back to the individual or the team that handles delivery, implementation, account management, or execution. Rarely does the salesperson address the emotional/personal experience the customer will have when dealing with the company after the sale.

The "feelings" associated with working together are just as important as the steps and deliverables, yet are rarely addressed. According to research by international consulting firm McKinsey, 70 percent of buying decisions are based on how the customer feels they are being treated.[1] If a salesperson fails to take the prospect's feelings into consideration, the organization will grow stagnant and die from lack of sales.

This typical organizational structure creates a functional disconnect between what drives and motivates the salesperson and what makes for a successful customer experience. This behavior is ingrained in the company's processes and procedures and in most instances leads to failed transitions.

The good news is that it's not hard to fix this problem.

The bad news is that it takes a shift in thinking and behavior within the entire organization, and specifically within marketing and sales. But don't worry. They can handle it!

PREFRAME YOUR PROSPECT

To avoid disappointment after the sale, the salesperson should "preframe" the customer experience—in other words: explain and demonstrate the look and feel of the experience after the sale, as well as set expectations for future interactions. The salesperson needs to paint a picture of what can be expected and then put the prospect at ease by detailing what will happen to make sure this image of life after the sale becomes a reality.

To preframe in a meaningful manner, have interactions during the sales process that show the prospect you've been paying attention. By making your attention to detail evident during the sales process, you send a clear message that the prospect will receive this level of focus *after* the sale.

DRINKING "BEERS" AT 9:00 A.M.

I recently attended a three-day seminar hosted by the financial advising firm Wealth Factory in Salt Lake City. The event was designed to introduce prospective clients—typically, entrepreneurs—to Wealth Factory's services and offerings. The goal of the event was to provide valuable information about managing all aspects of wealth and finances, and to position Wealth Factory as experts in the field. If the Wealth Factory team achieved their goal, they hoped attendees would sign up to work with them on an ongoing basis.

When I walked into the seminar room just before the 9:00 a.m. start time, the founder and chief wealth architect of the company, Garrett Gunderson, came up to me and said, "Joey, we're so excited to have you here with us."

"Thanks so much," I replied. "I'm excited to be here and learn more about your business."

Garrett then took the conversation to an unexpected place. "A little birdie told me that you like root beer," he said.

Someone had clearly done his homework.

I don't drink alcohol. I don't drink milk. If offered a Coke or a Pepsi, I decline both. When it comes to drinks, my typical choice is simply a glass of water. That being said, I love root beer.

In fact, I am a bit obsessed.

Garrett produced a six-pack of (very good) root beer and explained, "While we have refreshments throughout the event for everyone in attendance, we wanted to have these special ones just for you."

With a simple gesture before the event even started, Garrett made me both a fan of his and of the Wealth Factory's by extension.

Doing the "homework" to tailor the experience to your prospective clients is an incredible way to show them how much you actually care. By investigating the individual's interests, likes/dislikes, hobbies, and habits, you can easily craft a series of interactions that will light up the prospect on an emotional level.

My appreciation of Wealth Factory didn't stem from their providing me with a delicious drink, although that was a nice added bonus. I fell for Wealth Factory because they took the time to find out a little "quirk" about my personality and interests and then took action to show me they had done their homework. By giving me a root beer, Wealth Factory showed me they care about their clients.

While previewing the customer experience during the Assess phase is certainly about respecting the prospect and doing the homework, I think the more important goal is to quickly build rapport via personal and emotional connections. The fact that Garrett would do the research, procure the root beer, *and* have it ready for me at an unexpected time (9:00 a.m.?!) shows a level of dedication and focus on "the little things" that is not the usual customer experience.

Want to guess whether I'm a client of Wealth Factory's now? Yes, and a very happy one.

(In the interest of full disclosure, Wealth Factory became a client of mine as well. When we talked about systematizing prospect and client interactions, Garrett was excited. While he knew Wealth Factory did many things "right," like most exceptional business leaders, he knew there was always room for improvement.)

Too many salespeople are concerned with making the sale today and in doing so miss out on the long-term benefits of taking the time to build rapport. While it certainly requires more work and will likely take more time, the return on this investment of effort is incredible over the life cycle of the customer relationship. By helping salespeople see the benefit of moving beyond transactional relationships and implementing sales incentives that align with securing long-term customers, an organization can avoid customer turnover and instead bring in the right customers from the beginning.

Instead of concentrating on closing the next sale, the best salespeople focus on the long-term relationship—even if it means passing on an opportunity today in order to secure a deeper connection in the future. Evaluating whether a customer will truly benefit from your product or service, and sharing your recommendation with them—even if the recommendation is to *not* purchase your product or service—

helps establish trust before the relationship officially begins. Pointing the customer in the direction of a competitor's service or product that would serve them better is another way to ensure that the prospect comes back to you next time they seek a solution. These types of selfless acts prove to the prospect that you are interested in a long-term relationship as opposed to making a quick sale.

 ## Quick Takeaway

Do the homework. Investigate your prospective customers to discover ways to please and surprise them very early in the relationship. If you can find one or two key personal details, you can grab and hold the customer's attention. If your product or service isn't the right fit, make sure to let the prospect know. This level of honesty is rare and always results in the customer coming back when they need help in the future—because you've built trust, even though it came at the expense of getting a sale in the moment.

PREFRAMING WORKS INDIVIDUALLY AND ACROSS YOUR ENTIRE ENTERPRISE

Preframing works on multiple levels. This technique allows a business to go above and beyond the usual sales and marketing activities in order to make an experience memorable. By showing a prospect what to expect once they become a client, you can both set expectations effectively and hint at the good things to come.

Preframing is not about singing your own praises and telling the prospect why you're going to be a great fit for them. It's not about explaining why you have the credentials, experience, and expertise to help them solve their problem.

It's about making the experience all about the customer by show-ing them what it will be like to work with you once they decide to pur-chase your product or sign up for your service.

Some business owners begin to worry when they hear these stories.

What do we have to do to create these bespoke experiences? How do I teach my employees to do this? How much will all of this cost? How do I do this once I have more than two or three customers?

That's why I wrote this book, to teach you the answers to all of these questions.

Doing these things is much easier than you might expect. Identify-ing ways to create emotional connection with a customer can take as little as two minutes if you're willing to listen when they speak and/or spend a few minutes perusing their social media profiles.

Employees can be taught how to do this, and the first step is mod-eling the behavior by showing this level of interest and investigation into your employees' lives. It's almost impossible to expect an employee to "wow" a customer if they have never personally experienced being wowed.

That sentence bears repeating because I see it as one of the big-gest problems with customer experience initiatives today: It's almost impossible to expect an employee to "wow" a customer if they have never personally experienced being wowed.

The impact of an experience has very little to do with the cost of the experience. A single golf ball led to a five-figure consulting engage-ment. A six-pack of root beer led to a $3,000 per month ongoing retainer fee. It's not about the dollars; it's about the thoughtfulness.

Personalized communications and connections *can be system-atized and done at scale*. Certainly it requires more effort, but once the philosophy is adopted across the organization and investments are made to identify, track, and act on customer information, the effort to design remarkable experiences becomes minimal.

Stunning emotional effects can come from creating connection with your customers. When interacting with your business, the desire of your customers is actually quite simple. . . .

They want to feel special. They want to feel important. They want to matter. If you can make them feel this way, on a consistent basis, you will keep your customers for years.

THE UNIVERSE HAS A MESSAGE FOR YOU

Creating personal and emotional connections with customers doesn't need to be a "one-off" exercise where every interaction is customized at an individual level with a large investment of time, money, and effort.

There are easy ways to implement personalization and show a high level of care in your preframing, prospecting activities. At this stage in the relationship, the potential customer will happily volunteer some personal details—especially if this request for information seems innocuous. Once the prospect becomes a customer, you can use these details to personalize ongoing communications. The customer will likely forget that they shared the information during the Assess phase and will be amazed when you showcase your ability to recall their personal information.

Years ago, a friend forwarded me an inspirational email. I was so captivated by the message that I signed up to receive these daily missives.

Mike Dooley's "Notes from the Universe" started in 1998 as an email sent out weekly to 38 of Mike's friends. Since then it has grown into a daily message sent to more than 750,000 subscribers in 185 countries![2]

These email "Notes" are brief passages written to you by "The Universe." Personalized with your name and occasionally your personal goals and dreams, the Notes are designed to remind you of everything good in your life. The messages are encouraging, inspiring, thought provoking, and at times even emotion triggering.

To receive the "Notes from the Universe," an individual visits the TUT website (www.tut.com) and provides the following information:

- Name
- Email
- Country
- Nearest City
- Birthday

The site also asks you to complete the following sentences:

Goal 1: I "now" have my own _____.

(e.g., beautiful vacation home)

Goal 2: I will soon _____.

(e.g., help millions of people every day)

Once you hit Submit, from that day forward you receive an inspirational message in your inbox, a note from the Universe encouraging you to see the world a little differently and keep moving forward toward your goals.

I'm not 100 percent sure how I answered the questions when I signed up many years ago, but I do recall that at the time one of my personal goals was to someday end up on the cover of *Time* magazine, so I wrote that into the questionnaire. I didn't give it much more thought.

Day after day, I received inspirational messages from the Universe that put a spring in my step and a smile on my face. In a world where positive thoughts and feelings aren't often what one finds in an email inbox, the notes were a welcome respite from the typical business communications—encouraging and inspiring me along my journey.

About five months after subscribing, I opened my inbox to find the following message:

> Did you know, Joey, that your boldest dreams today, like a beach house and when you are on the cover of Time Magazine, will one day just be memories that make you smile, like learning to read, riding a bike, and Hula-Hooping.
>
> Dang, you're so "on it" this lifetime.
>
> Your biggest fan,
> The Universe[3]

Here we were, 129 days later, and the Universe had sent me an inspirational message specifically tied to one of my goals!

When I first read the message, joy and excitement crept over me as I thought, "Oh my gosh, the universe really does have this in store for me. This is actually going to happen someday!"

It wasn't until several hours later that I remembered *I had shared this piece of information as part of the Assess phase when I signed up to receive these emails.*

Preframing creates a stunning effect when a customer gets an emotional return later in the relationship. It makes the customer feel heard and understood, and that's exactly what happened to me with this particular Note from the Universe.

Even though *I* was the one who told them about the *Time* magazine cover, they remembered and fed that information back to me later. While it was a computer that created this personalized experience, it didn't feel that way to me.

I felt special. I felt important. I felt that I mattered.

⏱ Quick Takeaway

If you want to know about your customers, it's okay to just ask. Once they answer, you *must* use this information to make their future experience and interactions more personalized and meaningful. That means recording the information in a customer relationship management tool and then making sure to circle back to it later in the relationship.

THE PERILS OF PREFRAMING: WHEN EXPECTATION SETTING FALLS APART AFTER THE SALE

Preframing is a great tool to enhance the Assess phase and give the customer a glimpse into their future experience. However, when the expectations set in the Assess phase aren't met—whether due to the sales representative's exaggerations, their lack of policy/process knowledge, or simple oversight and failure to communicate something important to an account representative—the entire relationship is negatively affected.

You know what I'm talking about.

We've all had the experience where we explain to the salesperson *exactly* what we're looking for and they tell us the product or service is perfect to meet our desires.

But after we become a customer we realize what we told them we needed isn't part of the deal. We're hurt. We're frustrated. We're mad.

And sometimes we want to get even—launching a tirade on social media or in our conversations with friends and colleagues.

By the time we realize the early conversations were at best forgotten and at worst ignored, the salesperson from the Assess phase is no longer in the picture. Instead, we find ourselves in a conversation with a paid-by-the-hour, unhappy call center representative, trying to figure out why the promises made during the sales process aren't being fulfilled.

I experienced this firsthand recently when I lost my wedding band.

Anyone who has ever lost a wedding ring knows what a trying and sad experience this is. In addition to my wife's very understanding and nonjudgmental reaction, the small glimmer of light for me in this otherwise dark time hinged on the fact that I had purchased insurance for the wedding band.

I opted for the "show me the money" clause (my words, not theirs). It was my understanding that because I submitted an appraisal of the ring's value when I signed up for the policy, and because my policy was tied specifically to that amount, and my monthly premiums were based on that specific amount, I would *receive* that specific amount (with no depreciation—or appreciation, for that matter) in the event that I made a claim.

After spending weeks looking for my wedding band to no avail, I contacted the insurance company and made an official claim. The agent I spoke to on the phone was very polite and, after taking down the details of my loss, said, "The only other thing we need is an appraisal on the value of the ring."

I was caught off guard. "When I originally signed up for this policy about seven years ago, I submitted an appraisal from the jeweler, which should be part of the official file," I explained.

"Oh . . . I'm sorry, I'm not seeing that in our records, can you re-submit it?" the representative asked.

Ugh. Fine.

I called the jeweler who originally sold me the ring and got her to resend the original appraisal to me (thankfully, she still had it in her records). I then passed the appraisal on to the insurance agency.

The next day I received a call from the insurance agent. She quickly shared that my file had been processed and they "would like to replace the wedding band."

"That sounds great," I said. "I'd like to take the ring settlement payment for the amount it was insured for when I purchased the policy. You can just send me a check and we'll be all set."

"Okay," the agent replied. "However, the settlement will be forty-five percent of the insured value. Your appraisal was really inflated and that's not how much it would cost to replace the ring. We can either mail you a ring from our 'preferred jewelry supplier' or we can send you a check for the settlement value we're offering. It's up to you."

The sadness, frustration, and anger that I felt the day I lost the wedding band came flooding back and was now magnified by a factor of ten.

"No, no, no," I said, trying to keep calm. "When I originally signed up for this policy, I specifically requested a rider that would cover *actual appraised value*—not replacement value. I wanted to make sure that should my ring be lost, I could repurchase a ring of the same quality and craftsmanship, fashioned by the same jeweler who helped me personally design and select my wedding band. That's what we agreed upon, that's what the agent told me, and that's why I've been paying monthly premiums for seven years as an insurance policy against this very thing happening!"

"I'm sorry our salesperson misinformed you," the agent replied. "They really need to do a better job of explaining how this works."

Are you kidding me? After *seven years* of paying premiums, this is what I get when I file my very first claim?!

I won't bore you with the details of what transpired after that, but I will share that I learned two important lessons from this awful experience:

First, I immediately went out and found a new insurance agency to carry my property insurance. After seven years of paying monthly premiums, I left the first company because their behavior showed me they didn't care about me as a customer.

Second, I learned that when a salesperson fails to explain to the company what the customer wants, it can be devastating. When things go wrong, the customer is guaranteed a horrible experience.

The complete lack of handoff between the salesperson who sold me the insurance and the account manager who processed my claim was astonishing. The carefree and callous way the agent placed the blame on the salesperson for failing to explain the terms of the policy added insult to injury. Imagine the difference in my customer experience if the salesperson and the account manager communicated with each other. What if everyone on the team clearly understood my primary goal in purchasing the insurance? What story would I be telling now if the expectations I outlined in the Assess phase were actually met by the insurance company?

In this instance, the insurance company became a case study of what *not* to do, which is referenced in a book on customer experience and featured during my keynote speeches on stages around the world. I haven't shared the name of the insurance agency, but if I did, I promise you it would rhyme with Fiberty Futual.

⏱ **Quick Takeaway**

Honor the agreements you make in the Assess phase. Make sure the salesperson communicates the company's offering accurately to the customer *and* communicates the customer's desires to the company.

SUMMARY: PHASE 1—ASSESS

Creating Remarkable Customer Experiences in the Assess Phase

In the Assess phase, the prospect is considering whether or not to purchase your service and/or product offerings.

Potential assessment activities include evaluating your website, researching testimonials, considering online reviews, and reviewing your marketing materials. This period of time can vary from a few seconds (for an impulse buy at the checkout counter) to several months (for a large, multimillion-dollar software installation).

Most businesses are structured to make smooth handoffs between sales/marketing and account management almost impossible. Focusing on getting the sale isn't enough. You need to connect with the prospect, meet them where they are, and then follow through with a preview of what the experience will be like after they become a customer.

The Assess stage of the customer life cycle offers you the opportunity to preframe the prospect's expectations to be in alignment with your business operations. Not only does this offer the chance to create a remarkable experience early in the relationship, but by showing a prospect what they can expect as a customer, you set expectations while at the same time hinting at the good things to come. This helps combat any fears a customer has that your company lets customers fall through the cracks once they've handed over their money.

THE SIX WAYS TO COMMUNICATE IN THE ASSESS PHASE

Remember, you don't have to use every communication tool in each phase. Instead, just consider that it's *possible* to use each tool to create a memorable experience for a prospect during this phase.

 **IN-PERSON**

Establishing a face-to-face interaction at the beginning of the relationship can set the tone for future interactions while also giving you an early read on the prospective customer. Product demonstrations, "try before you buy" scenarios, and pitch meetings get you in front of the prospect early in the relationship and allow them to see your product or service offering in action.

Finding ways to look your prospect in the eye gives you incredible insight into their thinking, reactions, and emotional state when considering your products and services. The chance to connect, human to human, is often overlooked in an increasingly digital world—making any effort to create in-person connections that much more impactful and rare.

CHAPTER EXAMPLE: An in-person seminar (Wealth Factory) gives prospects the opportunity to assess the expertise of the team and the overall customer experience before signing up for the program.

 EMAIL

An educational email sent to prospects helps them learn more about your product or service offering by focusing on the educational aspects of your brand as opposed to just sales. In addition, email communications give you the opportunity to begin a dialogue with potential customers, which allows you to answer questions in advance and help them evaluate their options.

Taking care to gather any information the prospect shares during the exchanges gives you the chance to reflect that information back to the individual after the sale and prove that you were listening.

CHAPTER EXAMPLE: Properly designed intake questions (Notes from the Universe) offer the chance for a "wow" interaction in the future when the organization shares that personal information back with the customer.

 MAIL

Free educational newsletters and postcards can be sent to prospects to help them during their evaluation process. In the Assess phase, these mailings should focus on education as opposed to the typical hard sales pitch.

Free samples (where appropriate) allow the prospect to sample your offerings, reducing the risks associated with purchasing. The ability to customize mail pieces to the individual recipient further emphasizes a level of personal care and consideration.

CHAPTER EXAMPLE: The arrival of an unexpected FedEx package (Corporate Executive Board) gains immediate attention and emphasizes the level of care and attention to detail that is to come when joining a for-profit think tank's membership.

PHONE

Phone validation assists prospects in assessing your brand in a number of ways. By offering "call me now" features and free "ask the expert" call-in sessions, prospects can have questions answered directly by trained customer service members as opposed to salespeople.

Recording any concerns raised during these calls in the customer's record or file, as well as the answer provided in response, avoids future conflict by ensuring that expectations set during the sales process align with the experience delivered after the sale.

Educational teleseminars or recordings provide another way for prospects to sample your work, learn more about your offerings, and assess whether you will meet their needs.

VIDEO

Video brings a brand to life during the Assess phase of the customer life cycle. Short educational videos explaining your product and service offerings will answer prospects' questions and address any objections.

Videos can preframe the experience prospects can expect once they become customers. By "showing" the prospect what it will be like to work with you, videos give the customer a clear and specific understanding of future interactions.

Video communications can allow prospects to "meet the rest of the team" early on in the process—instead of just interacting with the salesperson.

PRESENT

Most prospects don't expect a free gift or present, which is why using this communication tool is often such a huge hit in the Assess phase.

When thinking about a present, go beyond the usual "free sample" of your product. While that is certainly an option, it doesn't usually feel like a present. To get around this hurdle, product and service businesses alike can offer associated gifts by partnering with similar or associated businesses. That way, the gift doesn't feel self-serving and yet is still relevant to the prospect's current wants and needs. A personalized gift will have a much greater impact on the prospect's experience and shows a level of commitment to the relationship right from the start.

CHAPTER EXAMPLE: Surprising your customers with gifts that demonstrate you did your homework in advance (Wealth Factory), or paid attention in an early conversation (Corporate Executive Board), helps to create a long-term fan before they even have the chance to sample the business's offerings.

YOUR ASSIGNMENT: PUT THESE IDEAS TO WORK

At the end of each chapter, I encourage you to immediately put what you learned and the ideas you had to work by answering a series of questions designed to get you thinking about how to use each tool to enhance the experience in this phase of the customer journey. You'll be tempted to skim them and move on to the next chapter, but to receive the greatest return on the investment you just made in reading the chapter, please take fifteen minutes to write answers in response to this series of questions. Don't worry—despite what you may have learned growing up, it's okay to write in this book!

Evaluating the Current Situation

Answer each question, then write two or three sentences explaining your answer. For bonus points, write down any ideas you have for changes that would make your answers "better."

- When prospects review your marketing materials, do they get a good idea of what their experience is going to be like if they become customers (not what they will receive from doing business with you, but how they will *feel* when doing business with you)?

- How long does the typical prospect assess your product or service before becoming a customer?

- Does your sales team effectively and accurately record customer desires and needs?

- Does your sales team effectively and accurately share customer desires and needs with the individual(s) responsible for maintaining the relationship once the sale is made?

- Do prospects receive a detailed and accurate preview of what the experience will be like after becoming a customer?

- Do you preframe the prospect's expectations to be in alignment with your business operations?

- Do you create remarkable experiences during the Assess phase?

- If so, what are they?

- On a scale of 1 to 10, where 1 is "pathetic" and 10 is "world class," how would you rate the experience your prospects currently have in the Assess phase?

Tools to Enhance the Future Experience

Answer each question by coming up with two or three ideas for using the specific tool to enhance the customer experience. For now, don't worry about how much it will cost, who will do it, or how to get it implemented in your organization. Dream big and be creative without limiting your options!

- How can you use in-person interactions during this phase to give a prospect a taste of what it will be like to interact with you after they become a customer?

- How can you make your emails more informative and informational— instead of being filled with marketing and sales speak?

- How can a customized mail piece stand out and get the prospect thinking about you in an unexpected way?

- How can phone conversations augment the sales process by introducing prospects to people in your company *other than* the salesperson?

- How can videos create personal and emotional connections between a prospect and the rest of your team?

- What present(s) could you give prospects that would really wow them?

Pick One Now

If you've answered the questions above (I hope you're not just reading along—seriously, slow down and answer the questions!), you have a clear understanding of the prospect experience during the Assess phase, as well as many ideas for how to make that experience better. Taking that into account, consider the following questions.

- What is one thing you can start doing tomorrow to make the experience your customers have in the Assess phase even better?

- Who would you need to talk to in order to make this happen?

- How would you know if you've succeeded in making this improvement?

- How would you measure the impact of the improvement on the overall prospect experience?

- How would you share this impact with the rest of the company?

FROM ASSESS TO ADMIT

Now that you have a clear understanding of what your prospect experiences in the Assess phase, let's consider what happens when they admit that they have a problem and think you can help.

Phase 2: Admit

📝 Overview of the Admit Phase

The Admit phase begins when the customer admits they have a problem or a need and believes your company or organization can solve it. As a result, they decide to buy your product or service.

WELCOME NEW CUSTOMERS BY STUFFING THE OPENING INTERACTION WITH EXPERIENCE

Having traveled to more than forty-eight countries around the world and interacted with people from every race, religion, creed, socioeconomic standing, and walk of life imaginable, I have come to realize an enduring truth:

Kids love stuffed animals.

Present any child under the age of four (and often "older" children as well) with a stuffed animal and they immediately want to hug it, hold it, play with it, dress it up, and give it a name.

You can witness this almost any Saturday afternoon by heading to a Build-A-Bear store.

If you've never visited one of their stores, Build-A-Bear is a retail operation that allows customers to build their own stuffed animal. The child selects almost everything about the teddy bear, including the kind of animal, the texture and color of the fur, the density of the filling, and the outfit the animal will wear once it's made. After navigating through the options where the child takes a hands-on role in the assembly, everything is sewn together, but not before the child places a little heart inside the animal with (for a small upcharge) a recorded, personalized message. This hands-on opportunity to create a stuffed animal is both rare (most toys today are preassembled purchases) and nostalgic (grandparents in the store likely remember sewing stuffed animals when they were little) and thus disrupted the toy industry by offering a single-category store with a participatory/creator format.

Once the bear is put together, the salesperson behind the counter presents the child with a personalized birth certificate for the stuffed animal. The certificate shows the date the stuffed animal was "born" and the name given by the child during the creation process.

The sales clerk then proudly announces to the store the "birth" and "adoption" of this new stuffed animal by the child.

By creating a milestone to celebrate the moment the child became the proud owner of this bear, and by providing a physical, tangible artifact (the birth certificate) to memorialize the moment, the child feels that Build-A-Bear is as excited about the new stuffed animal as the child is. The child playing a role in the selection and assembly creates a sense of pride and ownership in the "product." This commitment and buy-in extends the feeling of euphoria from the moment the child walks into the store to the moment they arrive home to play with their new toy.

Quick Takeaway

Co-creating an experience establishes buy-in quickly. Memorializing the moment with a physical memento of the new partnership ensures that the new customer won't soon forget the decision to work with you.

THE ADMIT PHASE: WHEN THE CUSTOMER RAISES
A HAND AND SAYS, "YOU CAN HELP ME"

The Admit phase starts when the customer signs on the dotted line, clicks Buy on the website, or pays for the service or product. The customer admits to themselves and to the business that they have a problem or a need and they believe the business's product or service offering can help solve the problem or fulfill the desire.

In most businesses, this phase can be identified by the exchange of money from the prospect to the company. Most businesses believe this is when the customer experience officially begins, when in reality, it started back in the Assess phase.

Once the sale is official, the customer transitions to a new emotional state. They transition from "skeptical" to "excited." They believe this new product or service will be the answer to their prayers and they are eager for the future.

At this moment of decision, a physiological reaction takes place in the body.[1] Brain science shows that when a prospect is moving from a state of assessment to making a decision, a chemical is excreted in the brain. Dopamine floods the gray matter, creating an emotional euphoria. The newly minted "customer" feels excitement and joy because the search is over. They believe they have found what they were looking for and are fully committed to the decision. It is a natural human state to seek congruence with the decisions we make. Feeling good about a decision is a way to convince ourselves we made the right choice; the fact that the brain assists this process with a healthy dose of dopamine is an added bonus.[2]

During this euphoric state, a customer is filled with hope and possibility about the new things that await. They are excited not only about the purchase, but also about the budding new relationship with the company that created the product or service offering.

I like to think of this state as the "new customer feeling." Similar to the smell of a new car, it triggers a feeling of excitement and enthusiasm about the purchase.

At this point the company, and specifically the salesperson who worked with the prospect, is excited as well. The courting process inherent in the Assess phase has reached its primary goal—the prospect has become a customer. In most organizations, the job of sales is now over.

In the typical business, the Admit phase is marked internally with celebrations. Bells are rung, high-fives are given, and rounds of applause honor the individual who closed the deal. The salesperson moves up the leaderboard and maybe even qualifies for the week-long trip to Napa! Everyone is excited, and the feelings the company employees have at this specific time match the feelings the customer is experiencing—at least for the moment.

While the business continues to enjoy the success of landing a new customer, the customer's physiological state starts to change. As the dopamine slowly recedes, the customer slips into a state of fear, uncertainty, and doubt. This will be discussed in much greater detail in the next chapter, *Phase 3: Affirm*.

To help associate the customer's excitement with the company's excitement, it is important to join the customer in celebrating the milestone inherent in the Admit phase. Similar to Build-A-Bear's announcement to the rest of the store, this shared emotional state is worthy of a shared experience.

Typically, the celebrations around landing a new customer are held in private, within the company. It is the rare company

Most businesses don't do anything to *join* the customer in these feelings of joy and euphoria.

that reaches out to a new customer to share in the excitement of the "admit" decision.

If there is a shared celebration, it's usually a single communication from the salesperson. Ironically enough, this can leave the new customer feeling even worse. While the salesperson shares in the excitement with the customer, the customer recognizes the salesperson's excitement may not be in alignment with their own. It's only natural for the customer to think, "Of course the salesperson is happy, they just took my money!" The customer knows the salesperson is excited about the sale and imagines the salesperson earned a commission and met a sales quota. The customer worries that their new "friend" is most likely unconcerned with and unmoved by the customer's own emotional state.

Most companies miss a golden opportunity in the Admit phase to honor the shared excitement and capitalize on the customer's emotional peak by matching or echoing the euphoria.

LADIES AND GENTLEMEN, START YOUR ENGINES!

For some reason, toy companies are better at honoring the Admit phase than nearly any other industry. The shared joy between the company and the child receiving the toy is easily marked and capitalized on by several companies operating in the industry.

Not too long ago, I visited Downtown Disney, an outdoor shopping center located at the Disneyland Resort in Anaheim, California, that caters to children and those who promise to never fully grow up.

I fit in just perfectly!

While chasing my nieces, nephews, and sons down the pedestrian mall, I spotted an eye-catching store completely new to me. I later discovered this store won the award for "Best Attraction Retailing" in 2008 in the Retail Store of the Year awards.[3]

Ridemakerz is a toy car heaven. Targeting the child (or the child at heart) whose eyes light up at the thought of a custom-built toy race car, the store lets the child (or "customizer" as they are called within the store) pick a chassis and decide on a custom body type.

From there, the child can choose from a variety of tires, rims, decals (including flames and racing stripes), spoilers, and even sound chips that mimic different types of engines. Ridemakerz estimates that more than 649 million different combinations are possible when customizing a "ride."

Once all the options are selected, the child joins a member of the Ridemakerz sales team (known as the "pit crew") at the assembly station. Here the child uses a real drill (with supervision, of course) to bolt the wheels and the body to the chassis, affix the spoilers, add any accessories to the vehicle, and insert the engine-sound microchip. For a small additional fee, the car can be programmed to refer to the child by name.

After the car is built, a member of the pit crew holds the race car above their head and announces in a booming voice to the store that the child (who is called by name) has just become the proud driver of this new vehicle. The pit crew member calls for a round of applause from the other patrons in the store to celebrate this occasion.

Ridemakerz aligns the emotional experience of the new customer with the emotional reaction of the organization, sending a message to everyone within earshot that this is a moment to be celebrated. Not only do they create a shared emotional experience with the child, but they also give a gentle nudge to other prospects in the store that, should they decide to purchase a vehicle, this celebration is available to them as well.

Creating a meaningful experience in the Admit phase is not limited to toy companies. Any business can create an experience associated with this important phase to make sure the relationship starts off on a positive note. The shared celebration is even more powerful when the company creates a memento to memorialize the experience.

 Quick Takeaway

Announcing the new partnership between the company and the customer shares the good news with the rest of the world. Celebrating and congratulating the customer with excitement elevates the interaction to an emotional high.

GET YOUR PICTURE WITH A CELEBRITY—FOR JUST $15,000!

While a company can ride the emotional high inherent in the product the customer purchases (as with Build-A-Bear and Ridemakerz), another option for creating connection is to design experiences that are ancillary to the purchase—but still emotionally satisfying to the newly minted customer.

Peak performance coach and internationally renowned speaker Tony Robbins hosts a quarterly event called "Unleashing the Power Within." This event introduces audiences to Tony's teachings and methodologies over the course of a three-and-a-half-day rock concert–esque spectacle. By the third day, the participants have "fire walked" across red-hot coals, Tony and his team have established credibility, and the event has delivered a great deal of personal development guidance and value. Then Tony's team tells the audience about the Mastery University program.

Mastery University allows students to continue their learning and their experience with Tony by attending three live events over the course of the following year that focus on health (Life Mastery), finances (Wealth Mastery), and designing the life they desire (Date with Destiny). With the "pay today" tuition priced at $15,000, the decision to join the program is not a small one.

As part of the pitch to join Mastery University, prospective participants are offered a bonus for signing up before they leave the event. In addition to a reduced fee, if an attendee registers for Mastery University, they get the chance to have their picture taken with Tony as a thank-you for enrolling in the program.

After spending countless hours (Tony's events are known for starting early in the morning and running into the wee hours of the night) watching Tony command the stage in front of thousands of cheering fans, the typical audience member is eager to get a photo with this leader who, in many cases, is now their newfound hero.

The number of people who jump to take advantage of this offer—and the accompanying memento—is impressive. Hundreds of people at each event rush to the back of the room to sign up for Mastery University. Given the emotional high of the event, it would be easy to assume that this euphoria creates the interest in the program. While the emotions certainly play a role, it's important not to overlook the smart engineering of the customer experience that prompts an on-the-spot $15,000 purchase.

After completing the purchase, audience members are given a receipt that allows them to go onstage with the other new enrollees to get a picture with Tony. The chance to do this in front of thousands of people not only adds a level of excitement to the experience (the audience cheers for the new enrollees), but results in a significant amount of FOMO (fear of missing out) for audience members who are undecided. More often than not, this ends up tipping the decision process as prospects view the spectacle and then rush to sign up. Strategically, the sign-up period stays open long enough for the audience to fully witness the photo sessions with new enrollees.

The photo session certainly requires an investment of time, money, and effort from the Mastery University team, but that investment pales in comparison to the priceless gift the new enrollees receive. The photo is a unique and special present that only Tony can give. The value to the recipient is much greater than the cost incurred by the organization.

Not long after the event, the company emails the photo to the newly enrolled student as a visual marker of the student's commitment to the Mastery University program and the time they stood onstage with this well-known speaker, coach, and businessman.

Creating a physical memento during the Admit stage not only marks the milestone that occurred in this phase, but when structured like the photo offer described above, gives a legitimate reason for ongoing and additional communication from the company after the sales transaction is completed. This physical artifact of the decision process reminds the customer of the choice they made and reinforces the wisdom of that choice.

Quick Takeaway

Celebrating milestones, sharing physical mementos, and providing the illusion of joining an exclusive club combine to elicit powerful feelings of inclusion and collaboration. Doing this publicly in front of thousands of people magnifies the emotions. Consider what you are uniquely qualified to offer your customers to mark the significance of reaching this milestone.

I BET YOU $100 YOU WILL CLICK ON
THE LINK AND WATCH THIS

Anyone who visits a gym knows the uncomfortable yet familiar feeling of approaching a workout machine only to find it drenched in sweat.

This problem served as the genesis for Paul LeBlanc to create single-use disinfecting gym wipes and, while he was at it, to found Zogics™ (pronounced "Zah-gics"—think "logics" with a Z) in 2007. Based in the Berkshire Mountains of Massachusetts, Zogics is one of the wellness industry's largest one-stop shops for fitness professionals. The company offers a comprehensive catalog of thousands of products and hundreds of brands. Serving more than twenty thousand gyms worldwide, Zogics isn't just famous for its fitness products.

Over the last decade, Zogics also built a reputation for stellar service. "We're super passionate about making our customers happy," explained Paul. "Everything we do is with our customers in mind." Zogics's commitment to remarkable customer experiences begins with the first interaction. When new customers go online and make a purchase on the Zogics website, they immediately receive a playful confirmation email outlining the items they purchased and setting the expectation for when those items will arrive. By incorporating enthusiasm and friendliness, Zogics gives customers a taste of its company culture without expending much effort or money. But things really get interesting when, several hours later, at the end of the day, the new customer receives the following email (see image on next page).

The most interesting aspect of this message is the thumbnail screenshot of the Zogics employee holding a clipboard that says "Thank you, Daniel!" The fact that the thumbnail for this video includes an image proving the personalization of the message results in a very high click-through rate for email recipients watching the video. Prior to sending the email showing the personalized thumbnail image, approximately 20 percent of new customers opened the confirmation email. Now more than 60 percent of new customers open the email—a 3X improvement in open rates. The number of customers who watched the video in the original formatting was 4.5 percent. Since adding the personalized thumbnail, that watch rate shot up to 20.7 percent—a 5X improvement![4] To have a video watch rate of 20.7 percent this early in the customer relationship is unheard of in any industry, let alone first-time e-commerce purchasers where click-through rates (let alone watch rates) range between 1.33 and 5.13 percent depending on the product being purchased.[5]

As if the click/play rate weren't reason enough to incorporate video confirmation messages, these videos take *less than one minute to create.*

Zogics doesn't overscript or overproduce the videos. It empowers its employees to focus on a high-energy video instead of worrying about high production value.

When the new customer elects to play the video, a browser window launches and takes them to a personalized YouTube page (see sample here: http://bit.ly/2yx1zME). The video starts playing as follows:

> *Hi Daniel! Laura from Zogics here . . .*
>
> *I just wanted to take a minute to thank you for your order and let you know we're here to help with anything that you may need.*
>
> *We love to see our products in action so please feel free to upload a photo or video to social media using the hashtag #zogicslove.*
>
> *Thanks again for your wipe and dispenser order. We hope to hear from you soon!*

This simple yet effective thank-you message, paired with a personalized video, sets the tone for the interactions Zogics will have with this customer going forward. This commitment to customer experience continues when the package arrives and the customer finds a custom-printed cardboard shipping box decorated with playful messages.

The top of the box includes an entertaining and thought-provoking message about the "magical" shipping box (see image on next page).

On one side of the box there is a predrawn tic-tac-toe board with the first *O* already placed.

On the other side of the box is a message from Zogics that warns:

> *"Hey! USE CAUTION: Knife blade may damage contents. And while we have your attention, do NOT take the wipes out of their bags! Need more? Reorder #Z1000"*

The box design is completed by a message on the underside of the box cheekily asking, "Checkin' out my bottom?"

As if the packaging weren't engaging enough, taped to the inside of the box is a YumEarth organic lollipop. This unexpected tasty treat aligns with Zogics's commitment to health and organic products, while at the same time offering a great moment of surprise and delight for the new customer.

The fact that Zogics works to make a significant impression this early in the relationship shows how much they value and emphasize a positive Admit phase. By showing the new customer how playful they can be, Zogics sets the tone for a series of positive interactions in the future.

"The best thing about this specific focus on customer experience," observes Paul, "is the amount of fun we have doing it. My feeling as a CEO is that when these initiatives are approached almost as a game, rather than 'we must increase the customer experience to increase the profits,' the end result is much more successful and genuine."

In the end, Paul notes, "The most important thing I can do as CEO is give permission and then get out of the way and let my team create remarkable customer experiences. We often say internally that 'it's not what we sell, it's how we sell it.' To the extent we've been able to make our customer experience improvements a game, the more we've had fun, excitement, and the reward of a continually growing business. All of these efforts have translated to increased share of wallet, increased retention rates, and customers who are always talking about us on social media. We've been averaging 25 to 40 percent growth per year. I can only assume that most, if not all of this success is driven by our ability to delight our customers."

⏱ Quick Takeaway

Use playfulness, humor, and unexpected surprises (that may have nothing to do with the actual product) to make the experience remarkable. Your customers are human, and so are you. Remind them with your actions and behaviors and in the process give them a taste of your company culture.

ONCE YOU TAKE THE GREEN PILL, LIFE WILL NEVER BE THE SAME AGAIN

Capitalizing on the natural fears of missing out on a good time, international entrepreneur organization Maverick1000 has a unique ritual for welcoming new members and celebrating their decision to join the group. What's more, Maverick1000 gives customers a vocabulary to refer to their new selves, recognizing that deep down, each and every one of us wants to feel a sense of belonging.

Maverick1000 is a collective of "maverick" entrepreneurs from around the world who have joined a group focused on growth, impact, and experience. Signing up to be part of founder Yanik Silver's crew allows a Maverick1000 member to attend live events, participate in online learning, and get special invitations to once-in-a-lifetime experiences, like flying a MiG fighter jet in Russia, climbing Machu Picchu, or having a beach party on Richard Branson's private oasis, Necker Island.

As part of the Assess phase, prospective participants in the program attend a live event where they experience firsthand what it's like to be a Maverick member. During the program, they meet current members of the group who tell the prospects about the program and provide feedback to the organization on whether they think a new prospect would be a good fit for the membership.

On the final night of the live event, if a prospect has shown interest in joining the membership and the members have voted to accept this individual, the prospect transitions to become a member in an entertaining and fun-loving ritual designed (and regularly enhanced) by the Maverick members themselves.

To celebrate the Admit phase decision, a newly minted Maverick member is invited to the front of the room at the closing of the farewell dinner. Stepping onto the stage, the new member is wrapped in green industrial-sized cellophane—along with the other new members who join the group that night.

Have you ever seen someone completely wrapped in green cellophane?

It's hard to keep a straight face. . . .

After being completely wrapped, the prospective new members are asked to recite the Maverick creed. The creed is a collection of powerful statements that speak to the caliber of individuals in the group. The statements add gravity to an otherwise laughable moment. The creed assigns additional meaning to each letter in *Maverick*, as follows:

M—I am a MULTIPLIER

A—I am ABUNDANCE MINDED

V—I am a VISIONARY

E—I am EXTRAORDINARY

R—I RE-IMAGINE, RE-INVENT & RE-CREATE

I—I am IMPACTFUL

C—I CONNECT, CATALYZE & CO-CREATE

K—KISS KISS, BANG BANG! (*an inside joke*)[6]

After reciting the creed, the new member is given a green pill (the brand color of Maverick) and told that the world will never look the same way again. The ritual is reminiscent of the movie *The Matrix*, where the main character, Neo, is given the option of taking a pill that will show him how the world really works. The remaining elements of the Maverick initiation ceremony (including how the new members get out of the cellophane wrap!) are top secret, but suffice it to say it's entertaining to witness.

This ritual is the exact behavior that the kinds of entrepreneurs who enjoy Maverick look for in their lives. While it may not work in a gathering of accountants or lawyers, in a group of hard-charging, adventure-loving, travel-seeking entrepreneurs, this is the perfect way to capture the admission moment with a ritual and experience that will always be remembered.

> ## ⏱ Quick Takeaway
>
> Mark new customer entry points by creating rituals and meaning. People search for (and buy) products that promise to transform them. Give customers the overt experience of a ritual that marks a change from one state (the time before they were customers) to another (their life going forward as a customer) and you go beyond the claim of "your life will change with us" to begin showing them how.

MEMBERSHIP HAS ITS PRIVILEGES

When you make newly minted customers feel like they are part of an existing community, you build affinity early in a relationship with your company and your existing customers. The slogan "Membership Has Its Privileges," popularized by the credit card company American Express during its 1980s ad campaigns, touched on this fundamental element of human nature.

We want to feel a sense of belonging, community, and commitment.* From an early age we seek "groups" to join in all aspects of our life. Whether you joined a collection of fellow children on the playground, a group of sash-wearing Girl Scouts, a team of fellow soccer aficionados, a team of special forces commandos, or some other collection of

All human beings want to be part of a tribe.

---

*For an incredible discussion of this concept, see Sebastian Junger's *Tribe: On Homecoming and Belonging* (New York: Hachette Book Group, 2016).

like-minded individuals, the lure of the tribe/team/club was too great to deny. This trend likely increased as you got older and found yourself singing in the choir, playing in the band, registering as a member of a political party, or joining a union. Regardless of age, income, or background, the desire to be part of a tribe is irresistible.[7]

Shared experiences build a strong bond and can connect a newbie with a similarly situated veteran of the organization. This model is proven time and time again, with strong initiation rituals serving as a catalyst for community building in organizations like fraternities, sororities, and military units.

I experienced this firsthand my freshman year of college when I auditioned for the Notre Dame Glee Club. At the end of the audition process I was told to be in my dorm room the next evening at 6:00 p.m. to learn whether I would receive an invitation to join the group.

At 6:00, a sharp knock caused me to open the door. I found three ominous-looking strangers who proceeded to lead me out of the building and into a waiting car. We drove in silence for twenty minutes until we arrived behind a building in a quiet neighborhood and entered through the back door.

Once inside I was greeted by fifty or so singers belting out the Notre Dame fight song. As it turns out, we were inside an Italian family restaurant and I was officially "in" the group. From that moment on, I was accepted as a full-fledged "brother in song."

Helping your new customers feel like they already "belong" to something bigger than themselves is a wonderful way to build a relationship early on. It allows for a fast start during the Admit phase and reinforces the decision on the grounds that others have a similar problem or need that the organization is addressing.

⏱ Quick Takeaway

The sooner you can build a connection between your new customers and your current customers, the stronger those bonds will be and the longer they will last.

DON'T PEAK TOO EARLY

While creating memorable experiences for a new customer in the Admit phase is important, and matching the new customer's level of enthusiasm is a great way to build rapport, the experience a business creates at this stage shouldn't be the pinnacle of the relationship.

Depending on your product or service, you want to be careful not to *overcelebrate* too early. Just like in dating, you don't want to peak too soon. If on the first date you offer to fly your companion to Paris for a romantic dinner, you're almost certainly going to scare them off. Instead of presenting yourself as a romantic, you end up exuding an aroma of desperation.

It's just too much, too soon, too fast.

The Admit phase works in a similar way. You want to match (and maybe *slightly* exceed) the joy, euphoria, and excitement the prospect is feeling. However, you do not want to reveal all your tricks this early in the relationship.

Creating excitement to match the thrill of a child getting a new stuffed animal or a custom-built toy race car is a parallel matching of the emotional experience of both parties. Anyone who has witnessed a child receiving a new toy knows you must work overtime to match their level of enthusiasm.

In the business world, where emotions are traditionally more subdued, it can be dangerous to be overly excited this early in the relationship. A gigantic party with balloons, dancers, and a DJ to celebrate signing up for a new car insurance policy would be the wrong message to send on so many levels!

Businesses must pay attention to the circumstances surrounding the "buy decision" and should create a celebration that fits the moment and the customer. Mark the decision that occurs in the Admit phase, make a memory, and celebrate it accordingly—but don't go overboard.

SUMMARY: PHASE 2—ADMIT

Creating Remarkable Customer Experiences in the Admit Phase

The prospect enters the Admit phase of the customer journey by giving you their hard-earned money. They "admit" they have a problem that they believe you can solve, or a need they think you can fulfill.

At this point in the life cycle the customer feels a sense of **hope** and possibility for the promised results of your product and/or service offering. A chemical reaction in the brain affirms the choice with a dopamine release, producing an energy high that may or may not be perceptible to the customer who made the decision.

The Admit phase of the customer life cycle gives you the chance to capitalize on the euphoria caused by the purchase and exceed expectations the instant the new relationship begins.

SIX THINGS TO DO IN THE ADMIT PHASE STARTING TOMORROW

I'm going to cover all six communication tools again—but you don't have to use all of them. Just challenge yourself to even consider what it would be like to use each of these tools in the Admit phase and see what ideas that generates.

 IN-PERSON

In-person celebrations offer a fantastic opportunity to connect during the Admit phase. The energetic exchange of an interaction with a person who is genuinely excited about working together and thankful for the opportunity to do so starts the relationship on a positive note.

CHAPTER EXAMPLE: Whether celebrating the adoption of a stuffed animal (Build-A-Bear), showing off a customized toy race car (Ridemakerz), wrapping an unsuspecting new initiate in green cellophane (Maverick1000), taking a celebratory photograph (Tony Robbins), or "kidnapping" the newest member of your tribe (Notre Dame Glee Club), creating in-person rituals marks the significance of the decision to do business together.

@ EMAIL

An email that is personalized and signed by the entire team (as opposed to a stock thank-you) allows you to thank the customer for their purchase and for their trust. This communication reinforces the company's core values, brand voice, and overall spirit by using unique and focused language.

CHAPTER EXAMPLE: Sending a memento after the fact (Tony Robbins) transports the recipient back to the moment they made the decision to work together and the excitement they felt around the choice.

MAIL

A personalized, handwritten thank-you note sent the same day the order is placed offers yet another surprise interaction for a new customer. Because most businesses never thank new customers—let alone in writing—a mailed piece further distinguishes your brand from the competition.

CHAPTER EXAMPLE: Creative packaging adorned with playful messages (Zogics) makes receiving a purchased item an experience in itself. Showcasing your story and company culture early in the relationship begins to build rapport and affinity from the first delivery.

 **PHONE**

Individual thank-you calls within twenty-four hours of a purchase differentiate your brand from almost every business. A call offers the opportunity to acknowledge the purchase, thank the customer for their trust, and answer any additional questions they may have. A high-energy, short voicemail message creates a great touchpoint as well.

 VIDEO

A short "Welcome to Our Family" video from the team can be sent to new customers shortly after their purchase. Ideally, this video has a very homemade feel, is customized for the specific customer, and captures the gratitude for the opportunity to work together. It should also exude excitement about the relationship ahead.

CHAPTER EXAMPLE: A personalized "thank you for your order" video (Zogics), where the thumbnail image reveals the name of the individual customer, all but guarantees the new customer will watch the video and join in the celebration of the new relationship.

 **PRESENT**

An unexpected treat to start things off on the right foot is always well received. Coupons for future purchases and company-branded promotional products are not gifts—at least not for the customer. Instead, focus on a thoughtful symbol of appreciation that has a perceived value corresponding to the perceived lifetime value of the relationship.

CHAPTER EXAMPLE: Sending a photo (Tony Robbins) capturing the decision to work together serves as an ongoing reminder of the commitment to the relationship. Unexpected treats and bonuses (Zogics) bring a smile to a new customer's face.

YOUR ASSIGNMENT: PUT THESE IDEAS TO WORK

Now that you have a clear understanding of the Admit phase, answer a series of questions that are designed to get you thinking about how you can use each of the communication tools to enhance the overall experience during this phase of the customer journey.

(You did a great job answering these in the last chapter, right? Wait . . . You skipped it?! Ugh—please go back and answer them quickly, then come back here and answer these questions. Oh, I know—you plan to answer them at the end? No! Please answer them now so the learning really takes hold and you have a clear plan for implementation of each phase in the customer journey.)

Evaluating the Current Situation

Answer each question, then write two or three sentences explaining your answer. For bonus points, write down any ideas you have for changes that would make your answers "better" if you did this evaluation six months from now.

- What happens when the prospect takes action to become a customer? (Hint: This is probably when they hand over money or sign a contract to work together—or something similar to those activities.)

- Describe in detail what happens at the moment of "the sale": How long does this time period last? What does it "feel" like? What does the customer need to do to make it "official"? What do you do in this moment?

- In your current business, do you create remarkable experiences during the Admit phase?

- If so, what are they?

- On a scale of 1 to 10, where 1 is "pathetic" and 10 is "world class," how would you rate the experience your customers currently have in the Admit phase?

Tools to Enhance the Future Experience

Answer each question by coming up with two or three ideas for using the specific tool to enhance the customer experience. I've said it before, but please don't worry about how much it will cost, who will do it, or how to

*get it implemented in your organization. Keep dreaming big and being
creative with your ideas!*

- How can you use in-person interactions during this phase to get the relationship started on the right foot?

- How can you use emails to let the customer know you're excited to work with them and eager to get started?

- How can a customized mail piece memorialize this transition from prospect to customer?

- How can a phone conversation create connection with this new customer?

- How can videos draw the new customer in and mark the moment when they transitioned from prospect to customer?

- What present(s) could you give these customers to memorialize the occasion?

Pick One Now

*If you've answered the questions above (I hope you're two for two now on
completing these end-of-chapter questions), you have a clear understanding of the customer experience during the Admit phase, as well as
many ideas for how to make that experience better. Taking that into
account, consider the following questions.*

- What is one thing you can start doing tomorrow to make the experience your customers have in the Admit phase even better?

- Who would you need to talk to in order to make this happen?

- How would you know if you've succeeded in making this improvement?

- How would you measure the impact of the improvement on the overall customer experience?

- How would you share this impact with the rest of the organization?

FROM ADMIT TO AFFIRM

Now that the prospect is officially a customer and has volunteered in the Admit phase that they have a problem or need, it's time to affirm their choice to work with you.

CHAPTER TEN

Phase 3: Affirm

? | **Overview of the Affirm Phase**

After experiencing the emotional high of the Admit phase, customers move into the Affirm phase—and their emotional state can take a dramatic turn. This phase is commonly known as "buyer's remorse." The customer likely feels fear, doubt, and uncertainty about the decision they just made, and the business must take steps to assuage those feelings.

INTRODUCE "BOB" WHEN YOU PROPOSE, NOT ON THE WEDDING NIGHT

For companies that operate in both online and offline interactions, keeping customer confidence high as things shift back and forth between the two communication mediums is imperative. The Canadian company Total Debt Freedom straddles the space between online and offline interactions in a way that builds confidence in their service and clarity in their process. By placing a high value on smooth handoffs between the salesperson and the account manager, and by connecting on a personal and emotional level that recognizes the customer as a human being instead of a number (an uncommon act in the world of debt and finance), Total Debt Freedom delivers a customer experience unfamiliar in its industry.

Based in Toronto and founded in 2004, Total Debt Freedom offers three ways to help Canadians deal with their personal debt: through do-it-yourself debt settlement, debt and finance coaching, and guidance in seeking legal counsel. The team at Total Debt Freedom helps customers go from a state of stress and uncertainty to a place of financial stability and security.

Because the team at Total Debt Freedom doesn't have the opportunity for in-person interactions that other organizations might have, they created a process for easing a new customer's fears. Once a prospect expresses interest in Total Debt Freedom's services, a sales representative schedules a call with the customer. The discussion focuses on identifying and clarifying the customer's needs, wants, desires, and expectations for the relationship, while outlining the service offerings that would help the prospect achieve their goals.

Immediately after concluding a successful sales pitch call, the sales representative walks from one end of the office to the other and shoots a handheld, selfie video with the account manager who will be responsible for handling the new customer going forward.

The video conversation goes something like this:

Hey Frank!

My name is Bryce and I'm the guy that's been taking care of you the last two weeks to get you signed up for our Debt Settlement Program. I'm here with my friend Joel and he's going to be your client care representative. He's been doing this for seven years now and is going to be working with you for the next four years—or less—depending on the speed of your progress. You save your money and we'll be able to get you out of debt sooner, buddy. . . .

I know you're ready to take action on this, you're tired of living paycheck to paycheck, and you want to get out of some of the bad debt you have so you can afford that dream house you want to buy for your family in the future.

Joel—what are your digits?

(Joel then shares his office number, his cell phone number, and his personal email—all of which appear on the video screen while he's speaking. He concludes by saying that he looks forward to speaking with Frank soon and working with him to help get him out of debt.)

Now right behind us here, Frank, you can see we have our Raving Fan wall—with lots of signatures from our happy clients. Hopefully one day you'll get in here and sign the wall as well. Our goal in the coming months or years is to provide such an incredible experience for you that you're proud and eager to sign the wall.

Take care, buddy, and we'll talk to you soon!

Bye-bye.

The interactive video provides concrete evidence that the customer's concerns have been shared. This smooth handoff allows the salesperson to repeat the expectations of the new customer and personally introduce the customer to the account manager who will be in charge of the experience from then on. The level of enthusiasm and confidence expressed by both the salesperson and the account manager confirms that the customer will be well taken care of throughout the process. Before any work has even begun, the new customer's decision to work with Total Debt Freedom is affirmed, and the customer moves through any feelings of buyer's remorse very quickly.

To understand just how important this handoff is, consider a key relationship from your personal life. Imagine meeting someone and thinking, "I'd like to get to know this person better." You go on some dates, meet the friends and family, and next thing you know, you're down on one knee asking this person to enter into a long-term relationship with you. To your delight, the person agrees and you begin planning a formal celebration of your new relationship. You gather all of your friends and family, publicly profess your commitment to each other, and after the celebration head to the newlywed suite.

Imagine what would happen if you opened the door to find someone standing in the room. Imagine what would happen if you said to your new spouse, "My love, this is Bob. I know you've never met him before, but he'll be taking care of you from now on. I need to go find someone else to chase!"

No sane person would *ever* do this to their spouse, and yet this is how most businesses treat their customers. The salesperson does all the courting, makes sure the agreement is finalized, and may even celebrate the new relationship. But then the customer is handed off to account representative "Bob" after the celebration is over. Bob wasn't on any of the dates! Bob wasn't at the dinners. Bob didn't hear any of your hopes and dreams. . . . Is it any wonder that this typical handoff is so jarring to our new customers? Here's a pro tip: If you wouldn't do it in your personal life, why do you think it's acceptable to do this in your professional life?

Quick Takeaway

Most customers assume (rightfully so) that the handoff between the salesperson and the account manager will fall somewhere in between shaky and horrible. By designing your business to include a smooth handoff, you can significantly improve customer confidence. Affirming the purchase decision with a transparent, clear, and effortless transition between the salesperson and the account manager showcases extra care and attention to detail, creating a positive customer experience in the process.

IT'S ALL FUN AND GAMES UNTIL SOMEONE STARTS TO QUESTION THEIR CHOICES

Despite the fact that a new customer assesses the options, admits there is a problem or need, and then decides to make a purchase, the customer can often doubt the decision they just made. The severity of the doubt can vary dramatically, but even when a customer seems okay with their decision, subconscious feelings of doubt often remain. The same chemical that produced feelings of euphoria during the Admit phase, dopamine, recedes from the brain during this phase, triggering buyer's remorse.[1]

It's easier to empathize with customers in this phase if you understand the psychological theory of cognitive dissonance: discomfort resulting from inconsistent thoughts and behaviors. Buyer's remorse is an example of postdecision dissonance. Stressed by their purchase decision and the implications it will have for their resources, customers usually need to take responsibility for making the decision while committing to continue with this course of action.[2]

In layman's terms, the buyer has to accept that they made the decision to spend time and money on something that may not provide ongoing value, and may end up requiring a long-term commitment. Worst of all, the customer may have selected the wrong product or service from a host of competitors.

Following a purchase, the mind starts racing with questions:

Did I make the right choice?

Is this really going to help?

Is this going to be the answer to my prayers?

Was I swayed by the salesperson's silver tongue?

What if it fails to work—will I get a refund?

What if it's not everything it was promised to be?

What if my spouse hates it?

Is this thing going to make me look like an idiot?

Is this decision going to get me fired?

Uncertainty and regret eat at the new customer, which can slowly destroy any faith or confidence they have, and in turn, their faith and confidence in the company providing the product or service they purchased.

As these feelings of doubt flow over the customer, the typical company fails to acknowledge any shift in the customer's emotions. I often think of this phase as the "tumbleweed zone," where the communications from the company to the new customer are like an iconic western movie scene, with empty buildings and a lone tumbleweed blowing across the street.

Am I doing this right?

Where is everyone?

Why am I all alone in dealing with this situation?

The most important thing a business can do to counter feelings of buyer's remorse is to offer ways for a customer to reaffirm their decision as quickly as possible. By reaffirming the customer's decision through a series of positive, high-energy communications, you can counter the chemically induced feelings of doubt. Whether it's a video that reminds the customer they made the right choice or a case study affirming that your offering can solve their problem, giving evidence of your ability to deliver can serve as a counterbalance to the customer's feelings of doubt and uncertainty.

SURE I'VE HEARD OF IT, BUT WHAT DO I DO ABOUT IT?

I must confess that while my research gives me a deep familiarity with the mental and emotional anguish new customers experience in the Affirm phase, it does not mean I am immune to experiencing buyer's remorse myself.

In fact, I experienced significant buyer's remorse while writing this book.

As a busy entrepreneur and speaker, I wanted to write my book in a "different" way. I knew that sitting down in front of a blank computer screen for hours on end, pounding away on the keyboard, trying to capture the importance of creating remarkable customer experiences, would not be an efficient way for me to produce a book.

I'd already attempted to write the manuscript in a more traditional way, and after countless starts and stops, it was clear I needed a different approach.

That's when I reached out to my friend Tucker Max. He cofounded a company called Book in a Box, which created a process for writing a book in a nontraditional way. Their process has several parts, but in short, it boils down to the author doing a series of phone-based interviews. As anyone who knows me will attest, I have no problem talking for hours on end! My parents could tell you stories of their child who never stopped talking. Given that I speak professionally for a living, I do my best to live up to my Irish-Scottish grandmother's comment/

curse/admonishment that I have a "gift for the gab." Needless to say, "talking the book" seemed like a good idea.

The process is pretty straightforward. First, a professional outliner helps the would-be author create a structure and outline for the book. Then an editor uses the outline as a guide to interview the author about everything the author wants to say in the book. These conversations are then transcribed and edited into the final manuscript—complete with the author's ideas, in their words and voice.

After signing up to work with Book in a Box, I had a kickoff call with Tucker and my outliner, Mark Chait (a well-known senior editor with past experience at most of the major business book publishers), where we outlined the premise and discussed my goals. We then developed a time line for creation of the book and started to work on an outline.

The Admit phase was fantastic. Emotions were high for all parties involved, and we started to dive into the outline on the very first call. But not long after that, I started to doubt myself and I began to question my decision to write a book.

Did I really have a good enough message that could carry an entire book? Would the readers find as much value in the eight-phase process as my clients had over the last twenty years? Would I be able to explain all the nuances of the framework properly in three hundred pages? Was I going to make myself look stupid?

As these thoughts of fear, doubt, and uncertainty flooded my mind, I grew distant. I started rescheduling planned phone calls with the team, pushing them off for both real and fabricated reasons alike. I used any excuse I could think of that would allow me to delay the next step in the process.

This went on for several *months* until one night when my cellphone rang unexpectedly. The caller ID indicated it was Tucker's cellphone, and a quick mental scan of my calendar let me know this was an unexpected call. I decided to answer anyway.

Tucker got me to open up, admit that I was having feelings of remorse and regret, and assured me that the emotions I was feeling were natural for any author. He told me a story about how he felt the same way when he released his first major book, which ironically enough went on to be a *New York Times* bestseller, selling more than a million copies worldwide since its release.

Tucker helped me see that I did indeed have a book in me and that he believed it would be valuable to many people. He persuaded me to trust the process, come back into the fold, and continue the work.

That is how powerful buyer's remorse is. Even though I deeply understood the perils of the cognitive dissonance that marks the Affirm phase, even though I *teach this* to companies, I could not separate myself from these emotions when I was in that position. Oops—I'm human too.

When a business doesn't take the time to build into its system and process ways of countering feelings of fear, doubt, and uncertainty, the new customer often grows distant and eventually leaves the business altogether.

Part of the reason I am sharing this story is because the Book in a Box team are avid students of my process—so much so that Tucker was able to spot it easily when I stalled in the Affirm phase. Since then, the team has worked very hard to implement specific steps to make sure that they anticipate the emotional journey and help authors avoid falling into an emotional abyss.

First, they added a "celebration" event, right after the author signs, where they celebrate *with* the author. In addition to a set of emails from the entire publishing team congratulating the author on signing with Book in a Box, they send an "author care package," which arrives a week or so after the new client signs, and usually right before the first call. This care package contains several fun and playful items, including a handwritten note from the editor working with the author, some celebratory treats, and a bottle of champagne—with specific instructions not to crack it open until the book is launched. The arrival of this package is unexpected and reminds the author that they are in the hands of professionals who won't let the author down.

On the very first call with the author, the publisher (who is like an account representative) initiates a conversation about this exact issue. The publisher asks the author how they are feeling, what their doubts and worries are, and then listens to the author explain their feelings. The publisher then does exactly what Tucker did in his call with me. The publisher explains that these feelings are normal, helps the author understand what the emotions mean, and offers suggestions on how to work through these feelings.

Not only does the Book in a Box team initiate this conversation early in the process, they refer back to it with the author whenever the author is feeling down or uncertain.

Instead of trying to push away the anxiety, Book in a Box uses a potentially negative emotional experience to build the relationship with the author, while also building a foundation of trust in the process.

⏱ Quick Takeaway

Understand and anticipate the customer's emotional journey. One of the best ways to handle shifting emotions is to open the door for the customer to talk about it and address any concerns head-on. While having a specific conversation to check in on the customer's emotional state might not be necessary for every business, it's definitely recommended for *most* businesses—particularly when the purchase is expensive (in the customer's frame of reference). Create space for the customer to share feelings and have strategies in place for countering any negative emotions.

THE EMAIL, THE JAPANESE PACKING SPECIALIST, AND THE GOLD-LINED BOX

Not all interactions in the Affirm phase need to be high touch like the efforts of Book in a Box. It is possible to address customers' feelings of buyer's remorse at scale, and in an automated fashion.

In 1997, a musician named Derek Sivers created a website to sell his own music that soon evolved into CD Baby, Inc., an online music store specializing in the sale of CDs, vinyl records, and music downloads from independent musicians.[3] Sivers infamously listened to every CD he sold on the website—something unheard of at the time and greatly appreciated by the musicians listed on the site. This brought a personal touch to the business that served as a welcome juxtaposition to the more "corporate" feel of his competitors.

As part of the CD Baby sales process, once an order was processed on the website, the customer received an auto-generated email confirming the details of the purchase.

At this point in history, e-commerce was very novel. Shopping online was brand new and Sivers recognized the importance of countering feelings of buyer's remorse, especially in a scenario where the customer interacted with a website, not a person. His goal was to instill confidence in the buyer that a CD was going to be delivered.

The original CD Baby email looked like this:

> Your order has shipped today. Please let us know if it doesn't arrive.
>
> Thank you for your business.

Short, sweet, and to the point—this certainly worked as a confirmation message.

The email told the customer that the order had been processed, encouraged them to reach out if there was a problem, and thanked them for the purchase. However, the statement "Please let us know if it doesn't arrive" actually increased the customer's fear and uncertainty—even going so far as to hint at a pattern of CDs never arriving!

As Sivers noted in a guest post on Tim Ferriss's blog in 2012, "After a few months, that [confirmation email] felt really incongruent with my mission to make people smile. I knew I could do better."[4]

According to Sivers, he took twenty minutes and wrote "this goofy little thing":

> *Thanks for your order with CD Baby!*
>
> *Your CD has been gently taken from our CD Baby shelves with sterilized contamination-free gloves and placed onto a satin pillow.*
>
> *A team of 50 employees inspected your CD and polished it to make sure it was in the best possible condition before mailing.*
>
> *Our packing specialist from Japan lit a candle and a hush fell over the crowd as he put your CD into the finest gold-lined box that money can buy.*
>
> *We all had a wonderful celebration afterwards and the whole party marched down the street to the post office where the entire town of Portland waved "Bon Voyage!" to your package, on its way to you, in our private CD Baby jet on this day.*
>
> *I hope you had a wonderful time shopping at CD Baby.*
>
> *We sure did.*
>
> *Your picture is on our wall as "Customer of the Year."*
>
> *We're all exhausted but can't wait for you to come back to CDBABY.COM!!*
>
> *Thank you, thank you, thank you!*

The difference between the two order confirmation emails is stark. What began as a transactional communication confirming an online purchase ended up as a hysterical narrative that not only delivered the key message, but surely left the recipient smiling and laughing.

When the customer was primed to experience the throes of buyer's remorse, CD Baby came to the conversation with levity and enthusiasm that countered any feelings of doubt.

This confirmation email set the standard for the best-in-class online companies and has been copied and used as inspiration by dozens, if not hundreds, of e-commerce businesses since then.

Sivers made the decision to stop doing the "normal" thing. He knew he couldn't send a boring confirmation email, as it wasn't in align-

Make the required remarkable.

ment with his brand, vision, or voice—nor did it properly address the feelings of buyer's remorse. Sivers realized that it's difficult to be in an emotional state of fear, doubt, and uncertainty when you're smiling and laughing. He decided to adopt a philosophy that I encourage all of my clients to incorporate into their business operations: Make the required remarkable.

Every company has aspects of its business that are "required elements" of operation. Confirmation emails, out of office auto-responders, contracts, invoices, voicemail messages, and email signature lines are but some of the required elements of doing business in the modern era.

When a company makes required elements remarkable, people start talking. This is particularly true in the Affirm phase. It's difficult to be in an emotional state of fear, doubt, and uncertainty when you're smiling and laughing.

Sivers authored the new confirmation email in 1998. By 2011, searching the phrase "CD Baby jet" on Google resulted in more than 20,000 hits, each of which represented a thrilled customer raving about this unexpected touchpoint. At the time of this writing in 2017, a Google search of "CD Baby jet" produces more than 2,560,000 results, and the number continues to grow.

Quick Takeaway

The best way to counter any feelings of buyer's remorse is to confirm the purchase as quickly and accurately as possible. By providing customers with a detailed review of the elements of the purchase you reassure them that everything is proceeding according to schedule and that things are happening as they would hope and expect. Infusing confirmation messages with the brand spirit reinforces the purchase decision and carries the customer experience past the point of purchase.

DON'T WORRY—YOU CAN GET YOUR MONEY BACK!

A money-back guarantee wipes clean the customer's fear that they will lose their investment. If the decision is in fact changeable in the future, you've just eliminated two major elements of postdecision cognitive dissonance (fear of money loss and fear of ongoing commitment).

Increasingly, money-back guarantees and lifelong warranties are becoming the hallmark of reliable and trustworthy brands. Online mattress retailer Casper is "so confident you'll love your Casper" that you have one hundred nights to try it out. If you don't like it, they will come pick it up and give you a full refund.[5] As a bonus, they donate the "used" bed to a homeless shelter near you—a nice way to provide positive emotional feelings to counter your feelings of regret.

When Zappos.com first started selling shoes online, customers were often concerned that the shoes wouldn't fit. From the beginning, Zappos eliminated this fear with its comprehensive and generous return policy. If, for *any* reason, you are unsatisfied with your purchase, you may return it (in its original condition) within 365 days for a full refund—no questions asked.[6] Zappos will even pay for return shipping.

Purchasing a used car can be even more stressful than buying new because you have no idea how the car was driven or cared for by the previous owner(s). CarMax, the United States' largest used-car retailer and a Fortune 500 company, not only offers "CarMax Quality Certified" vehicles, but they come with a free vehicle history and safety recall report, as well as a 5-Day Money-Back Guarantee.[7] You can drive a car off the lot and return it for up to five days with no questions asked *and* receive a complete refund.

Is it possible to eliminate the potential for buyer's remorse permanently? If so, Lands' End has probably done it. An American clothing company that specializes in casual clothing, luggage, and home furnishings, Lands' End has an extremely liberal return policy: love it forever or get a refund. And they do mean "forever." There is *no* time limit on when you can make a return. One would think this type of offer would subject Lands' End to dishonest people who would purchase an article of clothing, wear it once, and return it for a refund (known as "wardrobing" in the industry). That's not a problem for Lands' End. "Our customers are incredibly loyal, and we have such strong relationships with our customers that our return rates are really within an industry standard," notes senior vice president of employee and customer services Kelly Ritchie. "[I]t is just not a problem."[8]

If you have a money-back guarantee or generous return policy, you will want to reiterate that to the customer in the Affirm phase. Even if they knew about this policy at the moment of purchase, reinforcing it helps to soothe any rogue feelings of fear, doubt, or uncertainty.

IT'S EVEN BETTER WHEN YOUR CUSTOMERS
SING YOUR PRAISES

The importance of counteracting buyer's remorse increases as the overall cost of your product or service increases. It's rare to feel buyer's remorse for purchasing a pack of bubble gum. The more time, money, and effort invested in a purchase, the higher the customer's self-doubt. It is almost universal to feel buyer's remorse when purchasing automobiles and houses. As the cost increases, the affirmation message can remain the same, but shifting to a new messenger can dramatically increase effectiveness.

An organization that does a stellar job of countering feelings of buyer's remorse is CADRE, a networking group based in Washington, D.C., founded by husband and wife Derek and Melanie Coburn in 2011.

In a city known for its politicians, CADRE is a unique and exclusive networking group in which members pay a monthly fee in order to attend private events designed to help them manage and run their own businesses. CADRE hosts small group trainings on specific business skills useful to any enterprise and large, membershipwide educational events featuring top business writers and speakers from around the world.

Given that membership in CADRE requires a $3,000 initiation fee, followed by a recurring $499 monthly membership fee, it is important to provide value right after the purchase is made to counter the onset of buyer's remorse. Because the trainings and educational events occur once a month, it could be weeks or even months before a new member experiences a return on investment from the membership dues. This delayed gratification only exacerbates the feelings of buyer's remorse.

To counter these emotions and provide value as quickly as possible, all new CADRE members receive a welcome call from the organization after enrolling.

Let's be honest—that's somewhat normal. Many companies make welcome calls to thank new customers for signing up.

But what is not normal is that the CADRE welcome call does not come from the founders of the business. Nor does the call come from a member of the CADRE support staff. The new customer welcome call comes from a veteran CADRE member.

Early in the company's origins, the Coburns identified a small group of enthusiastic, highly active members and turned them into the CADRE Member Welcome Committee (in full disclosure, I am an active CADRE member and a proud participant in the Welcome Committee).[9]

Immediately after joining the membership, a new CADRE member is introduced by email to a veteran member of the Welcome Committee. The veteran member welcomes the new member via email and then requests a twenty-minute telephone call to get to know the new person. During this call, the member of the Welcome Committee reinforces the multiple benefits of CADRE membership and offers to serve as a resource for any questions or concerns the new member might have.

CADRE reinforces the purchase decision in a deep and meaningful way by having a fellow customer explain to the new customer the various nuances of the membership and how to maximize one's return on investment.

By separating this welcome call from an operation of the business and making it an activity of a fellow customer, CADRE removes any skepticism the new customer might have about self-serving commentary or an overly salesy communication early in the relationship. In addition, this process quickly introduces a new member to the "tribe," fulfilling the human need to belong to a group as discussed in the previous chapter on the benefits of an admission ritual.

Any organization that can put its best customers to work promoting the business has the chance to create unique and remarkable experiences for new customers. The typical business relies on written testimonials or will identify a current customer reference as part of the sales process. By incorporating veteran customer feedback as part of the Affirm phase, a business not only stands out from the competition, but addresses the new customer's emotional state in a powerful and compelling fashion.

The new member welcome call from a veteran CADRE member plays an integral part in helping the organization maintain an incredible *90 percent retention rate* on an annualized basis over the last six years.[10] "Our Welcome Committee does more to get the relationship officially off to a great start than any other initiative we've tried," notes Derek. "Creating these initial connections allows our new members to immediately experience our people and our culture. In doing so, they feel like part of the community before ever attending an official event, which reinforces their decision and increases the likelihood they will continue to be happily paying members."

The CADRE welcome call equally benefits both participants. The new member is happy to receive the call because they will now know at least one person when attending their first event. The veteran member is happy to make the call because CADRE is all about networking and the veteran gets to know a new member who has been vetted by the Coburns as a reliable business contact.

CADRE also surprises new members by sending a stack of books written by authors who have spoken at past CADRE events. This unexpected present early in the relationship not only creates a surprise and delight moment, but it also reinforces the caliber of CADRE event speakers. In doing so, CADRE encourages new members to attend future events while subtly reinforcing the organization's commitment to its members' growth and learning. Derek observes, "We started receiving amazing thank-you messages from our members when we incorporated this touchpoint into our First 100 Days onboarding strategy."

Quick Takeaway

Turn current customers into evangelists and then use their enthusiasm to counter a new customer's feelings of buyer's remorse. Connecting them with current customers is one of the most effective ways to make new customers feel welcome and confident about their decision.

SUMMARY: PHASE 3—AFFIRM

Creating Remarkable Customer Experiences in the Affirm Phase

The Affirm stage of the customer life cycle experience begins in the minutes and hours after the purchase and lasts until the first major interaction with the purchased product or service. This phase can last minutes, hours, days, weeks, and sometimes even months.

Despite the positive emotions at the moment of purchase (Admit), things begin to deteriorate in short order. An underlying current of doubt (which the buyer may not even be aware of) starts to counter any positive feelings. The longer this buyer's remorse goes unmitigated, the faster the customer's anxiety grips their emotions. The "quiet zone" between the purchase and the delivery of the product or service further exacerbates the problem as the void in communication is filled by the customer's self-doubt.

The Affirm phase of the customer life cycle offers you the opportunity to counter the natural feelings of buyer's remorse by reinforcing the purchase decision and reaffirming the elements of the offering that initially contributed to the customer's buying decision.

SIX THINGS TO DO IN THE AFFIRM PHASE STARTING TOMORROW

It's important to remember that you don't need to use every communication tool in each phase. Just consider the possibilities of using the different tools to create memorable experiences for the new customer during this phase.

 IN-PERSON

Often the mere presence of a representative from the company can assuage buyer's remorse. Just knowing that someone at the organization cares and is focused on a new customer can provide a level of reassurance that will carry the customer into the next phase feeling good about their purchase.

CHAPTER EXAMPLE: Salespeople who reiterate your generous return policy to customers (CarMax) help remove any fears or doubts about an investment because the customer knows they can change their mind about the purchase in the future.

 EMAIL

A "breaking news" third-party testimonial or case study offers validation of the purchase decision. When paired with a message noting the customer's "wise choice," this email can help mitigate feelings of buyer's remorse. Confirmation emails also help to affirm a purchase decision and give a customer confidence that the order is being processed.

CHAPTER EXAMPLE: A well-written confirmation email (CD Baby) that captures the brand spirit and makes the recipient smile or laugh can calm the customer's nerves and give them confidence the purchase is proceeding as planned. A message of excitement from the team to the customer (Book in a Box) reinforces the enthusiasm for working together. Reiterating money-back guarantees (Casper), no questions asked, free returns (Zappos), and lifelong warranties (Lands' End) reminds customers that they needn't suffer from buyer's remorse because they can always get their money back.

 MAIL

A mailed case study of a similarly situated customer, combined with a personalized note, can show a new customer what is possible now that they are working with your organization. The additional message of "We hope to have even better results with you" can further reinforce the team's excitement about working with the new customer.

CHAPTER EXAMPLE: A "care package" (Book in a Box) sets a tone for the relationship, reaffirms the commitment to personal attention, and exhibits a sense of professionalism that instills confidence in a new customer. A box of books from well-regarded experts (CADRE) cements the brand positioning and core values of an organization dedicated to growth and learning.

 PHONE

A call from a senior member of the management team affirms the purchase decision by delivering a "You made the right choice" confirmation paired with a "We care about you at the highest level" sentiment.

CHAPTER EXAMPLE: A call from a veteran customer (CADRE) invites the new customer into "the family" and begins to foster interactions between existing customers and new customers that will strengthen and increase the overall value of the tribe. A call from the owner (Book in a Box) helps keep projects moving forward when they are at risk of ending.

 VIDEO

A brief "Keep the Faith" video can be emailed to new customers between the time they place their order and when the order is "received" or the service is first delivered. Giving customers visual confirmation of the business's enthusiasm for the new relationship is a great way to reassure them about the decision to do business with you.

CHAPTER EXAMPLE: Personalized and customized handoff videos (Total Debt Freedom) reaffirm the purchase decision and allow the organization to subtly reference some of the key benefits and rationales the customer cited during the sales process to justify or explain why the customer needed this specific product or service.

 **PRESENT**

By offering a free, unexpected upgrade (faster shipping, free samples, preview of product before release, etc.), you can begin to overdeliver on the customer's expectations.

CHAPTER EXAMPLE: Unexpected gifts and surprises (Book in a Box and CADRE) create a feeling of joy and delight in a time otherwise marked by fear and uncertainty. This type of bonus is easily factored into the business operations as a pass-through expense without significant bottom-line impact, and yet the perceived value to the customer is tremendous.

YOUR ASSIGNMENT: PUT THESE IDEAS TO WORK

Now that you have a clear understanding of the Affirm phase, answer a series of questions that are designed to get you thinking about how you can use each of the communication tools to enhance the overall experience during this phase of the customer journey.

(By now you might be thinking, "I'll just skip this part and go to the next chapter." Please don't! I really want the learning to sink in and to set you up for success when it comes to implementing what you've learned.)

Evaluating the Current Situation

Answer each question, then write two or three sentences explaining your answer. For bonus points, write down any ideas you have for changes that would make your answers "better" if you did this evaluation six months from now.

- What happens during the "quiet period" between the customer's making a purchase or signing up for your service and your first major interaction? (Hint: Don't worry if the answer is "Actually, nothing." That's what happens in the average business. Yay, you're average! But not for long . . .)

- Describe in detail what happens between the sale and the first interaction. How long does this time period last? What does it "feel" like? What is the customer really thinking during this time? What are you doing during this time?

- In your current business, do you create remarkable experiences during the Affirm phase?

- If so, what are they?

- On a scale of 1 to 10, where 1 is "pathetic" and 10 is "world class," how would you rate the experience your customers currently have in the Affirm phase? (If you don't do anything, the answer you're looking for is "1.")

Tools to Enhance the Future Experience

Answer each question by coming up with two or three ideas for using the specific tool to enhance the customer experience. I've said it before, but please don't worry about how much it will cost, who will do it, or how to get it implemented in your organization. Keep dreaming big and being creative with your ideas!

- How can you use in-person interactions during this phase to make the customer feel confident about the decision to give you their hard-earned money?

- How can you use emails to let the customer know you're working behind the scenes and that they are going to see something very soon?

- How can a customized mail piece take a customer from a place of fear, doubt, and uncertainty to a feeling of calm, cool, and collected—knowing that they took the right action?

- How can a phone contact make the new customer feel that they are being taken care of and that you are excited about their business?

- How can videos offer assurance that the customer is going to get what they hoped for when making the purchase?

- What present(s) could you give these customers that would surprise and delight them?

Pick One Now

If you've answered the questions above (and I hope you're three for three now on completing these end-of-chapter questions), you have a clear understanding of the customer experience during the Affirm phase, as well as many ideas for how to make that experience better. Taking that into account, consider the following questions.

- What is one thing you can start doing tomorrow to make the experience your customers have in the Affirm phase even better?

- Who would you need to talk to in order to make this happen?

- How would you know if you've succeeded in making this improvement?

- How would you measure the improvement of the overall customer experience?

- How would you share this impact with the rest of the organization?

FROM AFFIRM TO ACTIVATE

Now that the customer's decision has been supported in the Affirm phase, the time has come to energize the relationship and start things off with a bang! Creating a remarkable experience and spectacle activates the relationship in an energizing, memorable way.

CHAPTER ELEVEN

Phase 4: Activate

⚡ Overview of the Activate Phase

The Activate phase begins with the first major postsale interaction with the product or service. The business must energize the relationship and propel it forward with an official "kickoff" of the relationship. The business also begins to deliver on the promises made during the Assess phase.

THE LASER X-10 SUPER BLASTER

Imagine it's early Christmas morning, or the first night of Hanukkah, or any similar holiday that finds children eagerly anticipating their gifts. You're six years old. You race into the room to find a large, wrapped package with your name on it. You rip off the paper, pull the box apart, and triumphantly raise the Laser X-10 Super Blaster above your head. You've wanted it for months and your imagination fills with thoughts of battling aliens!

You pull the trigger . . . and nothing happens.

There are no flashing lights. Only silence instead of the laser shooting sound. All of your excitement and anticipation is dashed.

No batteries included.

Because you have to wait for batteries, playtime is postponed. The delayed gratification has a crushing effect on your overall opinion of the value of this toy. Your excitement about the Laser X-10 Super Blaster wanes, even if someone eventually finds some spare batteries. If the batteries aren't found, it's even worse.

This situation isn't fundamentally different for adults. Missing out on the opportunity to impress customers at the moment when they have first contact with your product or service can be devastating.

THE POWER OF THE FIRST IMPRESSION

In the Activate phase, the business activates the customer's emotions at the first major moment of truth: delivery.

Although there are phases that come before activation, this milestone is often seen as the first real interaction after the sale. The importance of creating a remarkable moment cannot be overstated.

That first moment is when the customer receives the product they purchased, experiences the service they signed up for, or participates in the kickoff meeting that begins the project.

Activation by the very nature of the word implies a sense of energy, enthusiasm, and excitement. These emotions should be implicit in the interactions during this phase. With buyer's remorse successfully kept at bay, this moment is the opportunity for the brand or company to impress the customer with its performance. In the beginning, interactions with the prospect and customer were all about the company making promises and foreshadowing the experience and results. Now it's time to actually *do* something—not just talk about it.

But don't just deliver your product or service like a dead fish you can't wait to get out of your sight. Deliver it in an engaging and memorable way. The customer reaction upon delivery should be like the reaction at the theater when the curtain rises: an audible gasp followed by spontaneous applause.

Many organizations *do* pay attention to this phase; however, few fully capitalize on the opportunity to start things off with an incredible first impression. Maybe your company made some good impressions in the sales process, but this is the first true impression of the product or service.[1] It promises to be a lasting one—so you should make it count.

If the initial interactions are negative, a company will find itself playing catch-up. The organization will be digging out of a hole for the remainder of the relationship because the customer's excitement is dampened and he's shifted back into the emotions associated with the Affirm phase: fear, doubt, and uncertainty.

LET THEM PLAY AS QUICKLY AS POSSIBLE

Apple knows the importance of immediate gratification. In 2001, the introduction of the iPod was a revolutionary moment in the world of technology and music. Prior to this, no one had even considered the possibility of having access to their entire musical library everywhere they went, and Apple offered just that.

But Steve Jobs went even further. He demanded that Apple ship the iPod precharged so the new customer would immediately experience the joy of using it.

Tony Fadell, one of the original designers of the iPod, described the origins of the precharged iPod in his TED talk "The First Secret of Great Design Is . . . ."[2]

> Steve noticed that [almost every new product needed to be charged before you could use it] and he said, "We're not going to let that happen to our product."
>
> So what did we do?
>
> Typically, when you have a product that has a hard drive in it, you run it for about thirty minutes in the factory to make sure

that hard drive's going to be working years later for the customer after they pull it out of the box.

We ran that product for over two hours. Why? Well, first off, we could make a higher-quality product, be [sic] easy to test, and make sure it was great for the customer.

But most importantly, the battery came fully charged right out of the box, ready to use. So that customer, with all that exhilaration, could just start using the product. It was great, and it worked. People liked it.

Today, almost every product that you get that's battery powered comes out of the box fully charged, even if it doesn't have a hard drive. But back then, we noticed the detail and we fixed it, and now everyone else does that as well.

No more "Charge before use."

As Fadell observes, precharged electronic devices are now the norm. Very rarely will you buy a new electronic device that isn't fully functional and ready to use upon removal from the packaging.

At the launch of the iPod, however, this was revolutionary. Prior to that, all electronic devices needed to be charged from four to twelve hours before the customer could begin using them. Apple's decision to ship its iPods precharged ensured that the initial moment of activation was everything the customer desired and more.

 ## Quick Takeaway

Remove any barriers, no matter how small they seem, to your customers experiencing the product they paid for immediately upon receipt. Make it supersimple to engage.

GROWN-UPS LIKE TOYS TOO

International toy company Tech 4 Kids has a unique way of making new wholesale buyers feel special. As part of its new customer onboarding strategy, Tech 4 Kids sends a "shock and awe" brochure via overnight service. The beautifully designed mailer opens to reveal a built-in video screen that automatically starts playing when the brochure is opened. The video includes a customized message from the sales representative that summarizes the key elements of the brand's business pitch. The video then transitions to a series of sizzles (quick videos combining visuals, audio clips, and messaging to create a fast-paced, stylized overview of a particular product) and television commercials that highlight key toys in the product lineup. Control buttons allow the new customer to select which videos to watch and rewatch, as desired. The mailer also includes prints of all the relevant ordering materials—including quote sheets, product business plans, and anything else the customer could want or need—all conveniently located in one place.

Shortly after this, Tech 4 Kids follows up by sending a box of sample toys. Delivered in a custom box adorned with key words from the company's core values, this mailer stands out from all the other boxes of toys the buyer receives from competing toy companies. The design of the box helps bring even more attention to Tech 4 Kids' offerings and reinforces the company's guiding principles.

The technological novelty of the video brochure, paired with the high degree of personalization, makes for an incredible first interaction. It helps assure the new customer that Tech 4 Kids will look after the little details and can be trusted with additional shelf space in the store. This initial interaction establishes a rock-solid foundation for the relationship and previews what doing business with Tech 4 Kids will be like. No one ever forgets this meaningful and lasting first impression.

CEO/President Brad Pedersen estimates that this extra thoughtfulness has led to consistent double-digit growth over the past four years. Not a bad extra margin of revenues and profits for a company that does more than $50 million in annual sales. Founded in 2008, Tech 4 Kids recently merged with another U.S. toy company (and acquired another) as part of an M&A roll-up strategy. The new company has been rebranded Basic Fun, has sales in excess of $100 million, and now has offices in Florida (its headquarters), Canada, California, Hong Kong, and China—shipping toys to more than eighty countries around the world.

Quick Takeaway

Offering a highly customized, tailored digital experience to your customers makes the interaction remarkable. Officially starting the relationship with an unexpected, high-energy surprise mailing is a great way to create a feeling of "shock and awe" and set the stage for incredible interactions in the future.

YOU TOO CAN DO GENETIC SAMPLE COLLECTION!

DNA testing company 23andMe knew that science-driven brands face an especially large hurdle when it comes to the potential for user error. With this understanding, the company set out to design an unintimidating, foolproof first customer interaction that felt both accessible and familiar to new customers.

Because the 23andMe team does not have an in-person sample collection force, they rely on their customers to gather a proper DNA sa-

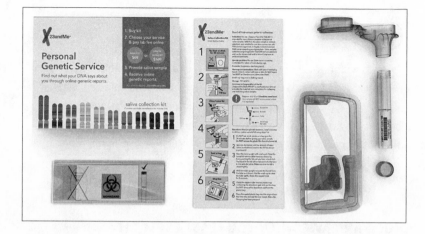

liva sample with an in-home testing kit. Given the scientific nature of this process and the potential for user/human error, the packaging for the 23andMe testing kit is personalized to emphasize the important role the customer plays in a successful sample collection. The directions are simple and clear so anyone can follow along and gather the necessary saliva. In addition, the genetic testing kit is visually engaging, with a series of colorful designs and playful messaging.

Receiving this personalized kit with sample-collecting instructions that even the most scientifically challenged customer can follow gets the relationship off to a great start. The sleek and user-friendly interactions that the genetic analysis company will have with the customer going forward are foreshadowed by the first major interaction. According to 23andMe vice president of business development–life sciences Emily Drabant Conley, designing the testing kit to gather a significant sample size of saliva ensures that if the first analysis procedure fails, there is enough to run a second procedure without going back to the customer to ask for another sample.[3] Helping customers have a successful first interaction that also mirrors the ease of use they will experience with the business sets the foundation for a long, thriving relationship.

⏱ Quick Takeaway

Emphasize the role your customers play in achieving their own success. Strive to make your early interactions accessible and familiar in order to avoid mistakes and mishaps early in the relationship. Explore ways to use design, color, emotion, and messaging to make your products and services engaging and experiential from the outset.

SHOCK AND AWE WHEN YOU LEAST EXPECT IT

The financial planning and wealth management firm Cornerstone Retirement, based in Las Vegas, welcomes new customers with a mailing to their home that is internally referred to as the "shock and awe kit."

Since its founding in 2009, the executive team at Cornerstone has pursued innovative ways to design experiences and trigger specific emotions at the beginning of the relationship with their new customers. By providing the customer with a host of resources, Cornerstone emphasizes a commitment to customer education. The quicker the customer learns about the firm's philosophy and approach to wealth management, the sooner the customer will see a return on their investment in a relationship with Cornerstone.

The "shock and awe kit" features Cornerstone's branding on a smooth, magnetic box with "Your Best Is Yet to Come" written on the cover.

Inside the custom package the new customer finds a personalized letter thanking them for joining the firm's practice as well as a series of documents and free gifts. A Better Business Bureau report highlighting the Cornerstone Retirement team and the great work they do in the community; a folder that includes step-by-step directions for what will happen next; and an outline of what to expect at the first in-person appointment with Cornerstone are but some of the items the new customer receives.

The kit also includes an annual report detailing Cornerstone Retirement's assets under management; a description of its business philosophy; and a copy of the book *Wise Money* by Daniel Wildermuth, whose philosophy of investing, wealth management, and asset growth is practiced by the advisers at Cornerstone.

Along with the documents and free gifts, the package also includes a DVD with a personalized video message to the new customer. While a DVD might be off-putting for a millennial, the fifty-five-plus-year-old demographic that comprises the bulk of Cornerstone's clients love receiving things they can easily watch on their home TV.

Cornerstone's mailing combines substance, gravitas, and personalized tone in a way that energizes the new customer. In addition, by providing a variety of educational materials, Cornerstone showcases its desire to have informed, prepared, and knowledgeable customers.

The team at Cornerstone Retirement understands that the greater the investment a new customer makes financially, the more significant and important it is to get the Activate stage right.

Quick Takeaway

Make the first impression a shocking experience. Combine your welcome with access (transparency), insight (here's the next step), and unexpected delight (resources for leveling up the relationship). Ideally, you want to paint a picture of what life is going to be like now that the customer is working with you.

FULL STOMACHS MAKE FOR HAPPY CUSTOMERS

Often the first interaction in the Activate phase does not come after receiving a product or signing on a dotted line, but instead happens at a kickoff meeting. While many organizations worry about the content and context of this initial interaction, there are simple ways to make it memorable and remarkable that require little monetary investment.

Years ago I found myself doing a project for the World Bank. As part of this project, I headed to a meeting at the bank's headquarters in Washington, D.C., to kick off a multimonth design project. The meeting was attended by approximately fifteen global economists, government experts, and development professionals.

These people were, to put it kindly, more comfortable operating in the world of spreadsheets and regression analysis than they were navigating kickoff meeting pleasantries. To help break the ice, I brought in a bunch of flavored sodas, a six-pack of craft root beer (I wanted something to drink too!), chocolate-covered raisins, and yogurt-covered pretzels. I arrived in the conference room twenty minutes before the meeting and arranged the food in the middle of the table so it was easily accessible to everyone in the boardroom.

When the economists arrived for the meeting, their eyes lit up. It was like a New Year's Eve celebration as they raced around the room to enjoy the snacks and drinks.

I was absolutely shocked. Who would have thought that thirty dollars of sugar-laden snacks could put a roomful of the world's top economists in the palm of my hand?

This simple tactic of providing fun snacks and interesting drinks as part of the kickoff meeting took the normal business interaction and made it something meaningful. It required only a small amount of time and thoughtfulness to execute. It was also inexpensive. Remarkable experience is not synonymous with really expensive.

⏱ Quick Takeaway

Don't forget the basics. It's not just about your products and services. People like food and fun. If you feed them, they will like you.

Now imagine what would happen if you took this "Just Feed the Attendees" approach one step further and tailored the snacks and drinks to the dietary needs and preferences of your kickoff meeting audience. This level of attention would leave the attendees telling a story about your thoughtfulness for weeks and months to come.

SUMMARY: PHASE 4—ACTIVATE

The Activate phase of the customer experience occurs when the customer receives the product or service they purchased in their initial order. This first impression (physical and emotional) sets the tone for future interactions and creates a baseline emotional reaction to your brand experiences. The customer engages with any packaging, inserts, or information associated with the product or service closely, as they have anticipated the arrival of this initial shipment or first meeting.

Think of the energy you need to bring to "activate" the relationship and create a remarkable experience for your customer. This phase of the customer life cycle offers you the opportunity to set the standard for future interactions while at the same time welcoming the customer to your brand or community.

SIX THINGS TO DO IN THE ACTIVATE PHASE STARTING TOMORROW

Remember, you don't have to use every communication tool in each phase. Just remember that it's *possible* to use each tool to create a memorable experience for your customers during this phase.

IN-PERSON

In-person interactions at this phase in the customer life cycle should be well thought out, prepared for, and extremely positive. High-energy exchanges, coupled with sincere connection and hospitality, make an indelible mark on a new customer during these first key interactions.

CHAPTER EXAMPLE: Bringing refreshments (World Bank) lays the groundwork for the relationship and adds an unexpected moment of surprise and delight in the first major interaction.

EMAIL

Email communication the day the customer receives their first product or service should address their emotional state and provide clear, concise directions for maximizing the customer's potential for success. Customization is key to creating a feeling of uniqueness and care from the outset of the first delivery or interaction.

MAIL

Depending on whether you offer a service or a product, mail can be used to create a special interaction. For services, a process map and success checklist (don't worry, we'll discuss these in more detail in the next chapter) in the initial interaction offer an artifact of the brand experience and help to build kinesthetic learning and behaviors into the process. For a product offering, enhanced packaging will get things off to a great start by reinvigorating the customer's excitement level.

CHAPTER EXAMPLE: The arrival via mail of an unexpected package filled with a personalized video brochure (Tech 4 Kids) or surprise gifts and marketing materials (Cornerstone Retirement) makes a powerful first impression to start a new relationship. Packages that are well designed (23andMe), easy to understand, and ready to use (Apple) make for fantastic first impressions.[4] Incorporating key elements of the brand spirit (Tech 4 Kids) into the packaging helps a business stand out from the competition.

 PHONE

A follow-up call confirming receipt of the product on the day it arrives—or checking in during a service call to make sure things are going exceedingly well—further anchors the brand experience. This call will also allow you to preemptively identify any problems with the initial order or service delivery, providing the opportunity for fast resolution.

 **VIDEO**

A personalized video helps bring a "wow" moment to the first interaction, especially if that video includes team members who may not be directly involved in the project who contributed to the initial delivery of the product or service. A video helps put a human face on the interaction at this key moment in the customer life cycle.

CHAPTER EXAMPLE: A high-tech, high-touch video brochure (Tech 4 Kids) creates an incredible first impression and sets the stage for many fantastic experiences to come in the future.

 **PRESENT**

In the tradition of the Cracker Jack free prize inside, the first shipment or exchange should include something special and unexpected. Potential prizes include: a sample of a product that wasn't in the order, a sample of a product that hasn't been officially released yet, or a card with a link to download a free tool that increases the likelihood of success.

CHAPTER EXAMPLE: Surprises that reinforce the key talking points of the kickoff meeting (Cornerstone Retirement) further establish a brand's credibility with a new customer. Precharged devices (Apple) allow the customer to start using the product immediately—delivering on instant gratification and creating a remarkable first impression.

YOUR ASSIGNMENT: PUT THESE IDEAS TO WORK

Now that you have a clear understanding of the Activate phase, answer a series of questions that are designed to get you thinking about how you can use each of the communication tools to enhance the overall experience during this phase of the customer journey.

(As a reminder, don't skim over these and move on to the next chapter. Keep doing the work so you receive the greatest return on the investment you just made in reading this chapter!)

Evaluating the Current Situation

Answer each question, then write two or three sentences explaining your answer. For bonus points, write down any ideas you have for changes that would make your answers "better."

- What is the first major interaction you have with your customers postsale? (Hint: If you mail a product, it's when they receive the mailing; if you do consulting, it's the kickoff meeting; if you run a membership organization, it's their first gathering; etc.)

- Describe in detail that first interaction: How long does it last? What does it "feel" like? How do you build rapport? Is the interaction special or memorable?

- In your current business, do you create remarkable experiences during the Activate phase?

- If so, what are they?

- On a scale of 1 to 10, where 1 is "pathetic" and 10 is "world class," how would you rate the experience your customers currently have in the Activate phase? (Again, be honest with yourself when assigning a score.)

Tools to Enhance the Future Experience

Answer each question by coming up with two or three ideas for using the specific tool to enhance the customer experience. I've said it before, but please don't worry about how much it will cost, who will do it, or how to get it implemented in your organization. Keep dreaming big and being creative with your ideas!

- How can you use in-person interactions during this phase to give the customer a taste of what it will be like to interact with you going forward?

- How can you make your emails more welcoming and enticing—instead of beginning with "to do" lists and tasks the customer "has to do" now?

- How can a customized mail piece thank the customer for their business and express excitement about the way the relationship has started?

- How can phone conversations augment the new customer onboarding process by making them feel welcomed and included?

- How can videos create personal and emotional connections between the customer and the key members of your team whom the customer will interact with in the future?

- What present(s) could you give customers that would really make them feel welcomed?

Pick One Now

If you've answered the questions above (and I hope you're not just reading along—seriously, slow down and answer the questions!), you have a clear understanding of the customer experience during the Activate phase, as well as many ideas for how to make that experience better. Taking that into account, consider the following questions.

- What is one thing you can start doing tomorrow to make the experience your customers have in the Activate phase even better?

- Who would you need to talk to in order to make this happen?

- How would you know if you've succeeded in making this improvement?

- How would you measure the improvement of the overall customer experience?

- How would you share this impact with the rest of the organization?

FROM ACTIVATE TO ACCLIMATE

Now that you've considered your first major interaction postsale and the customer experience that happens in the Activate phase, let's consider what happens as the customer starts to interact with you and acclimates to your way of doing business.

CHAPTER TWELVE

Phase 5: Acclimate

 Overview of the Acclimate Phase

In the Acclimate phase, the customer learns how the organization does business. The customer needs to get familiar with the various interactions that occur during the relationship. Businesses typically deliver their product or service dozens, hundreds, thousands, or millions of times, so they assume everyone knows their process and what will happen next. New customers don't have this understanding and need more hand-holding than you think.

VOMITING CAN BE PREVENTED

I live in Colorado, high in the Rockies, at an elevation of 8,500 feet. Acclimation is something that has a particularly personal meaning to me.

When friends or family members visit, I greet them at the front door with a large glass of water. This is not general courtesy. Guests arriving at our home are required to immediately drink at least twenty ounces of water to help them acclimate to the altitude.

Occasionally, someone will say they don't need the water. When we first moved to our home, I let them decline the drink. However, after 20 to 30 percent of our visitors found themselves struggling with the effects of altitude sickness (which can range from splitting headaches to vomiting), I made the water mandatory. The water is a vital aspect of their Acclimate phase, whether they realize it or not.

Companies need to do the same thing with their customers—holding their hands and guiding them to make sure they get where they want to go—even if the customer protests and says they're "fine."

SLOW DOWN AND HELP THEM ACCLIMATE

How do you achieve successful acclimation? By introducing customers to your organization's culture, people, processes, and systems in a way that allows them to get comfortable with the adjustment to a new environment.

This may sound like common sense, but most organizations don't do it.

Companies often assume a new customer already knows and understands everything about how the company works. They find themselves lulled into a false sense of security after a positive kickoff meeting or unboxing experience. The organization rides the wave of a good Activate phase into the Acclimate phase and expects the great experience to continue as the customer acclimates to the way the organization does business.

Plus, it's all clearly spelled out in the paperwork that gets sent out to the customer—whether it's a service contract or a proposal. And of course customers read that stuff thoroughly, right?

What do you think? When you become a new customer, do you read all the fine print?

I didn't think so!

So when you're on the delivery side of the equation, why would you assume your customers are any different? Companies fail to recognize that customers are inundated with messaging and information in every aspect of their lives. This bombardment of information is overwhelming. Companies often find themselves caught off guard when a customer they thought was paying attention asks, "What comes next?"

The company may believe that the process is clearly outlined and easy to follow, yet the customer is still getting used to working together.

This creates a huge gap between what the company expects and how the customer feels.

At this juncture the customer probably doesn't feel comfortable with the product or service, at least not fully. They are still learning the ropes and beginning to interact with the elements of the product, service, and support team. They are also starting to learn about the company's additional product or service offerings.

Acclimation is about making your customer feel comfortable with the people, processes, and systems of your business. If the entire process of onboarding customers is about creating a welcoming experience through a managed, structured series of contacts, then the Acclimate phase is where it is most important to help the customer settle into a new reality, one that you know more about than they do.

It's frustrating, I know, but this behavior exhibited by new customers (being focused on themselves instead of your onboarding process) is common across all humans. The hard reality of dealing with humans is that we are all insular and self-centered (at least to some extent), and when we are paying other people for products or services, we generally expect them to do the work for us. This is not meant as a judgment of anyone—I am like this as a customer as well—it's just a statement of fact.

Sometimes a company will respond to the unsure customer with anger and hostility. The company doesn't understand why the customer didn't pay attention, or read the contract, or review the manual. The customer said they did, but if that's true, why are they asking these basic questions? So the company offers no help while the customer is lost and desperately needing guidance.

You know what it's like to work with your company and you know the steps in your process. But your customer has barely absorbed this information. It doesn't matter that they've already signed on the dotted line, purchased the product, and participated in the kickoff meeting. They aren't caught up yet.

As a result, the distance between where you think your customer is and where they actually stand is huge. It is imperative at this phase that you do everything you can to bridge that gap and familiarize your customer with your way of doing business.

PULLING BACK THE CURTAIN TO THE DELIGHT OF YOUR CUSTOMERS

The secret to achieving success in the Acclimate phase is to guide and assist your customer as much as possible during the entire relationship. At each step in the process, you need to explain what is happening and what is going to happen next. In many instances, you'll need to reiterate why this step is necessary and how it contributes to the overall goal the customer seeks to accomplish.

International pizza provider Domino's does this well via an app that gives customers insight about their pending pizza delivery. After placing an order using the app, the customer is able to see exactly where the pizza is in the production process. They can follow along in real time as the pizza transitions from a plain dough crust, to a crust stacked with ingredients, to the oven, to the delivery person, to the delivery vehicle.

By guiding the customer through the entire journey of pizza creation, cooking, and delivery, Domino's keeps the customer informed and engaged. This level of communication not only keeps the customer aware of and acclimated to every step in the process, but it provides

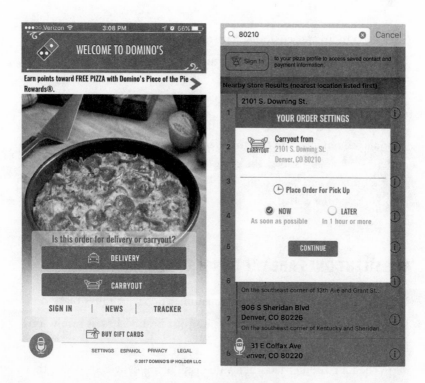

updates on the various "micro-accomplishments" that are necessary in order to get the pizza from the oven to the table.

Most people are familiar with the saying "No one wants to see how the sausage is made," and yet research from both Harvard and Stanford shows the opposite.[1]

> Customers want to know every step in the process. When they can see you do the things you've promised to do (i.e., you're "working"), it reduces uncertainty and allows them to plan their lives better, and it makes their overall satisfaction rate at the end of the engagement significantly higher.[2]

When customers can see you "working" for them, they feel more confident about their purchase and the care you are taking to deliver it.

This leads to greater customer satisfaction with the original purchase and more repeat business in the future.

(⏱) Quick Takeaway

Regular communication tied to key milestones eliminates uncertainty. There are no dead spots. The customer always knows where they are in the process and gains a feeling of satisfaction knowing that you are working on their behalf.

THE SILENT ONES ARE THE DANGEROUS ONES

It is important to remember that customer behavior takes place on a largely subconscious level and, despite your best wishes, is rarely spoken about or addressed.

When a customer feels like value isn't being delivered—value they were promised—they usually don't complain. Instead, they hope you will jump in to tell them what happens next. But when this hope turns out to be mistaken, when your communication becomes anything but regular and consistent, the customer disconnects, becoming more and more distant. They may be raising little red flags, muttering, "I don't know where I am," or even confiding in colleagues that they wish you would slow down. But because they rarely go so far as to raise their hand and say to you directly, "What? Whoa! Pump the brakes!," the company stays in a hard-charging, business-as-usual mode of operation—damaging the customer relationship with each passing day. Eventually the project stalls, dies, and the relationship that once held such great promise falls apart.

Even the customers who do complain or raise a concern often find their voices fall on deaf ears. At best, the company tries to reconnect and catch them up. At worst (and most often) the company shares the same time line or description in the proposal and expects the customers to figure out where they are in the process.

HAND-HOLDING AND MAPMAKING

While the previous phase, Activate, focused on creating an initial spectacle, the Acclimate phase emphasizes consistent performance above all else. During the Acclimate phase, holding the customer's hand, providing step-by-step instructions, and checking in regularly provides a feeling of security and certainty.

Each interaction should build upon the previous interaction. Not every interaction needs to be a spectacle filled with entertainment, but it should ease the customer's uncertainty and create a feeling of stability that is matched with a feeling of forward progress.

In the Acclimate phase, it's important to clearly communicate and provide the customer with a map that outlines the next steps. I mean this literally—an actual map, if at all possible, would be great. Why do you think I made this map:

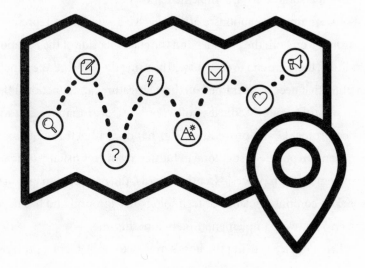

So that you could clearly see what the eight phases are, what each entails, and what comes next.

Your map should be a printed or online visual that the customer can use to easily identify their place on the path. It should also include regular reminders about what comes next and why it's imperative to stay in the flow. This is particularly important with more complex products or services and implementation time frames with a longer duration.

BUT YOU DON'T UNDERSTAND, OUR PROCESS IS TOO COMPLICATED TO SIMPLIFY

One of the most notoriously painful business activities is a software implementation.[3] The horror stories about software implementations going awry are well documented and voluminous. Companies have been known to spend hundreds of millions of dollars on software that they never use.[4]

It is with this understanding of the industry that PolicyMedical, a hospital records management software company in Toronto, embarked on an experience enhancement strategy to create a fun and easy-to-understand software implementation process.

Software implementations usually involve a number of representatives from IT on both the provider and the customer side of the equation. In addition, there are end users who will be using the software after implementation that need to be trained on the new features and functionalities.

Given that PolicyMedical's software is used to manage internal policies, protocols, and procedures (e.g., hand washing techniques and fall prevention policies), someone in human resources usually oversees the implementation process. In other words, the project manager usually lacks a computer science or technology background and has never overseen a software implementation before this one.

When a novice is using the boss's money to implement a project it never ends well. The lack of software experience often creates an even higher barrier to understanding and a greater level of stress and uncertainty on the part of the supervising project manager.

As if this weren't bad enough, in the typical software installation engagement, the executive management team makes the decision to purchase the software without the project manager's knowledge. Often the first time the project manager learns about the new software is when "volun-told" to attend a kickoff meeting, where it is revealed that the project manager will oversee the project as part of their now-expanded job responsibilities.

In discussing the Acclimate phase and exploring the standard implementation process with the PolicyMedical team, it became clear that while each installation was different, commonalities existed across projects. Working together we reviewed the implementation elements from a variety of prior client projects, identifying dozens of steps that were complicated, confusing, and rarely performed with any level of consistency—by either the customer or the PolicyMedical implementation team.

After reviewing the steps and combining or eliminating those that were ridiculous, redundant, or merely unnecessary, we arrived at a series of nineteen steps (and that was the simplified version!) that needed to be completed on every project, regardless of client size or the specific software configuration.

This step in the process is crucial, as you can only map out a process for your customer if *you* completely and comprehensively understand it.

SHOW, DON'T JUST TELL

Working hand in hand with the PolicyMedical team, we looked at the Excel spreadsheets, Gantt charts, email communications, and phone call agendas used in the old implementation process. Even though they used these tools every day, the PolicyMedical team was surprised by the complexity and confusion! It was clear there was no way a customer could navigate it.

In order not only to simplify implementations but to bring a sense of fun and playfulness to these stressful projects, we brainstormed a number of ideas for creating an engaging and informative process.

We decided that a puzzle could solve the problem.

With the creation of a puzzle that showed the sequential steps in the process, nontechnical project managers and implementation participants could clearly understand what came next. In addition, the puzzle gave project managers a fun and playful way of tracking progress that was consistent with the PolicyMedical brand image and helped to de-stress an otherwise exasperating time.

Working in close partnership with the PolicyMedical Customer Experience Team, as well as their Technology Implementation Team, we developed a custom picture frame with twenty slots for inserting mini-pictures. Each of the twenty "pieces" of the puzzle showcased a written description of the step in the process (e.g., "announce new software implementation to the entire hospital system") on one side and a glossy image that represented the step (e.g., a bright red megaphone) on the other side. Because their onboarding process had nineteen steps, we made the final step (#20) all about congratulating the customer on a job well done.

At the beginning of an engagement, PolicyMedical sends the customer-side project manager the frame and "puzzle piece" cards via overnight delivery to arrive the day of the kickoff call. During the video kickoff session, the PolicyMedical team invites the customer to open the package. Once the customer has the frame and pieces in hand, PolicyMedical explains the tracking process and gets the customer point of contact excited about this creative way to visualize progress during the implementation process.

PHASE ONE (1) Kickoff	(6) Schedule Best Practices Call	(11) Sys Ad Complete: Doc Tree Set-Up	PHASE TWO (16) Complete Site Set-Up
(2) Contact Sheet Filled Out	(7) IT Tasks To Be Completed	(12) Sys Ad Complete: Dept/User Grp. Set-Up	PHASE THREE (17) Power User Training Completed
(3) Training Dates Finalized	(8) IT: LDAP Set-Up (optional)	(13) Sys Ad Complete: Profile Management	(18) Host a Launch Party
(4) Announce Implementation	(9) Inventory of Policies	(14) Sys Ad Complete: Committee Mgmt.	(19) Go Live!
(5) Create Site for Application	PHASE TWO (10) Sys Ad Training Initiated	(15) Sys Ad Complete: Upload of Documents	Congratulations!

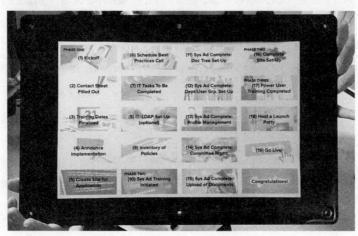

As the project proceeds, the PolicyMedical team sends emails that include headers showing the image of the step in the process that the customer is currently working on. The body text of the email explains the necessary steps to complete this piece of the puzzle. The email concludes by foreshadowing the puzzle piece that comes next.

As each step in the implementation process is completed, Policy-Medical encourages the project manager to place the puzzle piece in the frame so that over time the frame evolves to offer a visual representation of the progress to date.

When the implementation is complete, the customer installs the final "piece of the puzzle"—another card with a personalized message of congratulations that the customer can put into the final slot in the frame. The project manager now has a completed frame with twenty images that serves as a memento of the completed process. The achievement of this major milestone is celebrated when a member of the Policy-Medical team travels to the customer's location to host a "successful launch" celebration.

By making the process visual in nature, as opposed to a multipage document outlining the steps in the process in techspeak, PolicyMedical brings a feeling of creativity and fun to an otherwise onerous task. The implementation puzzle acclimates customers by giving them a clear map of the tasks, and it rewards their effort with an image they can proudly display in their office to memorialize a successful software implementation.

Quick Takeaway

You must understand your own process deeply. Take complex processes and break them down into bite-size pieces, being careful not to give customers all the information at one time. Turn technical and process-driven discussions into visual graphics to increase understanding.

WODS, RXS, AND BURPEES?

When San Francisco CrossFit was founded in 2005, it was the twenty-first CrossFit gym in the world (to put that in perspective, there are now more than fifteen thousand worldwide). Customers were still figuring out what CrossFit meant. "In the early days of CrossFit, it was so new that people would come in the door and join a class instantly. It was a serious initiation! Each class involves a ton of instruction, but to be a brand-new client and try to join in is like taking a nonswimmer, dropping them into the deep end of a pool, and hoping for the best," observed Juliet Starrett, CEO of San Francisco CrossFit.

Juliet didn't want the experience to be overwhelming for new clients, so she developed a fun, easy onboarding process.

Every prospect who comes into the gym receives a fifteen-minute "No Sweat" introductory tour. They meet a representative of the gym staff who answers any questions and allays any fears (Do I have to follow a Paleo diet to do CrossFit? How long will it take to learn the new workout routines? Do I have to tell everyone I meet that I do CrossFit?). The prospect then receives a complete tour of the facility, including directions on where to put their clothes and gear and where to hang out if they show up early for a class. While the prospect is learning about the gym, the San Francisco CrossFit team is learning about the prospect. The tour is designed to feel educational and informative as opposed to salesy.

If interested, the prospect signs up for an "Intro to CrossFit" series. During these three personal training sessions, the prospect is paired up with a coach who will work well with the customer's personality. For example, one of the coaches is known for being speedy in responding to emails—so she is paired with CEO clients who expect professional, fast responses to email communications. The "Intro to CrossFit" private sessions break down all the basics of CrossFit, from the Cross-Fit lingo (more on that later), to the safest, most effective approach, to the workout movements, to the location of equipment.

At the conclusion of the three intro sessions, the customer "graduates" (90 percent of series participants do), which allows them to sign up for regular classes. The coach notifies the gym manager of the graduation, and the manager then reaches out to the customer to offer membership options and share the calendar of social events. There is no obligation to become a member of the gym, but 73 percent sign up right then.

After the customer completes the first class as a graduate, the gym manager sends the "High Ten" email. This email congratulates the customer on finishing their first class. The message goes on to invite the customer to the next scheduled gym social event in an effort to foster and encourage participation in the community.

The commitment to making gym members feel included continues throughout the relationship. Every class starts with the instructor asking everyone in the class—newbies and veterans alike—to introduce themselves. Juliet notes that this has a "visibly calming effect" on the participants and creates an immediate bond with the other class members. The tradition of starting each class with introductions began when the gym first opened and has been adopted by CrossFit gyms all over the world.

San Francisco CrossFit—and the entire CrossFit industry—uses another fantastic tool to help acclimate customers and build community: they speak a distinct language. It's not unusual to hear a CrossFitter say, "The WOD (pronounced "WAHD") RX includes 5 WBs, 20 DLs, and 10 burpies, 5X." Translated for non-CrossFitters, this means that the Workout of the Day (WOD) as prescribed (RX) includes 5 wall balls (WBs), 20 dead lifts (DLs), and 10 sets of burpies, done five times in repetition. "We try to be as welcoming as humanly possible," notes Juliet. "The lingo helps build community—but you have to come and participate to fully get it."

While San Francisco CrossFit is a gym, they also consider themselves to be in the event business. Every week, something is going on in the gym or around town that a group of CrossFitters participate in collectively. The most anticipated event is the quarterly Taco Social, where the gym brings in "a taco guy," provides a cooler full of "crappy" beer (Juliet's proud description), plays music, and creates the space for people to meet one another. This tight bond has affected members' lives outside of the gym. More than twenty marriages have taken place between people who met at San Francisco CrossFit, and twelve members have been so inspired that they left to start their own CrossFit gyms.

"We have a 'shirt on' policy," observes Juliet. "Our gym isn't about showing off your abs—it's about community."

The emphasis on community has a direct impact on customer retention. A tremendous 73 percent of intro series customers sign up for memberships, and another 9 percent sign up for continued private training. Overall, 82 percent of customers transition into a formal, long-term relationship after being properly onboarded in the first three sessions. Over time, this produced a membership where 8 percent have belonged for more than five years, 60 percent for more than three years, and 22 percent for more than two years—incredible retention given that 44 percent of new members at the average gym leave within the first six months.[*,5]

Juliet attributes the gym's success to its systematic onboarding

---

*The staff tries to connect people into the community events as early as possible in the relationship. Juliet explains that "[w]e know that if we can get a new member to attend even one community event in the first one hundred days of the membership, we have a huge advantage to have him stick with us."

process. "We've learned about the importance of acclimating our clients to our way of doing business. Even though it's more expensive for us and can be intimidating to our customers, it has made a huge difference in our retention and the overall success of our business. We often take someone who is afraid and skeptical of CrossFit and turn them into a customer for life."

⏱ Quick Takeaway

Help your customers acclimate to your process by walking them (sometimes literally) through your world. If your company uses a particular lingo, introduce them to it early on so they feel included instead of excluded. Pair them with a well-trained, friendly employee who will shepherd them through the first few days of their experience. Don't forget that people crave community. When you give your customers the opportunity to find and create a community of like-minded people through their interactions with your company, it makes it easy for those customers to continue doing business with you.

I'M ON THE PLANE, WHERE ARE MY BAGS?

I spend a lot of time on airplanes (and by "a lot" I mean more than 100,000 miles flown per year), and from time to time I find myself rushing to catch a connecting flight. Recently my plane landed at the connecting airport twenty minutes late, which meant that I had to get from the international arrivals terminal to the domestic departures terminal as quickly as possible. I don't normally check a bag, but this time I had. As I patiently waited to be cleared through customs, I started to worry whether my bag would make the next flight.

Once I cleared customs, I rechecked my suitcase and sprinted through the terminal looking for my gate. As I ran, I thought to myself,

"I might not make this flight and there is no way my bag is going to make it."

I made it to the departure gate just in time. I was literally the last passenger to board the plane before they closed the door.

As I sat down in my seat and smiled at my good fortune in making the flight, my phone vibrated. It was a message from the Delta app telling me that my suitcase had just been loaded onto the plane.

When was the last time you heard a good airline customer service story?

I couldn't believe it. Not only had my bag made it onto the plane, but Delta had also taken the time to let me know.

I spent my three-hour domestic flight relaxing, knowing that when I arrived at my final destination my suitcase would be there. Instead of spending three hours in the air worrying about how I would be prepared for an early meeting the next morning when I landed without clothes or toiletries, I was stress free. My inflight experience became remarkable because of what happened before the plane even took to the air.

While this level of communication isn't necessary in every business, every customer has potential moments of stress when they interact with you. If you can identify when these stress points occur and then develop ways to alleviate the stress by communicating directly with the customer, it can turn a moment of strife and despair into a moment of surprise and delight.

Quick Takeaway

Anticipate things that might cause your customer to feel negative emotions (anxiety, uncertainty, frustration, etc.) and then figure out a way to address them before the customer even has a chance to ask you for help.

When companies take the time to truly acclimate their customers throughout the business engagement, it creates an entirely different level of experience.

These communications may seem small, but they are huge to the customer. Every organization should think about the little things they can do to hold their customers' hands through the entire process. They should figure out how to let their customers know the work they've promised to do behind the scenes is being completed, on schedule, as promised.

WHO SHOULD I TALK TO IF I HAVE A QUESTION?

At the award-winning affiliate program marketing agency Acceleration Partners (whose clients include Adidas, Gymboree, Reebok, Target, Warby Parker, etc.), the team noticed that while they were very clear internally about who would be working on a project, customers were often less sure. To remedy this situation, they realized they needed to educate the customer and provide them with specific details on the people who would be working on the project. In particular, the client needed to understand which member of the Acceleration Partners team to contact regarding specific issues and how to escalate a conversation to more senior members of the team if necessary.

Approximately two weeks after signing the contract to work together, while the relationship is still in its infancy, the vice president of client services sends a "Who's Who" email specifying the members of the team who will be working on the project. The email looks like this:

TO: CLIENT
SUBJECT: Who's Who on Your Team
MESSAGE:

Dear <<Client First Name>>:

I hope that all is well and that your work with Acceleration Partners is off to a good start. I wanted to take a minute to introduce myself and formally let you know who's who on the AP team and make sure that you have the right points of contact for any issues or opportunities that arise as we continue to build our relationship.

My goal is to ensure that all of our client relationships are successful and mutually beneficial; please don't hesitate to contact me at any point with any questions or concerns about your account. Your complete account team is listed below along with recommended points of escalation for common questions or issues:

Natasha Romanova, VP, Client Services: Executive-level client services lead.

Best contact for: Contract changes, major account opportunities or issues, senior point of escalation.

Steve Rogers, Account Director: Responsible for overseeing client relationship and success.

Best contact for: High-level account performance questions or concerns, major workflow issues or changes.

Clinton Barton, Account Manager: Day-to-day strategic and operational contact, overseeing account strategy and performance.

Best contact for: Day-to-day campaign opportunities or concerns.

Of course, you're welcome to reach out to me or anyone on your account team anytime and I'm personally glad to discuss any issue or opportunity, large or small. We will also reach out to you quarterly via Client Heartbeat, an important tool that we use to regularly monitor our client satisfaction levels. It only takes a minute to complete but our team uses it as an important pulse on how we're doing, so I really appreciate your response.

We look forward to a successful partnership!

Natasha Romanova
VP, Client Services

Not only does this email formally introduce the team members working on the project, but it outlines clear responsibilities for each person and under what circumstances they should be contacted. Giving a client this level of clarity early in the relationship eliminates uncertainty and, in the process, builds trust. If Acceleration Partners wanted to take things one step further, the email could share two or three hypothetical scenarios that happen regularly with customers and then clearly state whom the customer should contact in these situations. It never hurts to be overly specific in explaining internal processes—especially this early in the relationship. Finally, the email also hints at the Client Heartbeat, a tool the agency uses for quarterly check-ins to monitor overall client engagement and satisfaction. This shows an ongoing and formalized system for continuing to build the relationship and maintain a high level of trust and confidence.

Along with the email, the client receives a PDF recapping the various roles and responsibilities as outlined in the email:

WHO WE ARE

NATASHA ROMANOVA
SVP, Client Services

Natasha Romanova is the Senior Vice President of Client Services. Prior to working at Acceleration Partners, Natasha was a Senior Manager of Client Relations at Acme Corp. for over 7 years, growing retention by 24% and building relationships with key accounts. Before Acme Corp., Natasha worked as the Marketing Manager for an online home products website. Natasha earned a BA in government and international relations and a minor in computer programing from the University of Notre Dame. Outside of work, Natasha enjoys spending time with her family, going to Disney World, and watching the Notre Dame Fighting Irish play.

NATASHA ENJOYS...
Navigating the customer journey with our customers as it often requires tracking the emotions associated with various touchpoints

CONTACT INFO
202-854-1002
nromanova@accelerationpartners.co

SHE'S YOUR GO-TO FOR:
• Account Strategy
• Reporting & Analysis
• Client Service & Communication

◇ | ACCELERATION
     PARTNERS

The individual pages of the PDF profile the team members, showing photos and sharing a few details about their personal lives. The inclusion of the photos humanizes the interaction and creates connection as the new customer "sees" the team members working on their project. Because the customer may never have the opportunity to meet in person, this creates opportunities for connection and trust building. Given the information shared about Natasha (see image above), a customer can connect on multiple topics: including her background with Acme Corp., her international relations and computer studies, her love of Disney World, or her support of the Fighting Irish. These pieces of information should provide at least one point of commonality (I love Disney World too!) or contrast (You can cheer for the Irish as long as they aren't playing my team!) for the customer to engage with this key team member.

Due to the nature of Acceleration Partners' business, most customers commit to a minimum six-month engagement, taking them well beyond the first one hundred days of the relationship. Despite this contractual structure, approximately 10 percent of customers tried to exit the agreement or change the terms in the past. Since implementing the new customer onboarding strategy, not a single new customer has altered or exited their contract in the first six months—proof that trust is being established and the clients are more certain about the relationship.

"In the First 100 Days," observes founder and managing director Bob Glazer, "you're often working from a place of distrust. The customer is unsure if they can trust you 100 percent because you're a new partner and they are coming to the table with the baggage of past relationships and bad customer experiences. Your actions and efforts should be designed to help them realize they can trust you and that this relationship will be entirely different."

Quick Takeaway

Building personal connection is a vital element of relationship building. By explaining who is on the team and detailing roles and responsibilities, it's possible to reduce uncertainty and establish trust early in the customer life cycle. Customers need to know where they should go with questions, concerns, and problems that may arise in the first few weeks and months of working together. Offering personal details about team members that go beyond their duties and responsibilities creates possibilities for connection via points of commonality or contrast. By empowering your employees to play an active role in creating your customer journey touchpoints, you increase buy-in, implementation, and commitment to the process in the long run.

SUMMARY: PHASE 5—ACCLIMATE

Creating Remarkable Customer Experiences in the Acclimate Phase

The Acclimate phase takes place between the first major interaction and the point where the customer accomplishes their original goal when choosing to purchase your product or use your service. During this phase, the customer will be learning the ropes as well as interacting with your team members and additional product or service offerings.

The goal in this time period is to get early buy-in and habit formation before the novelty wears off and/or the customer slips back into old behaviors. Think of acclimating at altitude and be ready to hand customers your own version of a glass of water to make their transition smoother and more comfortable.

The Acclimate stage of the customer life cycle is your opportunity to introduce customers to the organization's culture, processes, or systems in a way that encourages them to adapt to this new environment.

SIX THINGS TO DO IN THE ACCLIMATE PHASE STARTING TOMORROW

You don't have to use each communication tool in every phase—but you should at least consider each tool as a way to create memorable experiences for your customers.

 IN-PERSON

Lending a friendly hand as a customer navigates using the product or service is key in the acclimation stage. By now, the customer understands most basic operations and interactions, but is probably becoming aware of nuances that weren't addressed in the early stages. By being regularly present, the brand can help address these and increase the customer's comfort and experience.

CHAPTER EXAMPLE: Teaching your "language" to new customers (San Francisco CrossFit) and walking them through your processes at the customer's pace guarantees that no new customer is left behind. In-person celebrations along the journey (PolicyMedical) further reinforce the success of achieving various milestones.

@ EMAIL

By tweaking the sequence of additional orders, meetings, or interactions to include regular check-ins on customer progress, communications with customers can go from a one-way, "push" mentality to a more fluid dialogue. Quick email surveys to individual customers allow for deeper segmentation, targeted assistance, and the identification of defection indicators over time.

CHAPTER EXAMPLE: Sending a PDF that gives background information on the entire team (Accelerated Partners) and includes their photographs creates connections between the account services team and the individual customer. Regular status emails (PolicyMedical) help ensure that the customer knows exactly where they are in the implementation process. Congratulating customers on achieving early milestones (San Francisco CrossFit) and encouraging them to continue lets them know you are monitoring their individual progress and have a vested interest in seeing them succeed.

 MAIL

As most businesses move into the Acclimate phase, direct mail communications slow and often cease, except for invoices and upsell flyers/catalogs. Instead of being in sales mode, use mail to send unexpected tools to help the customer succeed. Use this opportunity to further deepen their understanding of your brand, your culture, and your core values.

CHAPTER EXAMPLE: A well-designed puzzle (PolicyMedical)

can serve as a visual road map of the entire onboarding process, making implementation faster, easier, and even more fun.

 PHONE

A group call or teleseminar provides the opportunity for new customers to get personalized coaching or suggestions on how to experience early success with the brand. This clear commitment to the new customer's success establishes a sense of accountability and support and acclimates them to these business interactions.

CHAPTER EXAMPLE: Text messages (Delta and Domino's) can assuage any concerns about things potentially not going as planned. They also provide constant confirmation that things are on track for the expected outcome.

 **VIDEO**

A video from an expert (senior management, project lead, etc.) congratulating the customer on reaching the halfway point in the project will enhance the relationship by showcasing commitment to the customer's success. This also offers the chance to anchor customer behaviors to the brand mission.

![present icon] **PRESENT**

Surprise gifts and bonuses as the customer becomes more familiar with the brand keep the interactions exciting and engaging. Anything that would make the experience smoother, easier, or more efficient offers the chance for a surprise at this stage in the customer life cycle.

CHAPTER EXAMPLE: Celebrations along the journey (Policy-Medical) further highlight the significance of the customer's effort toward achieving milestones.

YOUR ASSIGNMENT: PUT THESE IDEAS TO WORK

Now that you have a clear understanding of the Acclimate phase, answer a series of questions that are designed to get you thinking about how you can use each of the communication tools to enhance the overall experience during this phase of the customer journey.

(You're doing a great job! This is a set of questions that you ABSOLUTELY want to complete, as the Acclimate phase is where most customers leave you. Answer these questions and stop the defections!)

Evaluating the Current Situation

Answer each question, then write two or three sentences explaining your answer. For bonus points, write down any ideas you have for changes that would make your answers "better."

- How do you hold your customer's hand while they are getting familiar with working with you? (Hint: Do you have product directions, Gantt charts, process maps, an online customer portal, regular check-in meetings, etc.?)

- Describe in detail various things you do to help customers navigate your process. How long does it take before they start to see results? What does it "feel" like? How do you mark milestones along the way? How do your customers know what happens next?

- In your current business, do you create remarkable experiences during the Acclimate phase? If so, what are they?

- On a scale of 1 to 10, where 1 is "pathetic" and 10 is "world class," how would you rate the experience your customers currently have in the Acclimate phase?

Tools to Enhance the Future Experience

Answer each question by coming up with two or three ideas for using the specific tool to enhance the customer experience. Again, please don't worry about how much it will cost, who will do it, or how to get it implemented in your organization. Keep being bold and audacious with your ideas!

- How can you use in-person interactions during this phase to make sure the customer is staying on the path and always moving forward?

- How can your emails guide customers through your process— keeping them informed of their accomplishment to date and clearly outlining what still remains?

- How can a series of customized mail pieces mark the steps in the process that the customer completes and those that are still being worked on?

- How can a phone conversation create a check-in and open a dialogue for addressing any uncertainty or confusion?

- How can videos guide the customer through key steps and tricky elements?

- What present(s) could you give customers that mark their progress and accomplishments?

Pick One Now

If you've answered the questions above (and I hope you're not just reading along—seriously, slow down and answer the questions!), you have a clear understanding of the customer experience during the Acclimate phase, as well as many ideas for how to make that experience better. Taking that into account, consider the following questions.

- What is one thing you can start doing tomorrow to make the experience your customers have in the Acclimate phase even better?

- Who would you need to talk to in order to make this happen?

- How would you know if you've succeeded in making this improvement?

- How would you measure the improvement of the overall customer experience?

- How would you share this impact with the rest of the organization?

FROM ACCLIMATE TO ACCOMPLISH

Now that you've helped your customers learn the ropes and they are familiar with your process, habits, and behaviors as exhibited in the Acclimate phase, let's consider how you can help them achieve the goal(s) that led them to choose to work with you in the beginning.

CHAPTER THIRTEEN

Phase 6: Accomplish

 ## Overview of the Accomplish Phase

The Accomplish phase of the customer experience occurs when the customer achieves the result they were seeking when they first decided to do business with you. Unfortunately, many customers never reach this phase and even fewer companies pay attention to this important milestone.

(SOMETIMES) IT'S A PIECE OF CAKE

At face value, the phrase "managed disaster recovery" may sound like an oxymoron, but not if you know the team at Ongoing Operations (or OGO, as their clients call them). OGO manages disaster recovery by offering a fully prepared, temporary offsite office space and server backup to credit unions and other companies that need extra space in a pinch. OGO is considered to be the industry leader in business continuity process and disaster recovery technologies, partly because it follows the previous five phases of customer experience—deftly bringing a sense of humor and playfulness to a high-pressure planning activity—and partly because it actively reminds its clients to celebrate their progress, an action clients might otherwise forget to take amid the stress.

A good disaster recovery partner has a facility located far enough away from the cities it serves so that any natural or manmade disaster in those cities is highly unlikely to affect the business's ongoing operations (see what I did there?).

Located in Hagerstown, Maryland (less than ninety miles from the major metropolitan areas of Washington, D.C., and Baltimore), Ongoing Operations is on a different power grid, far enough away that it experiences different weather patterns, and yet close enough to the customers it serves to allow for their employees to easily travel to a temporary headquarters in an emergency. Ongoing Operations has room after room full of cubicles that are preloaded with the necessary software and telephone solutions so that at a moment's notice, everything can mirror the technology and desktop footprint that a client experiences in its usual headquarters.

Handling this preparation and planning is not an easy task and requires a level of strategy and coordination that most businesses find foreign and challenging. The typical new customer onboarding process at Ongoing Operations requires thirty phone calls, fifty or more emails, and six to twelve in-person meetings across a two- to three-month implementation schedule.

When the entire project is completed and the business has been green-lit as ready for a disaster recovery situation (usually about sixty days after the project begins), Ongoing Operations sends a custom-made cake and a bouquet of balloons to the customer's implementation team.

When the customer receives these gifts and opens the enclosed card, they find a playful message. "You just finished this great big implementation project. While it wasn't a piece of cake, have a piece of cake on us!" This unexpected celebratory treat brings a smile to the faces of the customer's employees and leaves them thankful for the completion of this daunting, and at times extremely stressful, implementation program.

Founder and CEO Kirk Drake notes that "[i]t's a small investment that costs $100, which is almost nothing considering the average contract brings in between $20,000 to $30,000 a month in revenue." Taking the time to acknowledge the completion of the project with a cake doesn't require a lot of money, it just requires some thinking and planning ahead. "Clients who complete the install process and receive the cake at the end love us forever," observes Kirk. "The effort of making the First 100 Days memorable and pleasant puts us in a position to be more comfortable when asking for a favor later in the relationship."[1] (Stay tuned for a discussion of asking for testimonials and referrals in chapter 15.)

Kirk is convinced that proper onboarding leads to long-term client relationships. "We spend a lot of time communicating with our clients to make sure they understand the process, expectations, results, and anything in between . . . if we don't spend the time during the First 100 Days, we've found that customers walk out the door at the end of the contract."[2]

Quick Takeaway

Know the customer's primary goal and then celebrate with them when they achieve that milestone. You should strive to invest at least 5 percent of a project's profits back into experience enhancements for your customer. If you run into challenges along the way, acknowledge them and, where appropriate, add humor to the interactions to make them more memorable and reduce the overall stress level.

WILL YOU EVEN REACH THE ACCOMPLISH PHASE?

First of all, you need to know whether you've reached the Accomplish phase or not. Shockingly few businesses track whether or not customers achieve their desired results. Because it often takes so long to accomplish the goal, many customers forget why they decided to try your product or service in the first place.

If you don't track the goal and the customer doesn't remember the goal, how are you going to know when to celebrate the achievement of the goal? How are they going to know when to thank you for making it happen?

The Accomplish phase is tied to the entire reason the organization is in business and to the main promise the organization makes to any new customer during the marketing and sales process.

Reaching the Accomplish phase is not as common as one might think. When it comes to accomplishing the customer's goal, most interactions fall into one of three categories:

1. Mission Accomplished

The customer achieves the desired goal and has such a positive experience along the way that they will continue to purchase from and recommend this business going forward.

2. The Lukewarm Bath

The customer achieves the stated goal, but the feelings associated with the process were less than positive. In this scenario, while the customer achieved the initial goal or result, they are unlikely to purchase again or refer other customers to the business because of the feelings they associate with the company.

3. Mission Failure

The customer does not accomplish the desired result and decides never to do business with the company again.

Sadly, this last scenario happens often.

The Accomplish phase is regularly overlooked by businesses— probably because it seems so obvious to their very existence. Of course the product is meant to achieve the results!

And yet it doesn't always work out that way for the customer. In many businesses, it is the rare customer who reaches the Accomplish phase with the business/customer relationship intact.

This violates the maxim outlined by business consultant John Jantsch referenced earlier in this book: "A sale is not a 'finished' sale until the customer receives a result."[3]

YOU REACHED THE FINISH LINE, HERE'S YOUR DIPLOMA

After hearing a fifteen-minute speech I gave at an event called Master-mindTalks, Jon Goodman decided to redesign his entire customer on-boarding experience. Jon launched the Online Trainer Academy (OTA) program in 2016. As the first-ever certification program for online trainers, OTA offered an online video course in which Jon taught a business development methodology he created.

Jon combined old-school, offline customer interactions with smart, automated systems that made customers feel cared for at all times. "My goal was (and is) to help personal trainers make a bit more money in a bit less time with a bit better schedule, all while doing a better job," Jon explains.

Contrary to many online training programs, Jon wanted to incorporate a physical element to complement his Web-based video series.

To do this, he designed a program where he surprises and delights his new customers via unexpected items they receive in the mail (a strong contrast for customers operating in an online environment).

After the training course is purchased, Jon's team mails the customer a hardback textbook, a spiral-bound training workbook, and instructions for how to use these two items in conjunction with the online training videos. The fact that Jon's online training program has a physical textbook and workbook automatically distinguishes it from the bulk of online education programs. The fact that these books are beautifully designed and printed further cements the emotional experience customers have and supports the brand image/reputation of a high-quality, high-value program.

"Even printing a textbook and mailing it to the customer is different," Jon explains. "Nobody in my industry does this because it's cheaper to do digital fulfillment. My goal is to blow my students away with the quality and thoughtfulness of the original materials we send as part of the course (including book-quality workbooks and a metallic, imprinted bookmark)."

Receiving the guidebook and workbook in the mail is just the first of many touches. Special gifts, small mementos, and other thoughtful presents appear from time to time in the customer's mailbox as a way for Jon to stay in touch, stay top of mind, and continue to show his appreciation for his customers' investment in his online training program.

Custom-built training software allows Jon to monitor the progress of his students and provide them with gentle yet useful nudges should they slow or stall in any of the training modules. This allows Jon to acclimate his clients as they navigate their coursework.

The real magic happens, however, when Jon's students accomplish the goal of passing their online certification test.

This is the reason they signed up for the course in the first place. In fact, about 40 percent of Jon's customers complete all of the training modules *and* take the necessary test to achieve the Online Trainer Academy certification. In addition, about 20 percent of Jon's customers complete all of the training modules but don't take the final step of testing to become certified. This shows that the majority of his customers (60 percent) are achieving the result of completing the course, even if they don't take the final step to become officially recognized as certified online trainers. Compared with the fact that online courses typically see an average completion rate of 3 to 5 percent, Jon's results are incredible and more than ten times the industry average.

To mark the important milestone and accomplishment of becoming certified, Jon sends the graduated student an email filled with badges to add to their website and images for them to upload to social media announcing their online certification.

The real surprise comes in the mail about a week later when the newly graduated and certified trainer receives a beautiful graduation diploma signed by Jon and marked with the Online Trainer Academy seal of approval. This "suitable for framing" diploma mirrors the diploma one would receive in a traditional, "real world" training program. The fact that it comes to individuals who have completed an online program makes it stand out in the world of online training courses.

The benefits of this approach to creating remarkable customer experiences aren't limited to the students in Jon's course. The employees are energized by these activities as well. "My people friggin' love it! It makes what we're doing a lot more real for the team because they can see what we build for our customers in our customers' hands. I feel like the employees at most digital product companies get bored because they can't really 'see' people enjoying or using their materials. We don't have that problem."

This extra care for students and employees impacts the bottom line of the business in a significant way. "On average, there is a 20 percent refund rate for digital products within the first one hundred days," explains Jon. "And this is considered 'acceptable' by my competition."

Never being one to rest on his laurels, Jon wanted to raise the expectations of his team and students by striving for a single-digit return rate. "In our most recent launch, we experienced just a 2.9 percent refund rate," Jon shared. "Based on our sales, the increase in expense for all of the physical fulfillment and the difference between a 20 percent refund rate and a 2.9 percent refund rate meant that we made another $264,939.82 in profit."

By the time a customer reaches the Accomplish phase, the results from enhanced customer experiences are permeating every aspect of the business. The customers are ecstatic, the employees are engaged, and the bottom line is getting better with each program iteration.

 Quick Takeaway

Defy customers' preconceived expectations. Create contrast in experience. Online customers expect that every interaction will be online. Consider adding offline interactions to bring your company and experience into the tangible world. Sending something via mail feels almost old-school in comparison with online offerings, but this contrasting experience creates a remarkable interaction.

RUN THROUGH THE TAPE

When I was in junior high, I had an ill-advised stint on the track team. Let's just say that my top running speed was a little above that of a toddler who has just learned to walk. In fact, one time while running an

800-meter race (two laps around the track) I was so far behind the pack that the organizers turned off the stadium lights before I crossed the finish line. Granted, it was the last race of the night, but come on, people!

My running accomplishments (or lack thereof) aside, I learned a valuable lesson that is familiar to all track runners and should be mandatory teaching (in my opinion) for business leaders everywhere.

In practice, my coach always insisted that I "run through the tape." He explained that as they near the finish line, most runners focus all their energy on getting to the tape strung across the finish line. This tape was designed to help race officials determine who had won the race—not to mark the runner's focus.

Coach explained that if you run to the tape, you're actually slowing down in the final steps as your body is trying to "land" on the finish line. He encouraged me to take my focus farther out—to a spot ten feet behind the finish line. That way, as I was running I would keep accelerating *through* the finish line instead of slowing down to meet it.

Instead of trying to get your customers to reach the "Accomplished" finish line, focus on helping them make it past their deadline, goal, or desired result.

What is the customer really hoping to do? If you sell a weight loss product, the goal isn't just to lose twenty pounds—it's to fit into the suit for the wedding. If you know the actual desire behind the goal, you can help manage the customer to that outcome (e.g., ask them to send a picture wearing the suit at the wedding *after* losing the weight).

By running through the tape, you ensure that your team and your energies are devoted to going above and beyond the finish line, instead of simply arriving at the desired result the customer expected.

WILL YOU PLEASE JUST GO THE F**K TO SLEEP?

The acknowledgment of a customer achieving their desired results doesn't require a significant commitment of time, money, or effort. In fact, when done properly, it can be automated in an incredible fashion.

Audible.com, a global library and resource for purchasing audiobooks as digital downloads, accomplishes this with a fantastic email. In the process, they also perfectly time their upsell offer and all but guarantee another purchase.

Back in 2012, my wife Berit and I found out that we were expecting our first child. Not long after the birth of our son, a colleague called me and said, "Joey, I have a book that you need to read.

"But I don't want you to read it," he continued. "I need you to listen to the audiobook. Every parent needs to listen to this book. . . ."

"What's it called?" I inquired.

"*Go the F**k to Sleep*," he replied.

I must confess that I started laughing. . . .

He cut me off: "Every parent *needs* to know that the total sleep deprivation that comes with a newborn is normal, and it's okay to be frustrated with your child in those moments."

To make matters even better, he shared the pièce de résistance: "By the way, the audiobook is narrated by Samuel L. Jackson."

Having this playful children's book narrated by a movie icon known for his unique and commanding voice (and his propensity for swearing) brought the book to an entirely new level of experience.

What was most interesting to me, though, was not the hysterical story by the book's author, Adam Mansbach (which was wonderfully irreverent), nor the passionate narration by Samuel L. Jackson (which left me laughing out loud). I was intrigued by the email I received from Audible the day after I accomplished my goal of listening to the complete audiobook.

Audible sent an email that looked like this:

I found a number of things about this email fascinating. First, the email didn't arrive until after I had downloaded and completely listened to the audiobook. The Audible app has an automation that lets the company know when you've actually listened to the book so it doesn't email you before you've experienced the result you sought when you first made the purchase. Once you've finished listening, Audible sends an upsell email. Interestingly enough, this message is modified if the listener gives the audiobook a low rating. In that instance, Audible won't recommend the same author or the same genre and instead will recommend a different kind of audiobook.

Second, the email focused on a visual presentation instead of written text. The typical company would have sent this message:

Dear Joey:

If you liked *Go the F**k to Sleep*, you're going to love:

For grown-up children:

Bossypants—Tina Fey

Sh*t My Dad Says—Justin Halpern

Are You There, Vodka? It's Me, Chelsea—Chelsea Handler

For growing children:

Mr. Popper's Penguins—Richard Atwater

The Cat in the Hat—Dr. Seuss

The Three Little Pigs—James Marshall

Make Me Laugh

These are the exact same words as presented in the visual email Audible sent, but the experience of receiving a text-based email like this is completely different.

Finally, I loved the call-to-action button that said "Make Me Laugh." The fact that Audible knew (or could assume) my emotional state and took advantage of this state in the message further reinforces that simple communications (like a confirmation email) can have long-lasting impact.

Quick Takeaway

The mere fact that your customer achieved their desired goal or result is worthy of noting and celebrating. Not only does it show you were paying attention all along, but it lets you share in the successful achievement. Communications can be personalized or automated—as long as they are properly timed to the milestone. If the message coincides with a well-placed upsell offer, the likelihood of the customer purchasing again is significant.

YOUR SITE IS LIVE!

Anyone who has ever been part of a website development project (whether as a designer/coder or the client) knows what a painful process it can be. Projects have a tendency to go way beyond scope, cost more than anyone planned or budgeted, and miss deadlines as if they weren't even there. Often, getting the website "launched and live" is a minor miracle, leaving everyone relieved and eager to avoid reliving the memories.

Clients of Yoko Co in McLean, Virginia, feel very different when their websites launch. As a Web development firm, Yoko Co focuses on enhancing the online presence of organizations that are driven by a purpose beyond profit. From the very first meeting, the Yoko Co team is focused on clearly identifying the client's goals and explicitly defining what a successful website launch looks like—in the client's own words— a focus that has led founder Chris Yoko to grow the company to a dozen employees and more than $1.5 million in annual revenues.

After making introductions at the kickoff meeting, Yoko takes the new client through a process to identify and record the organizational objectives for the website, as well as the short-term and long-term success metrics. They use this information throughout the development process and all the way through the launch of the website. Not only does the Yoko Co team assist the client in promoting the launch, but Yoko Co supports the effort with their own press releases and social media plugs designed to celebrate the client's new website.

The Yoko Co team then conducts two surveys—one internal, one external. While many companies send surveys, Yoko Co uses them to objectively assess the project while also gathering information that is valuable for both internal operations and client conversations.

Experience Increased!

The internal survey asks all the members of the team who worked on the project to evaluate their own performance, as well as that of their peers and the client. The survey begins by asking four basic questions:

- What project does the survey pertain to?

- On a scale of 1 to 5 stars, 5 being the best, how much (or how little) did you enjoy working with our client on this project?

- Would you like to work with this client again?

- What is your name and title?

The responses measure current employee project satisfaction while also giving insight to future project assignments. Depending on how many "stars" the employee gives the client, the survey expands to ask more specific questions. For example, with five stars, the survey celebrates a great project and offers the employee the chance to write a testimonial for the client. If the employee gives the project one star, the survey acknowledges the frustration, creates space for the employee to vent their feelings, and then playfully asks what should happen next (ranging from "Let's put this behind us" to "Can I kick you in the crotch instead?").

By gathering honest feedback, Yoko Co is able to better select clients in the future, as well as share (usually positive) feedback with the client at the Conclusion Meeting.

Can We Give You a Hug?

The external survey asks everyone who took part in the project from the client side to share their feedback. The survey begins by asking three basic questions:

- On a scale of 1 to 5, 5 being the best, how much (or how little) did you enjoy working with us on this project?

- Would you recommend Yoko Co to your colleagues?

- What is your name and title?

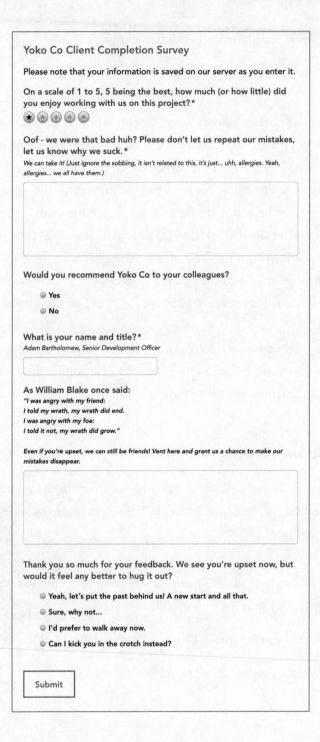

Yoko Co Client Completion Survey

Please note that your information is saved on our server as you enter it.

On a scale of 1 to 5, 5 being the best, how much (or how little) did you enjoy working with us on this project? *

★ ★ ★ ★ ★

Oof - we were that bad huh? Please don't let us repeat our mistakes, let us know why we suck. *

We can take it! (Just ignore the sobbing, it isn't related to this, it's just... uhh, allergies. Yeah, allergies... we all have them.)

Would you recommend Yoko Co to your colleagues?

- ○ Yes
- ○ No

What is your name and title? *

Adam Bartholomew, Senior Development Officer

As William Blake once said:

"I was angry with my friend:
I told my wrath, my wrath did end.
I was angry with my foe:
I told it not, my wrath did grow."

Even if you're upset, we can still be friends! Vent here and grant us a chance to make our mistakes disappear.

Thank you so much for your feedback. We see you're upset now, but would it feel any better to hug it out?

- ○ Yeah, let's put the past behind us! A new start and all that.
- ○ Sure, why not...
- ○ I'd prefer to walk away now.
- ○ Can I kick you in the crotch instead?

Submit

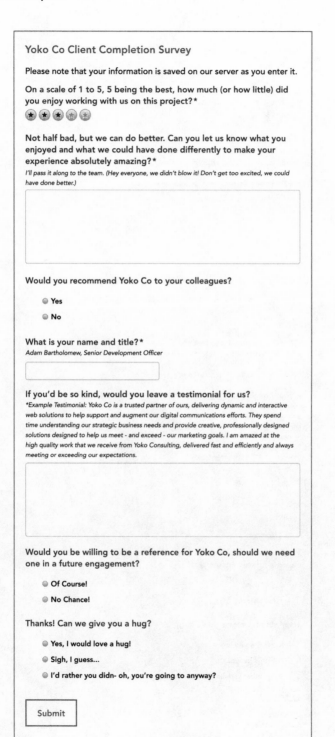

Yoko Co Client Completion Survey

Please note that your information is saved on our server as you enter it.

On a scale of 1 to 5, 5 being the best, how much (or how little) did you enjoy working with us on this project?*

★ ★ ★ ☆ ☆

Not half bad, but we can do better. Can you let us know what you enjoyed and what we could have done differently to make your experience absolutely amazing?*

I'll pass it along to the team. (Hey everyone, we didn't blow it! Don't get too excited, we could have done better.)

Would you recommend Yoko Co to your colleagues?

○ Yes

○ No

What is your name and title?*

Adam Bartholomew, Senior Development Officer

If you'd be so kind, would you leave a testimonial for us?

*Example Testimonial: Yoko Co is a trusted partner of ours, delivering dynamic and interactive web solutions to help support and augment our digital communications efforts. They spend time understanding our strategic business needs and provide creative, professionally designed solutions designed to help us meet - and exceed - our marketing goals. I am amazed at the high quality work that we receive from Yoko Consulting, delivered fast and efficiently and always meeting or exceeding our expectations.

Would you be willing to be a reference for Yoko Co, should we need one in a future engagement?

○ Of Course!

○ No Chance!

Thanks! Can we give you a hug?

○ Yes, I would love a hug!

○ Sigh, I guess...

○ I'd rather you didn- oh, you're going to anyway?

Submit

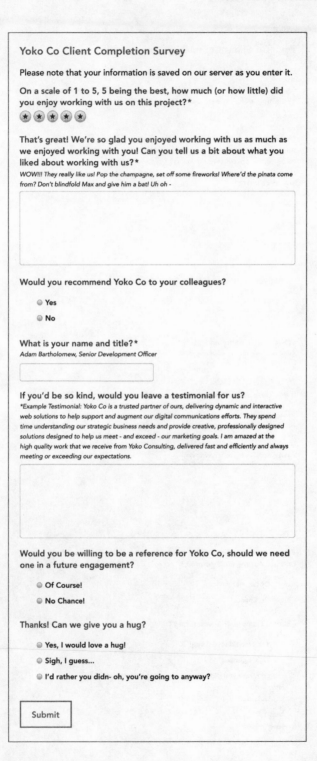

Yoko Co Client Completion Survey

Please note that your information is saved on our server as you enter it.

On a scale of 1 to 5, 5 being the best, how much (or how little) did you enjoy working with us on this project?*

★ ★ ★ ★ ★

That's great! We're so glad you enjoyed working with us as much as we enjoyed working with you! Can you tell us a bit about what you liked about working with us?*

WOW!!! They really like us! Pop the champagne, set off some fireworks! Where'd the pinata come from? Don't blindfold Max and give him a bat! Uh oh -

Would you recommend Yoko Co to your colleagues?

○ Yes

○ No

What is your name and title?*

Adam Bartholomew, Senior Development Officer

If you'd be so kind, would you leave a testimonial for us?

*Example Testimonial: Yoko Co is a trusted partner of ours, delivering dynamic and interactive web solutions to help support and augment our digital communications efforts. They spend time understanding our strategic business needs and provide creative, professionally designed solutions designed to help us meet - and exceed - our marketing goals. I am amazed at the high quality work that we receive from Yoko Consulting, delivered fast and efficiently and always meeting or exceeding our expectations.

Would you be willing to be a reference for Yoko Co, should we need one in a future engagement?

○ Of Course!

○ No Chance!

Thanks! Can we give you a hug?

○ Yes, I would love a hug!

○ Sigh, I guess...

○ I'd rather you didn- oh, you're going to anyway?

Submit

Again, depending on how many "stars" the client gives the project, the survey expands to ask more specific questions. For example, if a client gives it five stars, the survey asks for specific feedback about what the client liked and offers the respondent the chance to write a testimonial for Yoko Co. If the client gives the project one star, the survey acknowledges the frustration, creates space for the client to vent their feelings, and then playfully asks if they want to "hug it out."

Ending on a High (Five)

After gathering the survey feedback, the Yoko Co team conducts a Conclusion Meeting designed to mirror the kickoff meeting. The first item on the agenda is a review of the organizational objectives as well as the short-term and long-term success metrics. The Yoko Co team does an honest assessment, measuring the level of success on each of the metrics previously identified. The client also provides feedback on the metrics so that (a) any outstanding deficiencies can be addressed and (b) everyone is clear on whether the project goals have been accomplished. "As far as we're concerned, the project isn't complete until we confirm we've hit the mark and the client feels their goals are achieved," explains Yoko.

The meeting also offers the opportunity to review any problems the client experienced during the project, share the scores the Yoko Co team gave to the client, provide testimonials and endorsements for the client via online review sites and/or social media, *and*—only after a lot of giving to the client—ask the client for testimonials and reviews.

At the end of the meeting, Yoko Co outlines a plan for another three months of site monitoring (which is provided as part of the initial project fee), during which the team will make sure that the site continues to operate properly and the client remains happy. According to Yoko, "This is our attempt to mitigate 'website launcher's remorse' and to move them toward the adopt and advocate phases." This is also a great example of the "run through the tape" philosophy outlined earlier in this chapter.

Since adopting these onboarding strategies, not only have projects stayed on budget and on schedule, but client and employee satisfaction has skyrocketed. "I knew these systems would make for happier, more engaged clients," notes Yoko. "What surprised me was the impact on our employee experience. I've seen the team become more collaborative with clients, dramatically increase their personal engagement and involvement, and get super excited about surprising clients with thoughtful gifts. Not only are we accomplishing the clients' goals, but we are accomplishing my goal of creating a fun company culture, with engaging employees doing meaningful work."

 Quick Takeaway

It's not unusual for a business to think it has crossed the finish line with a customer, only to find that the customer feels six paces behind. Taking the time in the beginning of the relationship to collaborate with the customer and establish solid metrics for success makes it easy to know whether the finish line is reached. Using surveys (both internally and externally) at the completion of an engagement to gather information about how the customer and your employees feel about working together allows for a clear understanding of what went right or wrong, and a better experience for everyone in future engagements.

THANKS FOR DINING WITH US . . .

The best part about visiting the hopping Latin American restaurant Baro isn't its location in a gorgeous four-story, 16,000-square-foot building in the heart of Toronto's entertainment district. The best part is that from your second visit onward, you feel like you've been a loyal patron for decades. The restaurant manages to treat fairly new customers like family by having every employee—from food runners to bartenders to servers to partners—record your preferences in Baro's reservation software. So instead of hearing the blasé opening question "Have you dined with us before?" you can begin the evening by being asked, "Mr. Johnson, will you be having your Johnnie Walker on the rocks again?" In its first year in business, Baro booked more than C$10 million in revenue—an amazing accomplishment for a brand-new restaurant.

Baro's seamless dining experience begins with the hostess sending a subtle signal to the staff. Every customer receives either a blue or green menu—blue if they are an existing customer and Baro has customer intelligence on them, or green if they are a new customer with no record or prior booking in Baro's customer relationship management software.

The customer's interests, food and drink selections, and preferences not only are captured, but the experience coordinator reviews these daily. Before the restaurant opens for the evening, the coordinator talks to each server about the specifics of the guests who will be seated in that server's section. "Our goal is to constantly create micro customer experiences for our guests," Michel Falcon, one of Baro's partners, explains. "Small, subtle, memorable gestures that will resonate with them for years to come." The budget for creating these interactions is purposely kept lean—C$250 per month total, for the *entire* restaurant—to "keep the team creative."

In the days following the dining experience, Baro continues to connect with the customer. Customers receive a "thank you for joining us" call and an invitation to fill out a quick survey via email about their experience. Baro tracks these responses and receives a Net Promoter Score of 80+—astounding considering that the average Net Promoter Score in the restaurant industry is 0 (yes, you read that properly—zero).[4] Ironically enough, 10 to 15 percent of the customers who receive the thank-you call book another reservation while on the phone. To be clear, Baro doesn't ask the customer if they want to book a reservation— the customer takes advantage of the call to give Baro more business.

Once a month, the experience coordinator randomly selects ten customers to receive a very special thank-you from the partners in the restaurant. The partners film customized videos (incorporating references to the intelligence they have on that particular customer) that are then emailed to the unsuspecting diners. Needless to say, the response to these videos is incredible. "You can't imagine the state of shock and euphoria that customers experience when receiving these personalized messages," Michel shares with a proud smile on his face. "The additional word of mouth, online reviews, and increased business from these patrons is too difficult to accurately measure, but we know it's significant."

⏱ Quick Takeaway

Even in industries with the most transient of customers, it's possible to create a remarkable experience that gets them to come back again and again. By applying the collective powers of observation of all employees, intelligence on customers can be gathered, cataloged, and then used to create intimate feelings of nurturing and care. Following up with the customer after a successful (or unsuccessful) interaction not only will help improve your processes, but will bring your organization front of mind for the customer and spur the possibility of doing additional business.

IT'S OKAY TO ASK FOR MORE

Once you're sure the customer has accomplished their original goals, it's okay to ask for additional business. This can come in the form of an upsell, an extension of an existing service contract, or a new and improved product offering. Not only is pairing their heightened emotional state with a request for new business appropriate, but the likelihood of a successful sale is dramatically higher.

Successful upsell requests paired with heightened positive emotions after achieving the Accomplish phase can be seen in the long lines to purchase concert "merch" after a rock concert, the significant sales of postconference videos of the talks attendees witnessed, the photo of you in midscream that is available for purchase at the end of a roller-coaster ride, and in the likelihood that you will continue to spend money in the hotel and casino after winning a Vegas jackpot. In short, when a customer gets what they originally wanted, it is much easier to ask them to extend the feeling by making another purchase.

Keep in mind, however, that both you *and* the customer should feel that the previous engagement was successful before seeking new opportunities. The best way to do this is to identify the customer's goals at the beginning of the customer journey (ideally in the Assess phase but no later than the Activate phase) and then track your progress against completing those goals throughout the relationship.

Messaging an upsell at this point in the relationship doesn't require as much finesse as an earlier-stage ask, but that doesn't mean it should be an afterthought. Give careful consideration as to what the customer wants or needs now that the engagement is accomplished— instead of just trying to sell them anything you can.

SUMMARY: PHASE 6—ACCOMPLISH

The Accomplish stage of the customer life cycle occurs when the customer achieves the original result they were looking for when they decided to do business with you. This may be the time they use your product and achieve their desired impact, or the time that your service delivers on the hopes they had when deciding to work with you.

During this phase, the customer's initial expectation is met and they achieve the result(s) sought during the initial consideration of your product or service. Regrettably, not every customer achieves the results sought and thus not every customer completes this phase. By clearly identifying the customer's initial goal and then delivering that result in the Accomplish phase, you are able to make good on the brand promise shared at the beginning of the relationship.

The Accomplish stage of the customer life cycle offers you the opportunity to acknowledge the significance of this milestone, celebrate the achievement, and in the process remind the customer that this was the result they were seeking all along. Even if the customer remembers their original goal, they will probably forget to celebrate—and in the process acknowledge your contribution to their success—unless reminded.

SIX THINGS TO DO IN THE ACCOMPLISH PHASE STARTING TOMORROW

By now it should be clear—you don't need to use every communication tool in each phase. Just consider the possibilities of using a tool to create a memorable experience for the customer during this phase.

 **IN-PERSON**

Taking the time to celebrate the customer's achievement of their initial goal(s) honors this milestone and reinforces its significance. Hosting a party for the entire team or simply raising a glass in celebration with your main point of contact marks this moment as a memorable event, reminding the customer that their initial desire(s) came true with your product/service.

CHAPTER EXAMPLE: A Conclusion Meeting at the end of a customer engagement (Yoko Co) helps to mark the milestone and ensure that the customer's goals at the time of purchase or signing up have been met.

 EMAIL

An email congratulating the customer on reaching this result helps to acknowledge and honor the accomplishment. Highlighting the various steps along the path the customer traveled to reach this point further establishes the significance of the moment. With certain products or services, reaching this phase can be memorialized with badges, banners, and certificates for customers to proudly display.

CHAPTER EXAMPLE: Waiting until after the goal is achieved (Audible and Baro) lets you join in celebrating the Accomplishment before trying to convince the customer to make another purchase. Sending badges to display on social media (Online Trainer Academy) allows members of the "tribe" to publicly share their affiliation. Using surveys to gather both internal and customer feedback (Yoko Co) helps accurately determine whether the initial client goals have been accomplished.

MAIL

A handwritten note marking the accomplishment of the customer's desired goal or impact creates a lasting memento of the occasion. A celebratory card allows for the expression of heartfelt congratulations while showing that the company was aware of the customer's desired result and the fact that the result was obtained.

CHAPTER EXAMPLE: Sending unexpected, beautiful, physical items (Online Trainer Academy) is an unanticipated touchpoint for an online company. Following up these interactions with another personalized gift allows the organization to share in the celebration of a job well done (Ongoing Operations) when their customers reach major milestones and achieve their goals.

 PHONE

A congratulatory call and conversation shows the customer that the company was aware of the customer's expectations for the engagement/interaction and that it celebrates the milestone of achieving them. Genuine words of praise allow for the acknowledgment of the journey to date (noting both ups and downs) and help set the tone for any future interactions.

CHAPTER EXAMPLE: A thoughtful follow-up call to see if the customer enjoyed their experience (Baro) not only exhibits an "above and beyond" attitude, but it opens the door for the customer to share their honest opinions and, in some instances, suggest additional ways to do business with them even before you attempt an upsell.

VIDEO

A congratulatory video from the entire team allows for this milestone to be marked and celebrated at the same time. Making sure that the brand spirit and energy comes out in this video further cements the relationship and makes it clear that the customer's success is in direct alignment with the company's desired impact for its products or services.

CHAPTER EXAMPLE: A thoughtful video message (Baro) sent after the customer achieves their goal adds a level of remarkability to the overall experience and is a unique and memorable way to mark the milestone. This type of communication also builds a deeper level of connection and rapport between an organization and its customers as it is clear to the recipient that the sender went beyond the expected or required interaction to create something special.

PRESENT

The familiar practice of using gifts and presents to celebrate milestones and accomplishments in an individual's personal life makes transitioning this practice to the world of business fairly simple. Gifts that acknowledge the journey or the result further establish the importance of the moment. Celebratory food and drink can enhance the accomplishment and bring people closer together.

CHAPTER EXAMPLE: Sending playful presents (Ongoing Operations, Online Trainer Academy, and Yoko Co) to customers upon completion of landmark achievements brings a sense of levity and fun to an otherwise serious business engagement, while also adding a touch of celebration for a job well done.

YOUR ASSIGNMENT: PUT THESE IDEAS TO WORK

Now that you have a clear understanding of the Accomplish phase, answer a series of questions that are designed to get you thinking about how you can use each of the communication tools to enhance the overall experience during this phase of the customer journey.

(Show that you can "accomplish" the goal you had when purchasing this book and take the time to answer these questions that will help you implement what you're learning!)

Evaluating the Current Situation

Answer each question, then write two or three sentences explaining your answer. For bonus points, write down any ideas you have for changes that would make your answers "better."

- What is the goal your customer is trying to reach? (Hint: If you offer different types of products and services, there may be different or multiple goals. However, every customer has one primary goal that is the most important. If you don't know what that is, how will you know when or if they achieve it?)

- Describe in detail the goal that the customer seeks. Do you describe it the same way the customer does? What does it "feel" like for the customer to accomplish this? How does the customer know they have achieved it? How do you know that the customer has achieved it?

- What percentage of your customers do you think achieve the goal(s) they had when purchasing your product or services? What percentage of your customers are you *certain* achieve those goals?

- In your current business, do you create remarkable experiences during the Accomplish phase? If so, what are they?

- On a scale of 1 to 10, where 1 is "pathetic" and 10 is "world class," how would you rate the experience your customers currently have in the Accomplish phase? (Don't worry if you score yourself low—it just means there is room for improvement.)

Tools to Enhance the Future Experience

Answer each question by coming up with two or three ideas for using the specific tool to enhance the customer experience. I've said it before, but please don't worry about how much it will cost, who will do it, or how to get it implemented in your organization. You can worry about those things later!

- How can you use in-person interactions during this phase to celebrate the customer's achievement?

- How can you time your emails to celebrate as soon as the customer's primary goal is accomplished?

- How can a customized mail piece celebrate the customer reaching this important milestone?

- How can phone conversations add a level of personalization and sincerity to your message of congratulations?

- How can videos be used to infuse fun and humor into the moment a customer achieves their goal?

- What present(s) could you give customers that would really make them feel accomplished?

Pick One Now

If you've answered the questions above (and I hope you're not just reading along—seriously, slow down and answer the questions!), you have a clear understanding of the customer experience during the Accomplish phase, as well as many ideas for how to make that experience better. Taking that into account, consider the following questions.

- What is one thing you can start doing tomorrow to make the experience your customers have in the Accomplish phase even better?

- Who would you need to talk to in order to make this happen?

- How would you know if you've succeeded in making this improvement?

- How would you measure the improvement of the overall customer experience?

- How would you share this impact with the rest of the organization?

FROM ACCOMPLISH TO ADOPT

Now that you've helped a customer achieve their original goal(s) in the Accomplish phase, let's consider how to turn that customer into a customer for life.

CHAPTER FOURTEEN

Phase 7: Adopt

Overview of the Adopt Phase

In the Adopt phase, the customer adopts the business and proudly shows support and affinity for the brand. Having accomplished the original goal, the customer now decides to double down on the association and establish a long-term relationship. At this point the customer mentally and emotionally commits to continuing the business relationship even if another purchase isn't obviously imminent. Only after a customer has adopted the business's way of operating and taken a personal ownership stake in the relationship can they be considered "loyal."

A SPECIAL PLACE FOR PEOPLE WITH A SERIOUS BEAUTY ADDICTION

Sephora makes its most loyal customers feel incredibly special as it marks the Adopt phase with an invitation to join a powerful loyalty program. Headquartered in Paris, Sephora is a retail shop that sells makeup, hair products, and other beauty items at retail locations around the world. As part of Sephora's customer tracking program, it identifies which customers are the most loyal and invites them to be a part of VIB Rouge (Very Important Beauty Insider Rouge).

I learned about the VIB Rouge program when my wife came home and handed me a black padded envelope with red and silver printing. When I opened it, I found a smooth paper box with raised red print

lettering that read "Sephora VIB Rouge." I slid the box sleeve open and found an insert with embossed ink that repeated the "Sephora VIB Rouge" message along with an engaging invitation:

> *Welcome to the Top. There's a special place for people with a serious beauty addiction. It's called VIB Rouge.*

Below the insert card was a metallic card that said "VIB Rouge," along with a tube of lipstick.

The metallic membership card was polished to such a sheen that I could see my own reflection in it. The package also included a custom lipstick in a unique color available only to VIB Rouge members. This VIB Rouge package congratulated the customer on achieving a milestone of spending more than $1,000 at Sephora over the previous year, which my wife did after purchasing gift sets for all the women in our extended families (what can I say, I'm one of seven kids, so there are many gifts under the Christmas tree each year!).

By treating its high-end customers to a loyalty program that provides exclusive lipsticks, special access to new products, discount shop-

ping days, and multiple opportunities for gathering loyalty points, Sephora reenergizes and elevates the relationship with its most loyal and active customers.

In many ways, Sephora sees the transition to the Adopt phase as ushering in an entirely new customer relationship. By focusing on these power purchasers, Sephora cements the brand loyalty of its best customers and gets them to purchase even more products and services. In doing so, it ends up taking an existing customer and propelling them forward into a new type of customer—the loyal and steadfast adopter.

Quick Takeaway

Elevate good customers into even better customers by creating exclusive experiences and allowing them to earn unique rewards. By establishing an exclusive membership tier for your top customers, you build affinity and give them yet another reason to continue doing business with you (something the airline frequent flier programs have known for years).

THE CUSTOMER TAKES OWNERSHIP

The Adopt phase occurs when the onus for maintaining the relationship shifts from the company to the customer. The customer has accomplished the original goal and achieved their desired result, so they
"adopt" the brand, thus declaring their loyalty.

This declaration might be a formal, public statement of commitment,
a subconscious decision to stay loyal, or any number of stated or unstated
activities that evince an ongoing commitment. What matters is that the
customer has begun to regard your company with a new emotion.

To "adopt" means to take on an enhanced level of responsibility for
a relationship. When an individual adopts a child, in essence they raise
a hand and say, "I will be responsible for this person. I will make sure
they are taken care of and well provided for going forward."

In this phase of the customer journey, the customer says to themselves, "I will take a deeper responsibility for owning this relationship.
I will take a leadership role in communicating with the company to
make sure our relationship stays strong, and I will be loyal to the company for the foreseeable future."

At this point, the customer has acclimated to the organization and
understands most aspects of the way business is done. The customer is
now part of the brand and the culture. As a member of the tribe, they
are able to anticipate what comes next. They don't need to wait for you
to move the conversation forward.

The Adopt phase is wonderful. At this point, the customer is happy
to volunteer additional insight into your process, give unsolicited feedback on what is and isn't working, and may even preemptively schedule
calls with you to discuss your work together.

Regrettably, most companies never reach this stage. Somewhere
along the way (most likely during the Acclimate phase), the company

fails to take care of the relationship in a way that makes the customer feel significant. As a result, the customer drifts away.

When the company doesn't deliver on the customer's expectations and fails to fulfill the minimum threshold for a relationship, the customer isn't able to reach the Adopt phase.

When it comes to successfully navigating the Adopt phase, there are two key components: First, a business should make it easy for customers to express their brand loyalty. Second, once this loyalty is shared, the best businesses will step in to reward that loyalty on a consistent and ongoing basis.

EXPRESS YOURSELF—FROM THIRTY FEET AWAY!

In a corporate setting, the phrase "fan boy" or "fan girl" is most often associated with Apple. Though some would argue that Apple's standing in the marketplace has had its highs and lows, when Apple releases a new product, lines still form at their retail stores hours and even days before the "official" release. Many Apple customers will admit that they don't even care what the new product or service is. If Apple is making it, they want it. Founder and longtime CEO Steve Jobs observed, "A lot of times, people don't know what they want until you show it to them."[1] This level of adoption and commitment to the relationship, the products, and the services is not the norm in the corporate world.

When Apple first created white earbuds, it was a revolutionary moment in earphone/earbud design. Prior to that, the world of headphones could best be described by paraphrasing the famous saying attributed to Henry Ford when discussing the Model T: "Any customer can have any color that he wants, so long as it is black."[2]

When Apple introduced the white earbuds in 2001 (to coincide with the launch of the first iPod), it separated itself from the competition and gave a visual marker for what it meant to adopt its product. If you were riding on a subway, taking the bus, or walking down the street and you saw someone wearing white earbuds, you knew that person had an Apple product in their pocket.

The white earbuds sent a message about the customer's level of adoption, commitment, and fanaticism. If you were wearing white ear-buds, you were a buyer of Apple's products. If you were a buyer of Apple's products, you were almost certainly a fan.

This marker of adoption became so prevalent in the United States that it affected personal safety on public transportation. Thieves knew that if someone was wearing white earbuds, they likely had a $300-plus device in their pocket. The number of robberies increased, and police around the country began to warn customers of the consequences of their brand loyalty.[3]

With Apple's release of wireless earbuds (AirPods) in 2016, the conversation evolved once again; now the most loyal of Apple fans could be seen walking around with small white prongs sticking out of their ears.

AirPods are displayed as Apple Inc. CEO Tim Cook makes his closing remarks during an Apple media event in San Francisco, California, September 7, 2016.   *Source: REUTERS/Beck Diefenbach*

The first time I saw these earbuds "in the wild" I did a double take. Like most people, I'd grown accustomed to living in a world where I regularly saw individuals wearing headphones—but I expected to see wires connecting the wearer to the device. The new design of Apple's earbuds was both eye-catching and trend-setting, and it was just a matter of time before wireless earbuds became ubiquitous.

⏱ Quick Takeaway

Make it easy for your best customers to express their loyalty. If your customers are proud to associate with your brand, they will want others to know about their brand affiliation. Make showing their support easy and fun.

WHEN YOUR ACCOUNTANT GETS A TATTOO

When it comes to the world of motorcycles, most riders will happily agree that the Harley-Davidson brand is in a class of its own. The loyalty and commitment to Harley-Davidson demonstrated by riders and fans around the world has risen to such a level that often a Harley owner will get a tattoo of the brand logo. In many ways, this takes "branding" to the ultimate extreme.

For nearly every business on the planet, the likelihood of getting your customers to tattoo your logo onto their bodies is extremely rare. Yet time and time again, Harley-Davidson fans and customers show their adoption of and commitment to the business by branding themselves with a Harley tattoo.

What in the world would drive someone to tattoo a corporate logo on their body?

A belief that the logo represents their tribal affiliation. The most loyal of Harley-Davidson fans literally dedicate their own flesh and blood (at least a little bit) to show their affinity for the brand. For these individuals, their support has little to do with the logo and everything to do with the lifestyle the logo represents. It all comes down to what people think when they see the logo.

Harley-Davidson gives accountants, dentists, doctors, lawyers, and other professionals a way to be an outlaw, rebel, or badass for a few moments or a few hours. The Harley spirit, ethos, and brand story are clearly identifiable, and as customers come into the fold, they begin to see their brand loyalty as a commentary on their general life choices.

Harley-Davidson customers have a way to step outside their "usual" identity and become someone else. Associating with the brand (especially via a tattoo) gives customers a way to carry that relationship into every interaction. It also creates a sense of community, as customers can easily spot one another in a room (assuming the tattoo is visible).

Harley-Davidson owners take great pride in their reputation, which was put on the silver screen and cemented internationally with the release of *Easy Rider* in 1969. Starring Peter Fonda and Dennis Hopper, the movie tells the story of two bikers who travel through the American Southwest and South. Considered to be a "touchstone for a generation," the movie explored the societal landscape, issues, and tensions in the United States during the 1960s.[4]

Pairing self-exploration with the open road resonates with the experience of many current Harley-Davidson owners. Having come of age in the 1960s, Harley riders in their fifties and sixties today reflect back on their own self-exploration and open road experiences by connecting to the Harley-Davidson lifestyle. They take great pride in the fact that a motorcycle-riding, leather-wearing biker can also be an accountant, a doctor, or a lawyer. A current Harley rider/owner is able to live vicariously through the image of a rabble-rousing tough guy, even if their professional life follows a more conservative career path. As John Russell, former managing director of Harley-Davidson Europe, once said, "Harley Davidson sells to 43-year-old accountants the ability to dress in leather, ride through small towns, and have people be afraid of them."[5]

Any business that stands by its product and customer possesses the building blocks for creating a community around its offerings. By honoring loyal customers and giving them a way to self-identify, the organization establishes tight bonds within the customer base—to the point where customers may become so loyal that they seek outward displays of their brand affiliation.

⏱ Quick Takeaway

If you have a backstory and ethos with which your customers can identify, they will see their loyalty to you as a commentary on their life choices. Give your customers the chance to be part of a larger community and they will increasingly come back for more. Associating with your brand (regardless of whether it goes as far as a tattoo) gives customers a way to carry that community into every minute of their daily lives. It also creates a sense of belonging to the tribe, as they can easily spot another "tribe member" in a room.

ALL YOU LITTLE MONSTERS PUT YOUR PAWS UP!

A small but rabid percentage of readers threw their hands in the air when they read the subheading above this sentence. Unlike the average reader, these individuals are familiar with the phrase given their fanatical loyalty to the international music sensation (24 million albums sold and counting) Lady Gaga.[6]

In *Monster Loyalty: How Lady Gaga Turns Followers into Fanatics*, customer loyalty expert and best-selling author Jackie Huba does an incredible job of pulling back the curtain on the loyalty of Lady Gaga's listeners.[7] In the book, Huba uncovers a series of lessons learned from Lady Gaga that provide a guidebook for navigating customer loyalty. Some of these takeaways include:

Focus on Your One Percenters

Gaga spends most of her effort on just 1 percent of her audience—the highly-engaged superfans who drive word of mouth. She's famous for calling fans' cellphones from the stage and inviting them to come backstage for a drink, as well as creating personalized videos and sending them to her most loyal fans.[8] She makes her "Little Monsters" feel like they belong in a deep and meaningful way by sharing backstage, insider-only videos of her tours and music videos, as well as thanking them for their ongoing support. By building such strong connections with her supporters, Lady Gaga ensures their ongoing commitment and devotion.

Build a Fan Community

Gaga connects her most loyal customers to one another in a way that strengthens their bond to her as well. By creating spaces for her fans to engage with each other, she instills a feeling of collegiality and belonging that pairs nicely with the messaging in her music and her overall brand image.

Give Your Fans a Name

Gaga calls her fans her "Little Monsters" and in the process gives them a way to self-identify as being part of her tribe.

Not only is Lady Gaga's music catchy, powerful, and engaging, but her approach to building meaningful relationships is worthy of study by any organization that seeks loyal customers. Once a customer expresses loyalty, a business must do everything it can to reward that commitment—and in doing so, to amplify it. Like Apple and Harley-

Davidson, Lady Gaga created a system for continually acknowledging and rewarding brand adoption.

Quick Takeaway

Unique words and phraseology creates a sense of belonging within your customer base. By focusing extra attention on your most loyal fans and adopters, you increase their personal commitment to you while growing your word-of-mouth support and promotion. Giving your raving fans a special name and encouraging them to spend time together acknowledges their support and loyalty to your brand.

SMELLS LIKE LOYALTY TO ME

In living rooms throughout the world, more than two million independent distributors and salespeople introduce individuals and families to the incredible uses and benefits of essential oils. The world of multilevel marketing has long been known for the "hard sell," but few businesses in this space are known for their customer retention initiatives. dōTERRA is doing its best to change that reputation in the industry by valuing both its salespeople and its customers *after* the sale.

Known as "Wellness Advocates," dōTERRA salespeople are part of a multilevel marketing organization founded in Pleasant Grove, Utah, by David Stirling in 2008. Wellness Advocates sell the essential oils directly to consumers. Along the way, they are also expected to recruit other salespeople to join their "down line," increasing overall profits for the individual salesperson, the recruiter, and the company. In the interest of full disclosure, dōTERRA oils took over our home after my wife connected with my law-school roommate's wife (a successful dōTERRA Wellness Advocate) and became a customer and Wellness Advocate.

dōTERRA acknowledges purchases with a specific point rewards system and provides a new, free product each month for any customer who orders more than $125 in products. For example, a recent promotion gave a free tea tree/melaleuca roller ball for a $125 order, and a free Deep Blue roller ball and lotion combination (estimated value $94) for a $200 order. The fact that dōTERRA stacks rewards to encourage higher purchases is good for average order values, while at the same time rewarding customer behaviors it hopes to see repeated.

These free monthly bonuses introduce additional product offerings to the customers and encourage consistent ordering by pairing each purchase with a free gift that customers will find useful. After receiving the free gifts detailed above as part of a recent order, my wife made sure to hit the same order goal the next month to qualify for another bonus gift. This commitment to delivering a consistent, remarkable experience contributes to dōTERRA's impressive customer retention rate, which is nearly seven times the industry average.[9]

Quick Takeaway

Reward your customers for continuing to do business with you. If you have a product they love, consider gifting them another item in your product line that complements the items they already use. You'll be treating them to the feeling of excitement (everyone loves "free," high-quality goodies), and if they like what you give them, they'll come back for more.

STAY AT OUR HOTEL AND MEET JUSTIN BIEBER?!

How did Starwood Hotels attract an astronomical number of fiercely loyal Starwood Preferred Guests, including me?

As someone who averages 2.5 weeks on the road every month, I thought long and hard about what hotel affinity program to join early in my career.

I wasn't lured in by any of the little perks that are by now standard in "frequent guest" programs (free water, free Wi-Fi, larger rooms, etc.)—although these are nice benefits. I selected Starwood Hotels because they take things to the next level with the Starwood Moments program.

With redemptions starting at just one thousand Starpoints, the Moments program offers exclusive access to the biggest music, sports, and cultural events in the world. From private glamping (think camping but in a much more glamorous fashion) at Coachella, to Formula One racing, to attending Broadway shows and meeting members of the cast, Starwood Preferred Guests can bid on exclusive experiences. These experiences would be difficult for an individual to engineer on their own, no matter how much money they were willing to spend.

The irony of this model is not lost on me. A customer likely spends extra money for services in order to attend events and activities that they could have paid for directly. Despite this fact, the Starwood Preferred Guests program has 21 million members worldwide who will go out of their way to stay at Starwood properties.[10]

By creating an environment for Starwood's most loyal adopters to have access to special experiences, the business honors its top customers. In addition, Starwood often films these events and then shares them (along with testimonials from other customers) on the in-room entertainment channel that every Starwood hotel television is tuned to when you first step into one of its guest rooms. This subtle but consistent marketing effort further reinforces the benefits of loyalty to the brand.

⏱ Quick Takeaway

Creating incredible bonuses for your most committed customers builds affinity and gives them yet another reason to sing your praises. The more audacious your loyalty perks, the more your best customers will give you their loyalty. Honoring these top customers and using these interactions to create shareable content provides you with the examples you need in order to promote the benefits of becoming a repeat customer.

AND THE UMPIRE SHOUTS, "PLAY BALL!"

The Chicago Cubs are one of the most storied teams in American sports. After winning the World Series in 1908, the Cubs struggled to put together a season worthy of another championship. In 1945, William Sianis brought his pet goat Murphy to Game 4 of the World Series. When he was asked to leave, Sianis allegedly declared, "Them Cubs, they ain't gonna win no more," and thus began the Curse of the Billy Goat.[11]

Despite the ensuing years of mediocrity and failure, Cubs fans remained exceedingly loyal.[12] How, the owners and business managers wondered, could they continue to fan the flames?

In 2015, a phone call set in motion a dream come true for an expert in the art of "strategic appreciation." John Ruhlin, founder of Ruhlin Group, had chased the iconic Cubs for seven years. He specializes in developing unique, signature gifts for companies' best customers, and as a midwestern boy, John wanted to do a project with the Cubs.

During a call with a team representative, John heard that during the off-season the Cubs' locker room at Wrigley Field would be remodeled. All of the old wooden benches and lockers would be removed. Not one to miss an opening, John blurted out, "What if we made speakers out of the wood?" The Cubs were intrigued.

When John communicated with several speaker manufacturers to explain the project, the cachet of the Cubs' story didn't convince them. "This is the worst idea ever!" said one speaker company CEO. "It's old, warped plywood! You can't use old plywood to make high-end audio equipment." John eventually found some folks in his hometown of St. Louis who weren't speaker people—they were "mad scientists." Intrigued by the challenge, they relaminated the wood to preserve the dents and scuffs that gave the wood character. Partnering with another entrepreneurial company that was up for an adventure, they used world-class LSTN audio components to assemble the speakers. After a great deal of trial and error, they were eventually able to create four hundred Bluetooth speakers—made from "Wrigley Field wood"—that sounded amazing.

The Cubs gifted the limited edition (numbered 1–400) speakers to their top four hundred most important relationships—their premium seating holders, private suite clients, and top sponsors who committed $100,000 a year or more. This "useful artifact" was a purposeful, practical gift for the Cubs' most loyal customers. It was delivered via courier in February, the off season, when none of the top customers were expecting anything from the Cubs.

The feedback was incredible. Recipients begged for ways to get extra speakers. The owners of the team—the billionaire Ricketts family—felt it was one of the coolest gifts they had ever seen. The team exercised incredible discretion in not going back to create more speakers despite the overwhelmingly positive response. "We could have made more speakers for them and the Cubs could have sold them online for a fortune," notes Ruhlin. "But they wanted it to remain an exclusive item—something that couldn't be purchased. You needed to have adopted the Cubs into your life in order to qualify for this level of access."

Ruhlin lives the philosophy outlined in this book. "People think it's sexier to go chase new customer blood. They don't get it. The magic is pouring on gas to ignite existing relationships. I'd rather have a massive bonfire of my most loyal adopters than constantly light little sparks here and there."

In 2016, the Cubs ended a 108-year drought and won the World Series. Did the speakers created by Ruhlin and his team break the curse? The world will never know. But surely the sound of the cheering crowd coming out of the signature, limited-edition speakers will not soon be forgotten by the Cubs' most loyal adopters!

Quick Takeaway

Your most loyal customers deserve special treatment. Create something of unique value to them and not only will they feel appreciated, but they will see themselves as "part of a club." If there is the opportunity to add a dash of nostalgia, that will only heighten the experience. Exclusivity is a powerful feeling. Don't be afraid to create a limited-edition item or make a special experience available just to those customers who are most loyal and supportive.

HAVE A VERY MERRY SWIFTMAS!

With 85.8 million Twitter followers, 104 million Instagram followers, and 73 million Facebook followers, Taylor Swift knows a thing or two about social media. Over the years, her deft use of social media platforms has grown her fan base, sold millions of albums, and allowed supporters to interact with her in surprisingly personal ways.

Near the end of 2014, coming off a successful tour and getting ready to start another one, Swift took to social media and began to undertake a radically personal project. Later known as "Tay-lurking," she investigated every detail of a group of her fans—what they "liked," who their friends were, where they worked, and what was going on in their lives. Fans didn't know any of this was happening until, out of the blue, she posted a single Santa emoji on their social media profiles.

In the beginning, fans had no idea what this emoji meant—until the boxes started arriving. Enormous FedEx boxes (or SwiftEx boxes as she called them) were delivered to unsuspecting fans. Filled with handwritten notes from Swift and presents that had been hand-selected by her in accordance with the fans' interests, the "Swiftmas" (as it came to be known) was another instant hit.

A YouTube video of the first "Swiftmas"—Taylor Swift's Gift Giving of 2014—has been viewed more than 18 million times and shows Swift personally wrapping and packing dozens of Christmas and Hanukkah presents.[13] The video shows clips from her jubilant, crying fans as they received these unexpected gifts. Emotional outbursts and thoughtful thank-yous blend together to create a fan-favorite video. The specific references Swift makes in her notes to things her fans are going through and the personal names of their loved ones showcase the attention to detail she brought to her gifting.

Since this first experiment with targeted gifting, Swift has become a standout in the entertainment industry for how she rewards loyal fans. One fan received a check to help pay her college tuition.[14] During the summer, Swift crashed a fan's wedding after receiving a handwritten letter from the bride-to-be's sister.[15] Swift even traveled to visit her "oldest fan," a ninety-six-year-old World War II vet living in Missouri. They took selfies together—of course.[16]

One might assume that an international celebrity would outsource this type of investigating, gifting, and wrapping to an army of assistants. But Swift insists she does it all herself, noting, "I don't take it to FedEx, but I pack the box and tape it—I have so much bubble wrap in my house!"[17] This level of personal involvement serves as an example for organizations and executives around the world. You're never too big to connect in a meaningful way with your most loyal customers.

"[Sending presents] is fun for me," explains Swift. "I'm getting to know them on a person-by-person basis. When I pick people to send packages to, I go on their social-media sites for the last six months and figure out what they like or what they are going through. Do they like photography? I'll get them a 1980s Polaroid camera. Do they like vintage stuff? I'll go to an antiques place and get them 1920s earrings. Do they work out a lot? I'll get them workout stuff. When you actually get to know them on a person-by-person basis, you realize what you're doing is special and sacred and it matters."

Your most loyal customers deserve special treatment. Often companies worry about being "uniform" in their treatment, yet Swift's actions prove that this shouldn't be an inhibitor. She has millions more loyal customers than you do and still finds the time to randomly select a few dozen a year to receive special treatment. The word spreads, and all of her fans—whether recipients of gifts or not—feel closer to her.

⏱ Quick Takeaway

Take the time to get to know your most loyal customers on a deep and personal level. Whether through your personal interactions with them or by investigating their social media profiles, you can easily amass at least a dozen data points that can be used to create remarkable interactions. If you truly want a customer-centric organization, make sure that everyone in the company participates in these types of customer investigations and connections. Then take what you've learned and have fun with it! Any customer who receives a gift that combines this level of personalization with complete surprise is never going to cease being a fan. The relationship will shift from a one-sided, transactional interaction to a two-sided exchange.

SUMMARY: PHASE 7—ADOPT

Creating Remarkable Customer Experiences in the Adopt Phase

While most businesses stall out before reaching this phase, the Adopt phase of the customer experience occurs when the customer fully embraces a company's product or service and sees significant results. In addition, the customer is likely experiencing improvements in unexpected areas of their business or life as a result of the fulfilled outcomes promised in the beginning.

The Adopt phase of the customer life cycle is an opportunity to formalize a long-term relationship that goes deeper than a one-and-done purchase and results in the customer's seeing you as an important or indispensable partner.

SIX THINGS TO DO IN THE ADOPT PHASE STARTING TOMORROW

By now it's clear—you don't have to use each communication tool in every phase. However, if there was ever a time to expand your tool use it would be when customers have adopted your brand. Let's reward them for their loyalty with creative tool use!

 IN-PERSON

By the time a customer reaches this phase, they should have already experienced at least some personal interaction with brand representatives. If not, at this point an effort to connect on a personal level will augment the overall brand relationship. Special training sessions and non-work-related outings provide the chance to deepen the interactions.

CHAPTER EXAMPLE: Whether sporting white earbuds (Apple) or donning the corporate logo as a tattoo (Harley-Davidson), giving your adopters the chance to publicly profess their love of your brand confirms adoption very quickly. Inviting them to participate in special experiences and difficult-to-access gatherings (Starwood Hotels) further acknowledges their status as VIP customers.

@ EMAIL

A more in-depth "success survey" allows for data collection about the individual customer to be used in personalizing future communications. In addition, larger data sets from these surveys will identify trends within the customer base and could alter early sales messages, systems, and processes for future prospects.

 **MAIL**

"Expert User" guides and veteran tips help seasoned customers further adopt the product or service offerings. Now that the customer has taken on a sense of personal ownership for the use of the product or service, they are ready for the most advanced interactions. They are ready to use the product or service in unexpected ways to truly maximize success. Recognizing and rewarding loyalty with well-designed mail pieces adds a sense of physical permanency to the interaction and further cements the relationship.

CHAPTER EXAMPLE: Beautifully designed, exclusive perks (Sephora) reward your most loyal and steadfast customers for their continued commitment to your brand. Sending unexpected items in appreciation of your most loyal fans (Chicago Cubs and Taylor Swift) creates personal and emotional connection, while also providing for a moment of surprise and delight when the package arrives at an unexpected time.

 PHONE

A personal call from a very senior executive acknowledging this milestone reinforces the brand's commitment to the success of individual customers. These conversations also offer insight into customer behaviors and habits, which can be used to adjust communications going forward.

CHAPTER EXAMPLE: An unexpected call to your most loyal customers (Lady Gaga) that comes with an exclusive, unique offer or experience creates extreme loyalty and increased word-of-mouth marketing.

 **VIDEO**

A key milestone or anniversary celebration video showing the entire team celebrating the customer's "___-Day Commitment to Success" showcases the brand spirit while acknowledging this important milestone in making a long-term behavioral change.

CHAPTER EXAMPLE: Creating custom, personalized videos for your top adopters and fans (Lady Gaga) builds a personal connection that reinforces their overall brand loyalty.

 **PRESENT**

A memento or artifact commemorating this milestone offers an unexpected surprise. By welcoming the customer into the highest echelon of active customers, you place a great degree of significance on their contribution to the overall success of the brand, while giving them a sense of ownership over the relationship/engagement.

CHAPTER EXAMPLE: Unexpected high-end gifts (Chicago Cubs), exclusive products (Sephora), useful "free" samples (dōTERRA), hyper-personalized presents (Taylor Swift), and access to unique events (Starwood Hotels) show a loyal customer that you appreciate their commitment and want to acknowledge it in a meaningful way.

YOUR ASSIGNMENT: PUT THESE IDEAS TO WORK

Now that you have a clear understanding of the Adopt phase, answer a series of questions that are designed to get you thinking about how you can use each of the communication tools to enhance the overall experience during this phase of the customer journey.

(You've made it all the way to the Adopt phase—don't start cutting corners now! Keep at it and you'll have even more customers shifting to becoming customers for life.)

Evaluating the Current Situation

Answer each question, then write two or three sentences explaining your answer. For bonus points, write down any ideas you have for changes that would make your answers "better."

- What needs to occur in order for a customer to adopt you?

- Describe in detail what adoption looks like. How quickly could it happen with a new customer? What does it "feel" like? What metrics (if any) do you use to identify and recognize adoption?

- In your current business, do you create remarkable experiences during the Adopt phase? If so, what are they?

- On a scale of 1 to 10, where 1 is "pathetic" and 10 is "world class," how would you rate the experience your customers currently have in the Adopt phase? (Not everyone will reach this phase, but you should have at least a few.)

Tools to Enhance the Future Experience

Answer each question by coming up with two or three ideas for using the specific tool to enhance the customer experience. If ever there was a time to stop worrying about cost, team support, or implementation, it's now. These customers are loyal, and their commitment should be acknowledged and honored accordingly.

- How can you use in-person interactions during this phase to show a customer how special the relationship is?

- How can you make your emails more personal and familiar now that the customer is a significant member of the family?

- How can a customized mail piece thank the customer for their loyalty and introduce new and special perks for their continued dedication?

- How can phone interactions with company leadership send a signal to the devoted customer?

- How can videos showcase the personal and emotional connections between the customer and key members of your team?

- What present(s) could you give customers that would mark their commitment to you?

Pick One Now

If you've answered the questions above (of course you have—you're a pro by now!), you have a clear understanding of the customer experience during the Adopt phase, as well as many ideas for how to make that experience better. Taking that into account, consider the following questions.

- What is one thing you can start doing tomorrow to make the experience your customers have in the Adopt phase even better?

- Who would you need to talk to in order to make this happen?

- How would you know if you've succeeded in making this improvement?

- How would you measure the improvement of the overall customer experience?

- How would you share this impact with the rest of the organization?

FROM ADOPT TO ADVOCATE

Now that the customer has expressed personal commitment in the Adopt phase and is going to stay with you for the foreseeable future, let's consider what can be done to turn your steadfast supporters into raving fans.

CHAPTER FIFTEEN

Phase 8: Advocate

 Overview of the Advocate Phase

In the Advocate phase, the customer becomes a raving fan (not to be confused with a regular fan) and referral engine all in one. The customer acts like a built-in marketing representative, singing your praises to other potential customers who might benefit from your product or service.

WAIT—WE WANT TO SAVE IT!

Several years ago, I was in the delivery room as my wife gave birth to our first child. It was an incredibly significant moment for both of us (in hindsight—in the moment, it was pure mayhem), and mere minutes after our son was born, I stepped away from my wife and son to ask the nurse if she could help us out.

"Could you please make sure to save the cord blood and tissue?" I asked. No, we weren't planning to take it home and perform any number of activities you may have heard about or done yourself. Instead, we were hoping to save it for potential future use. The blood within a newborn baby's umbilical cord contains young stem cells that can help heal the body and have been used in transplant and regenerative medicine for nearly thirty years.

In planning for this moment, we researched our options and decided to work with ViaCord—a cord blood banking service based in Boston. This service allows new parents to save the cord blood from a child's birth, cryopreserve it, and then use it in the future.

Thankfully, ViaCord doesn't require a huge investment of time or effort to coordinate. You pay a one-time collection fee and an annual storage and blood banking fee thereafter.

ViaCord also has a well-thought-out referral program. Very early on, ViaCord recognized that new parents who would be interested in this technological service were most likely running in peer groups with other prospective new parents with similar interests. Every new paying customer referred to ViaCord generates a one-year credit on the cord banking storage fees of the referring customer. The more people existing customers refer, the more free years of storage they receive.

ViaCord's referral program works for a number of reasons. First, the referral doesn't happen until the customer has successfully experienced the ViaCord service. In our case, a courier came to the hospital and picked up the cord blood. The next day I received a phone call confirming successful receipt of the specimen. Within the week I had documentation of our storage records and the peace of mind that comes from knowing we accomplished our goal of banking the stem cells.

Making a referral to another prospective parent is extremely easy for the current customer. The customer simply talks to friends or colleagues who are expecting, explains the benefits of cord banking, and either makes an email introduction to an account representative or sends a link via email that allows the prospective parent to sign up for the service. Once the new customer enrolls in the service, the veteran customer receives an email stating that the referral is complete and shows a credit applied to the veteran customer's account equaling one year of storage fees. It's quick, easy, efficient, and valuable—the gold standard to strive for when establishing a referral program for your customers.

One of the most common ways to acknowledge a referral from an existing customer is through financial incentives. Referral fees, bonuses, and commissions can be an effective tool to drive referrals—but only where the fee is significant enough to spark action on behalf of the veteran customer and commensurate with the scale of the referral. If I get someone to purchase a luxury SUV from a dealership and the dealer rewards me with a $5 gift card, it will likely be the last time I make a referral. On the other hand, if the dealer gives me a year's worth of free oil changes, my interest has surely been piqued, and I'll probably think fondly of that referral experience every time I take my vehicle in for service.

Quick Takeaway

The best referrals come from happy current customers. Make your referral program easy to understand, even easier to participate in, and worthwhile for the referring customer's investment of time and effort. Your best customers most likely spend time associating with your ideal prospects. Creating the opportunity for customers to talk with their friends and colleagues about your offerings feels natural when you give customers the necessary information to make it easy for them to refer people to you.

IF YOU'RE GOING TO ASK FOR A REFERRAL, YOU NEED TO DO IT THE RIGHT WAY

By the time a customer reaches advocacy, they have enjoyed extensive personal contact with the company. The interactions and touchpoints have hopefully left the customer feeling confident associating their name with the brand and recommending it to others.

This is advocacy, and it is the holy grail of business. Why? Because advocacy creates word-of-mouth referrals, which is the very best marketing available.

Most businesses, however, will never reach the stage of advocacy with their customers. Though they make valiant efforts to convert the customer to an advocate, they're usually unsuccessful because they ask for referrals too soon, destroying their chances of ever getting one. Even if a customer feels confident associating their name with a brand earlier in the relationship, it's only after the relationship has been fully experienced that they're ready to give a referral.

Here's a great example of the wrong way to seek referrals. If you've shopped online in the last five years, you have likely found yourself, just moments after a purchase, face-to-face with a pop-up message that says "Please refer us to two or three friends who might also like to know about our software, product, or service."

In the hundreds of times I've seen this message, I've never *once* provided a referral. First and foremost, it's asking for too much, too soon. To ask someone to recommend or refer a product or service immediately after they purchase it is an unfair expectation and an unfair ask. They need to experience the benefit from the purchase in order to make a referral or introduce someone to a new company or product. The new customer wants to know the product or service does what it says it will do before sharing the product or service with friends and colleagues.

Furthermore, it's inappropriate to ask a new customer to provide the personal contact information for their colleagues to a nameless and faceless corporation. It presumes a level of familiarity that doesn't exist at this stage in the relationship.

By immediately focusing on the next customer, the company sends a not-so-subtle message that it doesn't care about the current customer. All it cares about is increasing the customer base. In this scenario, the new customer is just a number on a balance sheet. True advocates are not just a number—they are part of the tribe.

ACHIEVING ADVOCACY

Achieving the advocacy stage is the ultimate goal in the customer life cycle. Customers who reach this pinnacle are worth their weight in gold.

Not only is an advocate loyal and committed to the brand, but they do business with you (year in and year out), participate in upsell opportunities, offer product feedback and suggestions, and grow the share of wallet that they are willing to give your company.

The advocate doesn't just spend more. The advocate becomes your unpaid marketing and sales force.

When you have raving fans or advocates, you decrease spending on marketing and sales. You don't have to spend money on acquisition because your loyal advocates are out in the world encouraging others to sample your offering. People show up at your front door without you needing to draw them in.

When these new customers show up, they are preframed. They know how your business operates, what you offer as your value proposition, and how much the engagement will cost. In the perfect advocate model it makes the discussion of price an afterthought. The product or service has been presold so well by the referring customer that the new customer is committed to getting the benefits with very little care or consideration about the overall cost.

By focusing on the advocate, companies can cut their expenses, increase profits by reducing the cost of doing business, and increase overall customer retention.

THE LOYALTY OF A DOG (LOVER)

One of the most fantastic clients I've worked with is a company called 4Knines, LLC. Cofounders Maggie and Jim Umlauf make high-end seat covers for vehicles to prevent a dog from scratching the upholstery, shedding fur all over the backseat, staining the seats, etc. Granted, to a non–dog owner, this isn't life-changing stuff. But for a dog owner, 4Knines® provides a very important product.

Where 4Knines really shines is in its ability to garner customer reviews during the Advocate phase. In the world of Amazon sales (one of 4Knines' largest sales channels), the quality of the review (one to five stars) and the number of reviews (the more the better) contribute significantly to the overall success of the product. While Amazon's specific ranking and search algorithms are not public, it is well known within the community of Amazon sellers that reviews matter—almost more than anything else. You want as many reviews as possible and you hope that the majority are four and five stars.

From the very beginning, 4Knines realized that it couldn't ask for a written review or testimonial until customers had accomplished their point-of-purchase goal—driving down the road with a dog in the backseat sitting on a properly installed seat cover, feeling not a hint of worry about damaged upholstery or backseat messes. An automatically generated email (auto-responder) is sent to the customer approximately thirty days after purchase, when 4Knines is fairly certain that this goal has been achieved.

In the average month, a whopping 24 percent of customers who open this email click through and write a review. This is incredible and stands far above the industry's average customer review rate of 8 percent.[1] Why is the 4Knines review request so valuable and effective? There are several reasons.

First, 4Knines waits until the customer has accomplished the goal they had when making the original purpose.

Second, by the time the customer receives this email, they have already received several communications from 4Knines (designed to align with the customer's emotions as they pass through each of the phases in the customer journey). At this point, the customer feels like they know the 4Knines team (more on that later).

Third, the language of the email is specifically designed to elicit a review. It begins with an innocent question: "Can we ask a favor?" This friendly inquiry is almost certainly going to lead the customer to keep reading. The message then quickly follows up with an estimate of the time it will take ("about 3 minutes"), showing that while it is asking the customer to do something, it's not a large or difficult ask. Next, the message reiterates the brand story, spirit, and ethic (i.e., small, family-owned business that cares deeply about the customer experience, providing high-quality products and top-notch service).

Finally, 4Knines makes the "ask," providing a link to easily upload the review.*

It's that simple. The ask is quick, direct, and honest. It doesn't say

---

*For an excellent discussion of the value of customer reviews—and recommendations on how to get more of them—see Bill Tancer's *Everyone's a Critic: Winning Customers in a Review-Driven World* (New York: Portfolio/Penguin, 2014).

"give us a five-star review" or "tell us why you love us" or anything else that could be seen as trying to influence the review. It's a clear and basic request seeking honest feedback. And it works—as I mentioned before—24 percent of the time! As if the message couldn't get any better, it's signed by Jim and Maggie Umlauf (the founders) as well as their two dogs—Ares and Ana, the 4Knines mascots. Dog lovers go bonkers about the paw-print signatures.

The Umlaufs knew this request for reviews was working well but had no idea just how important it was until they sold their business to a private equity fund in 2016. For whatever reason (please don't get me started), the new management team decided to turn off all of the autoresponders, including the one asking for reviews. Things went south in a hurry. 4Knines, which had been doing more than $260,000 per month in sales, quickly saw sales plummet. In less than a year, sales fell by 73 percent to $74,000 per month. Realizing that it was on the brink of losing the company, the private equity fund asked (I say begged, but that's just me) Jim and Maggie to come back and run 4Knines again. The Umlaufs agreed, and one of Jim's first acts was to turn the autoresponders back on. Immediately the reviews started to pour in again and sales began to climb once more. Within two months, sales were back up over $120,000 per month and climbing steadily. Within six months, sales were over $175,000 a month and the business was back on track.

"We had believed it for some time, but now we had evidence," observes Jim. "Amazon is all about social proof and the reviews are the driver. We knew they were helping us to grow sales and customer loyalty, but we had no idea just how much."

During the time period when the review request was turned off, multiple aspects of the business were dramatically affected. Prior to this, 4Knines had over one thousand more reviews than its closest competitor. Now that lead had dropped to just over one hundred reviews. As sales fell, so did the product's ranking on Amazon (meaning where it would show up on the list of products when a consumer searched "seat cover"). Having held the coveted top listing for years, to fall in the rankings meant fewer prospects viewing the listing and thereby fewer sales. Thankfully, 4Knines got back on track and in short order was communicating regularly with customers and delivering remarkable customer service once again.

What is fascinating is how many of the reviews—of a dog seat cover purchased on Amazon—specifically reference the CEO Jim by name:

★★★★★ **Best Service, Amazing Product!**
By ▮▮▮▮▮ on July 17, 2014
Size: Regular | Color: Black | Verified Purchase

First let me start by saying this is a BEAUTIFULLY designed and luxurious dog liner for the back seat! I spent a good week researching all different manufacturers and reviews about the pluses and minuses and THIS IS ALL (A+++)

I ordered this and decided to mention that mine had a slight manufacturing defect. Nothing too serious. It happens with everything in life. Nevertheless I got a response in 3 MINUTES!!!!

I sent pictures of the mistake and spoke to "Jim" who I believe is the owner and wow, he's sending me out a full replacement and no hassle at all! I sent him pictures around midnight and "BAM" in 10 min he's packaging a new one up!!!!

This is customer satisfaction at its highest level. I wish I could say I'm a customer for life, but the "seat protecter" is so well made I don't think I'd go though a lot in a life time! But I will definitely tell everyone who I know that has a dog to buy this!! Save yourself the guessing game! Buy right the first time!!!

★★★★★ **Great Cover**
By Amazon Customer on February 17, 2015
Size: Regular | Color: Black | Verified Purchase

We received this cover and immediately installed it. Went in easily and looks great. We bought it for our small dog with back issues so that she doesn't slip around on the leather seats. However, when were adjusting it, we noticed one of the plastic clips had broken for the front passenger seat strap. We only used it one time. The clip still seems to operate, but if the other side goes it will no longer hold. I've included a photo of the clip. Great quality cover, but the plastic clips seem cheap to break for no reason.

UPDATE: I just received a message from Jim at 4Knines. He's taken into account what I said about the buckle and is sending me a replacement buckle! This is fantastic customer service and because of that, I've changed this from a 4 star review to a 5 star review. Couldn't be happier! I highly recommend this cover and this company.

I regularly encourage businesses to create *remarkable* customer experiences—that is, experiences that are "unusual or special and therefore surprising and worth mentioning."[2] The fact that so many customers comment on 4Knines products, and make note of Jim specifically, proves that their business is creating remarkable experiences and, in the process, customers whose loyalty rivals that of their dogs.

> ⏱ **Quick Takeaway**
>
> Asking for referrals requires thoughtful timing and a sincere ask. The goal should be an honest assessment of how you are performing. This feedback not only provides the data to enhance operations, but can serve as a marketing tool to draw in prospective customers. Used properly, testimonials drive sales in a meaningful and measurable way.

GARNERING AND GATHERING TESTIMONIALS

There are dozens of ways that a company can ask its customers to advocate for its brand. One of the most common requests is to ask for testimonials. As the 4Knines example above illustrates, the trick is to make it as easy as possible for the customer to advocate.

When asking for a testimonial, the company should give the customer specific guidance on what it's looking for. It's not enough to email the best customers and say, "We have a new website launching. Would you be willing to write a testimonial?"

That's not how you treat an advocate. That's putting the onus on them to do the work.

The better approach is to go to the customer and say, "We've worked together a long time. You've had some massive success and changes within your organization as a direct result of your relationship with us. Would you be willing to share the impact of our work together?"

Once the customer shares the success, the impact, and the significance of the relationship, you can produce the written testimonial—using the specific, tangible takeaways that come from the relationship.

To make giving a testimonial even easier, you can also say to the customer, "Look, I recognize that you're busy and have a lot on your plate right now. With your permission, I'd like to draft a testimonial for you. You can then feel free to edit or amend it as you see fit."

Most customers will be thrilled by this offer because, while they're happy to support you and give a testimonial for your company, staring at a blank white screen with a blinking cursor feels like a daunting task. Getting a customer to schedule the writing of a testimonial into their already busy calendar is a request that will not get a high level of priority, no matter how much they like you.

When preparing the testimonial, you should focus on clearly outlining the benefits the customer received from working with you. All too often, companies try to showcase features when they should be focused on outcomes and results. If there is a way to add a little "spice" into the testimonial (if, and only if, that is in alignment with your brand *and* your customer's voice), it can make for a fantastic review that will catch the eye of your ideal prospect. One of the best testimonials I ever received from an audience member stated, "Joey Coleman presents with a level of enthusiasm and energy normally reserved for Mountain Dew commercials!" While this testimonial doesn't share a word about my presentation content, it clearly outlines the impact I have on the audience—something that is incredibly important to event planners who hire speakers.

When you provide the customer with tools to write an effective testimonial for you (whether that is talking points, key observations, or the actual text of the endorsement), you make the customer's life easier (which should be your goal throughout the entire relationship) and ensure that the result will describe the experience of working with you.

The easier you make it to refer people to your business, the more customers will be happy to advocate for you. When you give your customer a brochure or a link to a video that highlights their experience with your brand and the benefits achieved from working with you, you give them an easy way to pass on the good word about your company.

By prewriting the testimonial, you are in control of the outcome. You can create a level of customization and personalization that the customer might not have created on their own. The testimonials become tools in your toolbox that make this long-standing and loved customer an advocate even when they're not in the room.

ADVOCACY IN ACTION

Advocacy, when done properly, is beautiful to witness and can have an incredible impact on your organization.

In the world of software as a service, online storage company Dropbox implemented a level of advocacy early on in its business operations that significantly bolstered the growth of its business. When Dropbox first launched its online storage service, customers could sign up for free. As part of signing up for a free account, they received 2GB of storage.[3]

Given that Dropbox was launched in Silicon Valley, most of the people who first signed up were tech-savvy computer users. They quickly used up their free allocation of online storage space.

When a customer hit that barrier, Dropbox sent an email with a link to a page on their website outlining options for purchasing more space:

Source: https://blog.kissmetrics.com/dropbox-hacked-growth/

At the bottom of that page there was a unique offer. Instead of purchasing additional space, the customer could get 500MB of "bonus space" for every friend who joined and installed Dropbox. By referring Dropbox to their friends, customers could avoid paying extra storage fees and get the benefit of extra storage.

Source: https://blog.kissmetrics.com/dropbox-hacked-growth/

The number of people who took advantage of this offer exceeded Dropbox's wildest dreams.* The company grew at an exponential rate over its first year. Within twenty-four hours of announcing the service, Dropbox had 75,000 people signed up for the waiting list. It slowly extended beta invites and reached one million users just seven months after publicly launching the service. Roughly a year later, Dropbox had registered over 10 million users—an incredible achievement.[4]

I know you're probably thinking, "But Joey, you said we shouldn't ask for referrals too early!"

Not so fast. Let's look at the expectations of the customers when they signed up for the service, when the request came in the relationship, and how the "ask" was framed.

The early adopters of Dropbox were already fans and practitioners

---

*In fact, Dropbox adopted its referral program after realizing that its Google AdWords customer acquisition was costing the company $233 to $388 per customer—for a $99 product!

of online storage. Many had already cobbled together their own form of cloud storage over the years, and this was the first time they were getting it in a commercially available, consumer-friendly model.

They expected they would be able to store their data in the cloud for free. After they used 2GBs, customers knew how easy it was to use the service. Enough time had passed for Dropbox to prove that the service worked and worked well. Founder Drew Houston once outlined the customer journey in a presentation.[5]

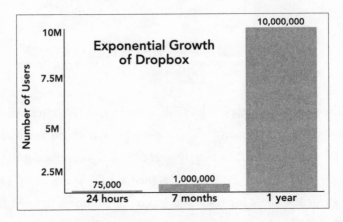

Once the service proved to be effective, the customer expected to pay—so Dropbox sent an email: Here are the payment terms . . . but wait—you can get more storage for free! All you have to do is refer our service to a friend, and you both benefit.

See what they did? When properly messaged and targeted, giving referrals turns into a win-win scenario. In the case of Dropbox, the referred prospects were excited to learn about the new software service, and the existing customers got a bump in their online storage.

Dropbox allowed customers to make referrals by providing an email address or by merely sharing a link. The goal was to make the referral process easy, efficient, and effective. The fact that the referral

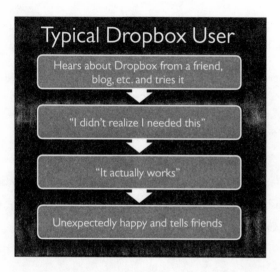

program increased overall Dropbox sign-ups by 60 percent proved that the referral process achieved its goal.[6]

Dropbox quickly made the referral even more alluring. It added bonus storage to the referrer's account and to that of the referred friend as well. So your referral was a bonus for your friend too! Had Dropbox decided to reward referrals with cash incentives instead of additional storage, the program would almost certainly have been less successful. In order for a cash incentive to be meaningful, Dropbox would have needed to spend enough money that it would likely take a significant amount of time to earn back the incentive via payments from the new customer. Instead, Dropbox gave its "power users" even more exposure to the service (i.e., additional storage), which in turn made them more dependent, which led to them being bigger fans, which resulted in even more referrals. Thus, an almost infinite, perpetual behavior loop was created, fostered, and encouraged.

Quick Takeaway

Reward your customer's positive behavior in a way that brings new customers into the fold. Give customers more of what they are already getting and more of what they would need to buy anyway and they will want to stay with you forever.

By integrating advocacy into the structure of operations, businesses can build and cultivate an environment focused on advocates from the very beginning.

IT'S ALL ABOUT THE STATUS

To create effective referral bonuses, a company must build a program that gives the type of gift or bonus the targeted advocate will find most valuable.

As a proud customer of American Express and Delta Air Lines, I found the cobranded opportunity with the Delta credit card by American Express too good to pass up. I signed up for this program more than a decade ago and quickly experienced the benefits of supporting both brands.

Every purchase I make using my American Express credit card earns miles on Delta. Whenever I fly Delta, I'm able to check my bags for free as a benefit of being an American Express cardholder. While I began to enjoy the benefits of being a cobranded Delta/AMEX customer immediately, my relationship became more interesting approximately a year after I signed up when Delta sent me a marketing message about referring other people to the Delta/AMEX credit card.

While I'm not completely sure, it wouldn't surprise me if somewhere in their tracking algorithms Delta made certain that I was the kind of customer from which they wanted to receive referrals. I was the type of customer that used the Delta/AMEX as my primary credit card for business and personal charges. I used it frequently and paid it even more frequently.

Once they confirmed that I fit the profile they desired, Delta/AMEX sent me a special offer where, if I referred new customers to the credit card and they signed up, I would receive bonus miles. Delta took this one step further by offering me the opportunity to obtain status-qualifying miles as part of my referral.

For those who may not be familiar with the operation of airline frequent flyer miles, you can accrue miles that can later be cashed in for upgrades, free tickets, and other perks. To be honest, it turns into a game where people earn miles for all sorts of behaviors. Rent a car? Get some miles. Stay in a hotel? Get some miles. Eat dinner at a participating restaurant? Get some miles. Shop at an online retailer? Get some miles. The chase for miles is enough to instill personal loyalty and make a customer *adopt* a specific airline as their carrier of choice. This leads to the kind of customer loyalty most companies envy—where dedication trumps rational decision making. I regularly pay more to fly Delta (versus other carriers) because I know I will get my miles.

However, mere miles aren't enough. To maintain status on an airline, you need to accrue a very specific type of mile—status-qualifying miles. Delta's Diamond-level status, which at present requires 125,000 status-qualifying miles, is the equivalent of six roundtrip flights between New York and Sydney. If you're going to be on an airline this much, you deserve a "diamond"—but Diamond-level status will do.

Usually, the only way to accrue status-qualifying miles is by flying actual miles on the airline. This can lead to insane behavior—including the infamous "mileage run." In this scenario, a customer desperately seeking status-qualifying miles boards a flight, flies a great distance (usually halfway around the world), and then flies back (without even bothering to stay the night) just to accrue the miles and earn the associated "status."

Delta/AMEX helped me avoid making mileage runs thanks to its generous offer. I was given the opportunity to obtain status-qualifying miles as part of a mileage bonus awarded when I referred a new card user to sign up for a Delta/AMEX card. It worked. Less than forty-eight hours after receiving this offer, I made my first pitch to a fellow entrepreneur. Much to my delight, weeks later, status-qualifying miles for my friend's business card and his personal card hit my account.

By offering status-qualifying miles, something that both Delta and American Express knew I would find particularly enticing, they ensured that I would make the right referrals and make them quickly.

 Quick Takeaway

Offer your best customers something that will be personally meaningful to them. If you know the customer doesn't have what they need or are going to fall just short of something you can provide, you can earn your company a zealous advocate if you deliver in that moment. There is desirable social prestige associated with "status." By helping your best customers achieve your highest "status," you help them attain the next level of customer segmentation. You can also trigger ongoing dopamine rushes by having your customers "win" games. Collecting points and achieving new levels can gamify loyalty and result in strong connections with your best customers.

HANGING OUT WITH SIR RICHARD

Maverick1000, the entrepreneurial membership discussed earlier, ran a referral campaign where the top referring member to the group received an all-expenses-paid trip to Necker Island with Sir Richard Branson.

Branson, by any measure, is one of the top three most famous and successful entrepreneurs in the world. Enticing a group of Maverick entrepreneurs with the opportunity to spend time with Sir Richard on his private island in the Caribbean guaranteed a high level of participation in the referral campaign. To date, this specific campaign has been the most successful referral campaign the Maverick organization has ever run.

Now you may be thinking, "But Joey, I don't know Richard Branson!"

Fair enough, but that's not really the point. The secret to creating great referral campaigns that get your customers to actively bring you new customers is to incentivize them with something they (a) want and (b) would have a hard time obtaining on their own. Knowing what your customers "want" is all about identifying things they will find exciting. This hinges on how well you know their likes, dislikes, interests, and hobbies (we'll discuss how to determine this in the next chapter). Identifying something they would have a hard time obtaining on their own requires you to look at your own network and resources to identify how you can bring your connections to bear when creating a magical moment for your customers.

For example, if you are a luxury high-rise owner trying to get your current tenants to refer new tenants to fill your unoccupied penthouse, you could consider offering the winning "referrer" the chance to host an all-expenses-paid party in the penthouse before the newly referred tenant moves in. If you are friends with a senior member of the Egyptian government, you could arrange for an after-hours, private tour of the Museum of Egyptian Antiquities for your top referring clients (I once had the opportunity to enjoy this rare privilege as a guest of the person who had the connection, and yes, it was as amazing as you might imagine). If you know that your customer is a fan of a famous author, movie star, or celebrity, you can purchase a unique experience for your customer to enjoy through a charity auction site like Charity buzz.com. One of my good friends has delivered some out-of-this-world experiences for his top referring clients by actively monitoring the experiences offered on this website and then purchasing them as gifts.

The referral bonus doesn't need to be expensive as long as it's memorable. I once received a referral fee (one of the more common ways to acknowledge a customer referral) from a colleague who made the experience remarkable by not only unexpectedly giving me the fee, but by presenting it in a metal briefcase delivered by a courier. Separately, he sent the combination to me in a message, saying, "You'll know what to do with this when you find yourself needing a combination." When I opened the combination lock I was shocked to find the briefcase filled with money. The total amount represented approximately 10 percent of the value of the referral I made—a somewhat standard referral fee— but the presentation was breathtaking. Stack upon stack of bills (he made the volume of cash that much more impressive by paying the fee in one-dollar bills) made me laugh out loud and put a grin on my face that I couldn't wipe off for days. Needless to say, I couldn't help but tell people about it as well—and immediately started thinking of other people I could refer to him.

⏱ Quick Takeaway

The best customer rewards offer exclusivity and rare opportunities—
and sometimes both! Look for things that you can give away that cost
very little to you compared with how much your customers will value
them. For your best referrers, go above and beyond to actively seek
out special experiences that they wouldn't easily be able to arrange
on their own.

GOLDEN TICKETS, CELEBRITY SIGHTINGS, AND PUSH-UP CONTESTS

While many companies make referrals online, most business referrals
are made through word-of-mouth marketing. Word of mouth is what
a satisfied (or unsatisfied) customer says about a product or service to
a potential customer.

MastermindTalks, an annual event founded by Canadian entrepreneur Jayson Gaignard, is an intimate gathering of entrepreneurs
from around the world. Over the course of three days, high-end learning and networking occur at this event (held at an exclusive resort)
where no more than 150 attendees are allowed. In the few short years
since its inception, MastermindTalks has become one of the hottest
event tickets in the industry.

At one point after the first year, MastermindTalks had a forty-two-
hundred person waiting list (more than sixteen thousand people have
applied since the event first began) for an event that cost more than
three thousand dollars to attend. At the time of writing, tickets to this
invitation-only event are now priced at ten thousand dollars, and people are still begging to get in. Because reviewing the number of appli-
cants from the waiting list would be a daunting if not impossible task,

Jayson implemented a new referral program. His program took the form of a golden ticket. Attendees at the event were told they could refer *only one* person to the next year's event and that their referral would be able to jump to the front of the waiting list. The referred prospect would still need to go through the same application process every attendee went through, but holding a golden ticket would guarantee consideration.

While most businesses want as many referrals as possible, MastermindTalks realized the importance of the *right referral*. Getting in front of the ideal candidate was more important than trying to get as many referrals as possible. By positioning this opportunity as a golden ticket available only to raving-fan event attendees, MastermindTalks created a feeling of scarcity and urgency. Attendees wanted to make sure their golden ticket was the one that led to a new attendee the following year.

At the annual event the next year, the room was filled with past attendees as well as a handful of new attendees who came in through the golden ticket referral program. Prior to this, MastermindTalks had never mentioned a referral bonus. The attendees were so excited to bring more people to this life-changing, incredible event that the opportunity to extend an invitation was viewed as enough of a bonus and benefit.

However, recognizing the importance of rewarding advocates in unexpected and experiential ways, Jayson drew names from the list of referring attendees and awarded prizes on the spot in front of all the attendees. These prizes were interesting, fascinating, and substantial. He gave away products with price tags in the hundreds of dollars. He gave away services and subscriptions that would have cost thousands of dollars on the open market. He gave away unique access that is almost impossible to come by—including a behind-the-scenes tour of Airbnb with cofounder and chief product officer Joe Gebbia and a hike with Lululemon founder Chip Wilson. Providing these types of experiences to a room filled with international entrepreneurs had people jumping out of their seats when they "won" the experiences. One of the more interesting spectacles came when Jayson gave away an all-expenses-paid, eight-day safari in Africa as a thank-you. Jayson drew the names of two referrers and then had them do a push-up contest onstage to see who won the safari (I swear, I can't make this stuff up)! Needless to say the cheering crowd only bolstered the experience and left everyone in the room thinking that they should make sure to be in shape for the next year's event—lest they lose a physical challenge like this!

This level of referral acknowledgment carried out in front of the entire customer base made the request for referrals the following year that much easier. MastermindTalks moved to nominations instead of applications (it became impossible to get in if you weren't nominated by a former attendee), and it produced 378 nominations from within the community—for 75 spots. When your customers become your referral source, not only do your marketing expenses go to zero, but the quality of your incoming customers increases dramatically. Not only did the conversion rate on these nominees skyrocket (81 percent of extended new member invitations purchase the premium-priced ticket), but 74 percent of that year's attending members attempted to purchase a ticket for the next event—even though it was almost a year away and the specific date and location hadn't been announced when tickets went on sale!

All too often organizations build referral programs where the prizes are not meaningful to the referring customer. You should develop programs that encourage and excite your most loyal customers to spread the word about your product and service offerings. Doing this will help create lifelong advocates.

⏱ Quick Takeaway

The right referral is much more important than just any referral. Thinking of your customers as your community or your family helps to make you more protective of them, and they will return the favor by bringing the right type of prospect to your door. Enrolling your customers as your marketers helps accelerate your business while also maximizing the likelihood of gaining new, quality, qualified customers. Using unexpected rewards to heighten the referral experience ensures that if you seek referrals, your customers will rush to bring them to you.

SUMMARY: PHASE 8—ADVOCATE

Creating Remarkable Customer Experiences in the Advocate Phase

The Advocate phase of the customer life cycle offers you the opportunity—via case studies and testimonials—to strengthen bonds with existing customers as well as work with customers to identify prospective clients.

Because of the customer's extensive personal experience at this point in the relationship, testimonials are more meaningful and the results of using your products or services are more easily quantified and qualified. In addition, the customer has established enough trust in your company that they will be more likely to share their network with you for potential leads and referrals.

SIX THINGS TO DO IN THE ADVOCATE PHASE
STARTING TOMORROW

While you don't have to use every communication tool in each phase—you can. Getting creative about making memorable experiences for your best customers should spark ideas and leave you eager to implement.

 IN-PERSON

Inviting your most-valued customers to come on sales calls, meet other customers, and mingle with prospects is a way to have your best customers become your best salespeople. When you create unique and engaging reasons to participate, customers will be eager to join in and will likely transfer those positive feelings into their conversations and interactions.

CHAPTER EXAMPLE: Providing top customers with incredible, once-in-a-lifetime prizes (Maverick1000 and MastermindTalks) is a great way to get them to refer new business while driving participation and excitement in the process.

@ EMAIL

Well-timed emails that are easy to act on allow your best customers to support, strengthen, and grow your business. When crafting these messages, consider how your customer will randomly receive them in their email inbox and make sure that the "ask" is something they can do quickly and easily. Make sure that the benefit of participating is a compelling reward, clearly outlined and effortlessly achieved.

CHAPTER EXAMPLE: By offering additional benefits to customers who get their friends to become customers (Dropbox and Delta/

AMEX), you can grow your customer base at an exponential rate. Recognizing peer group similarities of your customers (ViaCord) and giving substantial discounts on an ongoing service that nearly all of your customers want and need keeps the referrals coming in. Often the simple act of asking for testimonials (4Knines) is enough to drive customer engagement and boost sales.

 MAIL

The arrival of a free gift in the mail allows for a unique touchpoint (especially this long into the relationship) that marks the customer's arrival at the Advocate phase—an important distinction for your top customers. This communication should be highly personalized, handwritten, and feel as if it was custom-made for the recipient.

CHAPTER EXAMPLE: Offering breathtaking surprises (suitcase of cash) to your top advocates shows your appreciation for their help, while also creating a remarkable touchpoint that they will surely talk about with friends and colleagues.

 PHONE

A congratulatory call from the CEO or chairman of the board will emphasize the importance of the customer's status as an advocate. This interaction once again offers the company the chance to thank the customer for the ongoing patronage and support.

 **VIDEO**

Asking customers to share video testimonials is not only appropriate given the length of the customer relationship, but it has a greater chance of gleaning positive testimonials as these customers have significant personal experience with the brand. Giving prizes for the most creative videos and showcasing them in various brand channels will increase participation as well.

 **PRESENT**

A strong referral campaign at this point in the customer life cycle is both appropriate and meaningful—especially to those who reached this stage in the relationship. By offering the most successful customers free products or services to gift to friends and colleagues, the personal testimonial will take on entirely new meaning as they will be able to help their friends "sample" the brand.

CHAPTER EXAMPLE: Sweetening the incentives for making referrals (Delta/AMEX) by providing something that your top customers crave is a way to keep them active and engaged. Giving any referral a relevant bonus or benefit (Dropbox and Maverick1000) drives referrals while building loyalty on the part of the veteran customer. Shocking your top customers with incredible prizes (MastermindTalks) helps to drive enthusiasm and guarantee referrals for many years to come.

YOUR ASSIGNMENT: PUT THESE IDEAS TO WORK

Now that you have a clear understanding of the Advocate phase, answer a series of questions that are designed to get you thinking about how you can use each of the communication tools to enhance the overall experience during this phase of the customer journey.

(This is the last set of questions—don't fade on me! You're too close to the complete payoff to skip this section now!)

Evaluating the Current Situation

Answer each question, then write two or three sentences explaining your answer. For bonus points, write down any ideas you have for changes that would make your answers "better."

- What is the first signal that a customer is now an advocate for your company or offerings? (Hint: The customer might be making unsolicited referrals to you that are ideal prospects.)

- Describe in detail what advocacy looks like to you. What does the customer need to do? What does it "feel" like? How do you acknowledge the contribution? Does the referral lead to the right kind of business? Does the referral lead to the right kind of customer (in terms of personality/demeanor)?

- In your current business, do you create remarkable experiences during the Advocate phase?

- If so, what are they?

- On a scale of 1 to 10, where 1 is "pathetic" and 10 is "world class," how would you rate the experience your customers currently have in the Advocate phase? (If you don't currently have any advocates, score yourself a "1.")

Tools to Enhance the Future Experience

Answer each question by coming up with two or three ideas for using the specific tool to enhance the customer experience. These are your very best customers, so it's worth it—no matter the investment of time, money, or staff. This should be the place where your creativity runs wild!

- How can you use in-person interactions during this phase to make the customer feel like they are your most important customer?

- How can you make your emails feel like personal messages from a dear friend as opposed to corporatespeak?

- How can a customized mail piece mark the milestone of this customer being considered one of your very best?

- How can phone conversations add a level of personalization and familiarity that is commensurate with the status of your most valued customers?

- How can videos shift from marketing messaging to shared communications between friends?

- What present(s) could you give customers that would really make them feel appreciated as "most valued" customers?

Pick One Now

If you've answered the questions above (this is the last set of questions—I promise!), you have a clear understanding of the customer experience during the Advocate phase, as well as many ideas for how to make that experience better. Taking that into account, consider the following questions.

- What is one thing you can start doing tomorrow to make the experience your customers have in the Advocate phase even better?

- Who would you need to talk to in order to make this happen?

- How would you know if you've succeeded in making this improvement?

- How would you measure the improvement of the overall customer experience?

- How would you share this impact with the rest of the organization?

YOU'VE MADE IT THROUGH THE EIGHT PHASES— NOW IT'S TIME TO IMPLEMENT

You've now traveled from the first time a prospect considers doing business with you, through the eight phases of the customer journey, to arrive at the point where the customer is a raving fan of both you and your business.

Congratulations! If you've completed the questions at the end of each chapter along the way, you now have a detailed and clear understanding of how your business is currently performing, a treasure trove of ideas for enhancements and improvements, and some specific steps for what to do next. Now let's consider how to implement this new way of thinking across your organization. . . .

CHAPTER SIXTEEN

Get Started: How to Stop Losing Customers Today

I once believed that knowing about the eight phases was enough for people to understand how to create amazing customer experiences. For many people, that was all it took for them to take action and change the way their businesses operated.

But as I brought this method to wider audiences, I realized many business owners needed more than just information. They would tell me they loved the concepts, but had no idea how to apply the eight phases to their business or their customers' experiences. They wanted and needed step-by-step guidance.

In an effort to make my methodology as easy to implement as possible, this chapter outlines a step-by-step plan to learn more about your customers, determine the current experiences they are having, and enhance operations so you can deliver remarkable experiences on a consistent basis.

I developed a four-step process to help you understand your customers and position your business to roll out an enhanced customer journey across the eight phases. These four steps are:

1. Investigate

2. Observe

3. Personalize

4. Surprise

INVESTIGATE—*Learning Everything You Can About the People You Serve*

Dale Carnegie is famous for saying, "You can make more friends in two months by becoming interested in other people than you can in two years by trying to get other people interested in you."[1] The typical business approach to interacting with customers is to jump up and down and scream, "Look at me! Look at me! Look what I have!" Instead of asking questions and learning all about their customers, businesses have a tendency to focus on themselves.

The more we know about our customers, the easier it is to wow them in our interactions. While many different types of data are useful, the bits of information that offer a personal and emotional connection to customers are the most valuable. A personal data point is something specific to that individual (as opposed to the public at large)—for example, *where* they attended college. An emotional data point is something they have a strong and ideally positive feeling about—for example, their *experience* at college. As such, for some people, a discussion about their alma mater can be both a personal and emotional connection.

When it comes to investigating current customers, the first place you should start is with their name. Names matter. Carnegie noted that "[t]he average person is more interested in their own name than in all the other names in the world put together."[2] Carnegie believed so much in the power of a person's name that he referred to it as *magic*:

We should all be aware of the magic contained in a name and realize that this single item is wholly and completely owned by the person with whom we are dealing and nobody else. The name sets the individual apart; it makes him or her unique among all others. The information we are imparting or the request we are making takes on a special importance when we approach the situation with the name of the individual. From the waitress to the senior executive, the name will work magic as we deal with others.

Remember that a person's name is to that person the sweetest and most important sound in any language.[3]

Research has shown that hearing the sound of your own name being spoken lights up unique areas of your brain.[4] And yet most businesses fail to use this very simple technique to connect with their customers. In fact, in many businesses one of the first tasks is to assign new relationships a "customer number." It is no wonder that many customers feel like they are being treated as a number instead of as an individual. They are!

Once you have identified the names of your customers, there are a number of ways to begin your investigative research. But first, let's make sure what you learn doesn't go in one ear and out the other.

INK FADES SLOWER THAN MEMORY

When it comes to investigating your customers, it is important to get clarity on (a) where to store the data you collect, and (b) who is in charge of maintaining it. There are dozens of customer relationship management (CRM) software programs, and the best advice I can give is to choose the one that you will actually use.* The features and functionalities pale in comparison with the uphill battle to get employees to adopt a CRM tool as an integral part of their day-to-day habits.

Once you've selected your software tool, decide on the types of data and information you want to seek out from your customers and use when interacting with them. To assist in this process, I've included a list of *Audience Information Categories* in the Appendix that details potential data sets to record. You can do a quick assessment of your current tracking efforts by marking whether you collect a specific piece of information always, sometimes, rarely, or never.

Use this list to select the fields you would like to include in your customer relationship management program. To be clear, it is not recommended that you track all of the items given in the *Audience Information Categories* list. What is recommended is that you aim for completed data fields (for every customer) in the specific categories you do choose to track.

When evaluating which data to track, you may want to consider how you will use it. For example, by tracking favorite sports teams, you can plan to send a text message or email congratulating the customer when their favorite team wins. This is easily done by creating a "favorite team list" and then using a tool like Google Alerts to keep track of team wins. At certain key points in the year (a customer birthday, special holidays, the end of the sports season, etc.), you can give them something branded with the logo of their favorite sports team as a gift. In addition, give thought to selecting data points that will create both personal and emotional connections.

In the beginning, make sure to select five to ten fields you "must

---

*For a current review (I update it regularly) of some of the best CRM software on the market, visit: *www.JoeyColeman.com/CRM-Review*.

start tracking now." Then select five to ten fields you "would like to start tracking" once you're six to twelve months into your investigate endeavor. Make sure the CRM is formatted to include fields where you can populate specific data once your research efforts start to bear fruit.

Once you identify the desired data fields and start investigating/tracking them, it's time to start adding the data to the CRM to create completed records.

INVESTIGATE: A STEP-BY-STEP PROCESS

The different tools and techniques described in this section offer a variety of ways to gather insight and learn more about your customers. By approaching research efforts in this order, you can maximize your findings while operating efficiently and effectively. In addition, the more information you can gather without asking your customers for the answer, the more impressed they will be when you connect on something that is important to them.

Making Personal and Emotional Connections

Many people praise the power of making connections with customers. But the potency of the connection hinges on the type of data you have. Some data points are personal in nature while others are emotional. If you can find a data point that is both, you can make a more meaningful connection.

Historically, gathering customer intelligence was a difficult and time-consuming task. Now we live in a day and age when people are publicly sharing volumes of information about their personal lives, their interests, their hobbies, their desires, and their activities on social media. Many, if not most, of these profiles are open to the public.

Learning more about your customer is often as simple as spending ten minutes reviewing their social media profiles. Status updates, photos, and comments provide wonderful insight about the personal and emotional elements of your customers' lives.

Things You Know but Don't Write Down
When you think about your customers, there are often many things you know that haven't been captured in your CRM records. Begin by reviewing the missing data fields in your CRM for each customer and filling in any information that you know off the top of your head. If you're not 100 percent sure, fill it in and confirm using another source in the subsequent steps of the investigate process.

LinkedIn
Find the LinkedIn profile for the customer in question. This will offer insight into your customer's current job position and entire work history. The most robust profiles on LinkedIn also share information such as where the individual attended undergraduate school or graduate school, the languages they speak, the popular leaders and entities they follow, and in some cases their birthday. Review the page to complete any missing data fields in your CRM. Don't forget to review activity, articles, featured skills/endorsements, recommendations received, etc. Finally, make sure to copy the URL of the LinkedIn profile page and paste it into your CRM to make future research faster and easier.

Facebook
Facebook is also a treasure trove of data and information. Seen by many as the more personal side of their online profile, Facebook gives you the opportunity not only to see stated hobbies and biographical

facts, but also to see photos of this specific customer (from which you can learn how they like to spend their leisure time). A profile photo will give you tremendous insight into your customer. Is the photo a traditional headshot? Is it a glamour shot? Is it professional? Is it informal? Are there props or clues in the photo that give you an idea about your customer's interests, hobbies, or travels? Is the photo recent or a throwback to yesteryear? The old adage that "a picture is worth a thousand words" holds true when reviewing customer profile headshots. Finally, make sure to copy the URL of the Facebook profile page and paste it into your CRM to make future research simpler.

Company Website

In addition to researching social media profiles, company websites often have extensive "About Us" sections where team members are profiled. The closer your customers are to holding C-suite positions, the more likely you will find information about them on the company website. Don't forget to review any company newsletters for team member profiles. Finally, make sure to copy the URL of the company website and record it in the CRM.

Google Searches

After exhausting the obvious resources, a simple search on Google or another search engine will find any mentions of the person in traditional media, blogs, and other websites. It never ceases to amaze me how much I can learn by merely spending five to ten minutes investigating online. Search for the individual customer in question by searching their name within quotation marks. Depending on the familiarity or commonality of the name, you may need to add additional terms to the search, including the name of their employer, the town where they reside, etc. Click through the links to confirm the link refers to your customer and then use any data you find to complete any missing data fields in your CRM.

Customer Surveys

If you find there is a specific piece of information that is lacking across your CRM, a customer survey may be an efficient way to gather that data for every customer you serve. When conducting these surveys, remember to be short (ask only a few questions), relevant (ask questions the customer can imagine you need to know), and efficient (use an online surveying tool) to increase the likelihood of completion and decrease the likelihood of annoying your customers. If you think surveys will be necessary for you to fill in your knowledge gaps, coordinate this effort across your entire organization to make sure you aren't constantly asking customers to share information and respond to surveys.

The Direct Ask

When all else fails, you can ask your customers specific questions to complete their customer profiles. Consider doing this in an "I tell, you tell" format. For example, when trying to discern a favorite sports team, you can share the team you cheer for and then ask the customer if there is a particular team they support. By sharing your personal and emotional connection first, it helps to put the customer at ease and greatly increases the likelihood that they will volunteer personal and emotional information.

The Focused Listen

By practicing a commitment to focused listening, you can quickly gather information on your customers. Pay attention to side comments and subtle references in order to learn valuable information. For example, if you're on a call with a customer and their dog is barking in the background, you may hear them say, "Rover—be quiet!" By following up and saying, "What kind of dog is Rover?" you can enter three useful pieces of data into your CRM: (1) The customer has a dog, (2) named Rover, that is (3) a German shepherd. This research is ongoing and represents a commitment to continually learning more about your customers.

YOU'RE LEAPS AND BOUNDS AHEAD

Presuming you completed the tasks outlined above as part of the Investigate process (as opposed to just reading the book and saying, "I'll get to that when I'm done"), you're ready to move on to the next element of the process—Observe!

OBSERVE—If You're Willing to Watch and Listen, You Can Learn Almost Anything You Want to Know About Your Customers

The next step in the customer experience enhancement process is to observe your customer in their natural habitat. By observing our customers' interactions, we create unique opportunities to build connection and rapport. Allow me to share a great example of a time when someone observed me in order to create a remarkable experience.

HOW DOES HE KNOW?

Years ago I traveled to Toronto to give a keynote speech. After a long day of travel, I was already several hours behind schedule as I sat in a taxi in front of the Omni King Edward Hotel and tried to settle up with the driver.

If you've never traveled to Canada, you might not realize that if you pay by credit card, you (the customer) handle the credit card approval process. For Americans, this is a foreign concept. The driver handed me a portable credit card processing machine, I inserted my credit card, and I slowly navigated my way through the screen prompts.

To complicate matters, the processing machine offered both English and French options. Of course, I accidentally selected the French option. Did I mention I don't speak French?

It was a disaster.

I noticed out of the corner of my eye as the bellman came forward and walked down the hotel stairs toward the taxi. I started to get anxious because, knowing how hospitable Canadians are, I imagined the bellman would be opening the taxi door while I was still trying to pay. As a result, he would end up standing there waiting for me while I fumbled around to complete the credit card processing.

Much to my surprise, when I next glanced out the window the bellman had reappeared at the front door. Only this time he was holding my suitcase. He had walked down to the taxi, retrieved my luggage from the trunk, and carried it to the front entrance of the hotel.

Once again, the bellman started walking toward the taxi. When he arrived he merely placed his hand on the door handle and stood waiting next to the cab. The moment I finished processing the credit card and handed the machine back to the taxi driver, the bellman opened the car door and in a welcoming voice said, "Good evening, Mr. Coleman. Welcome to the Omni King Edward."

I was astounded. How did this bellman know who I was?

The hotel's information regarding my flight and my arrival time was completely off because my flight had been delayed by several hours. Certainly my reputation couldn't have preceded me. . . .

Eventually I asked him. He said he knew my name because he read the luggage tag on my bag. This incredible bellman had taken the time to read my name off the suitcase so that he could address me by name. When I asked him why he did this, he explained, "It's really pretty simple, to be honest. I've found that people really like it when I call them by their name."

This level of personalization (calling me by name) in the first interaction was unexpected. By observing my name tag, the bellman enhanced my experience with the hotel. Needless to say I hold a very fond spot in my heart for the staff at the Omni King Edward in Toronto.

A WEARY TRAVELER'S NIGHTMARE SCENARIO

I once took a multiweek speaking tour that ended with my arrival for an event in Las Vegas only thirty minutes before the kickoff reception began. The event was held at the Mandarin Oriental—a Forbes triple five-star luxury hotel that is unlike any other venue in the city of Las Vegas. It has no slot machines and no gaming tables. In fact, the hotel is located eight stories above the Strip and has a beautiful view of Las Vegas Boulevard without subjecting guests to its craziness.

After I checked in, I went up to my room to quickly drop off my bag before heading to the kickoff reception. I opened my suitcase and removed my toiletry bag. Unzipping the toiletry bag, I witnessed a traveler's nightmare. . . .

My cough syrup had exploded in my toiletry bag.

I'd been on the road for several weeks and developed a cold during my travels. At my previous location, I had grabbed a bottle of cough syrup before jumping on the plane and quickly chugged a swig of the medicine. I painfully realized that I had not tightly closed the cap on the bottle prior to putting it in my bag and, as a result, cherry cough syrup had spilled everywhere.

It coated everything. My toothbrush was sticky. My deodorant was sticky. My shaving cream and razor were sticky. Everything in my toiletries bag was coated in a sticky pink goo.

Cleaning up this mess was going to be on par with cleaning up the *Exxon Valdez* oil spill.

I didn't have enough time to wash everything, so I left the bag in the hotel bathroom and raced downstairs for the welcoming reception, figuring that I would deal with the mess when I returned.

Two and a half hours later I came back to my room and found an incredible surprise. The housekeeping staff had done a turndown service, and I found my toothbrush, deodorant, razor blade, and shaving cream were all cleaned and laid out to dry on a pristine, white towel.

The bottle of cough syrup, which had been an absolute disaster, was sparkling, as was the complimentary dosage cap that came with it.

But what impressed me the most was the written note I found under the clean bottle of cough syrup.

To say I was both shocked and moved by this touching and thoughtful gesture would be an understatement.

Do you think the management from the Mandarin Oriental, Las Vegas, conducts a training for their housekeeping staff in which they detail a specific set of procedures and policies for handling a situation where a bottle of cough syrup has not been properly closed and as a result leaks all over a customer's luggage? Absolutely not.

Instead, the Mandarin Oriental trains its employees to do everything possible to make customers' visits remarkable. A key practice in this commitment is to *observe* the customer. In this particular case, the housekeeper, Kelly, went above and beyond to make me feel comforted after observing the cough syrup disaster. Not only did she clean all of my items (a daunting task that I wouldn't wish on my worst enemy), but her thoughtful note left me feeling cared for in a way that I had not before, and have not since, experienced at a hotel. By observing my behaviors and then acting on that information, Kelly was able to create a meaningful moment that I'm still raving about years later.

OBSERVE: A STEP-BY-STEP PROCESS

Investigating your customers provides a great foundation, but all too often companies stop there and miss the opportunity to catch the nuances of their customers' behaviors. By incorporating observation into your customer intelligence gathering, you can add new insights about your customers and the way they use and interact with your products and services. This in turn can give you ideas on how to further enhance the overall experience of your customers.

Watch Your Customers in Their "Natural Habitat"
It's not enough to consider your customers from afar; you must get up close and witness their actions, comments, and behaviors. When was the last time you watched a customer use your product or partake of

your service? If it was more than a month ago, it's been too long. Examine your customers' day-to-day lives and see how your offerings affect and influence their interactions.

Walk in Your Customer's Shoes

In the literary classic *To Kill a Mockingbird*, the protagonist Atticus Finch gives advice to his young daughter in the famous line "You never really understand a person until you consider things from his point of view . . . until you climb inside of his skin and walk around in it."[5] Try to interact with your product or service in a way that takes you back to a time when you didn't know anything about how to use it or how it worked. Is the experience effortless? Do you know what to do at each step in the process? The better you get at regularly seeing your business from your customers' eyes, the more you will appreciate their experience and be able to make it better.

Study the Little Things

Pay attention to the microinteractions your customers have with you and your products or services. Consider the little things that seemingly have nothing to do with you but upon further examination are connected. Often it's the littlest observations that have the biggest impact.

Record Now, Review Later

It's often difficult to observe, consider, analyze, and improve in the same sitting. Give yourself permission to record your observations and then set up a time shortly after (within one to two days) to review your findings. You'll be surprised how much additional insight comes from giving your subconscious mind time to process what it witnessed.

Listen (and Look) for the Golden Nuggets That Drop from the Sky

On several occasions as a child and as a practicing attorney, I had the chance to sit at counsel's table in the courtroom next to my father—a well-known and highly successful criminal defense trial attorney. He regularly encouraged me to "listen for the golden nuggets that drop from the sky." He believed that in every trial, there were two or three moments when a witness, the opposing counsel, or the judge would say something that could change the course of the trial, but you would catch it only if you were paying extremely close attention. I've incorporated this philosophy into my customer observations as well. I can't give advice about what specifically your customer may say, but I can promise that if you listen closely, you will learn things that can change the course of the customer journey.

ALLOW ME TO MAKE AN OBSERVATION

Presuming you completed some, if not all, of the recommendations outlined above as part of the Observe process (you're a pro by now, always doing the exercises—I love it!), you're ready to move on to the next step in of the process—Personalize!

PERSONALIZE—*Making Every Interaction with Your Customers Meaningful*

The third step in the process of enhancing customer experiences is to personalize your interactions. Building on the investigations and the observations you've made in the previous two steps, you are now better positioned to customize your communications.

Any piece of information you can learn about a customer offers the potential for a tailored interaction.

Imagine learning that your customer attended the same undergraduate university you attended. Now you have the opportunity to create a connection that will most likely result in an instant and strong bond.

Imagine learning that one of your customers was born in the same small town that you were. Relating over where you were born and raised offers an immediate connection between two otherwise unknown individuals.

By learning about your customers' hobbies, you have the opportunity to discover if you share any similar hobbies. At the very least, knowing your customers' hobbies allows you to more effectively select gifts and target your interactions.

When it comes to potentially overlapping interests that you have with your customers, you must be honest. If you share a common interest, it's great to share that with your customer. If you don't, don't try to. If the conversation goes beyond the initial disclosure (as it surely will if you've hit on a true interest), you will quickly be out of your element and the customer will know it immediately. Your lack of honesty combined with the veiled attempt to build rapport when there actually wasn't any common ground will set the relationship back and may even end it. Better not to say anything at all, or even admit that you don't have the same level of interest, than to pretend or, even worse, lie. When you are honest with your customer, the relational dynamics click into place in unprecedented ways—creating strong bonds and clear connections.

After discovering one of my clients was a fan of photography, I recently found myself walking through an exhibit at an art gallery showcasing the work of a world-renowned photographer whose expertise is black-and-white photos of animals in Africa. I knew this was something my client would appreciate. I decided to send the hardcover show catalog to my client as a gift; I thought it was the perfect way to let him know that I was thinking of him. I took the extra step of personalizing it myself and having the photographer personalize and sign the book as well.

Within minutes of receiving the package, the client sent me a text message thanking me for the wonderful gift. He let me know that he had gained a newfound appreciation for the possibilities of photographing animals in the wild.

Anything that truly matters to your customers is a chance for you to connect with them in a way that can build instant favor and rapport. Whether their hobbies include the culinary arts, musical theater, interpretive dance, college football, pro hockey, astronomy, collecting *Star Wars* memorabilia, or heavy metal, knowing more about your customers allows you to personalize communications with them.

Given that many of your customers will likely fall into a similar demographic, you can batch your personalization moments and create communications that apply to several of your customers all at once. The opportunity for connection is only limited by your willingness to investigate and observe the things that matter most to your customers.

PERSONALIZE: A STEP-BY-STEP PROCESS

Once you've completed the missing data fields in your CRM for all of your customers using the techniques outlined in the Investigate and Observe steps detailed above, and you have a system for getting complete data early on in any new customer relationships, you are ready to use this information to create personalized touchpoints that strengthen the relationship with your customers.

Personal Wows

The easiest way to create a remarkable customer experience is to use personal and emotional connections when communicating with individual customers. This can be as simple as asking, "How is your daughter Lauren doing at Iowa State University?" (where your CRM tracks the names of your customers' children and the schools they attend) or as complex as giving the customer an issue of *Adventure Comics* #48, the first appearance of Hour-Man, to celebrate their retirement (the perfect gift based on your discovery that your customer loves this superhero and is missing a key issue in their comic book collection).

Wow Groups

When multiple customers have a similar interest, you can design communications that allow you to create a personal and emotional connection with multiple customers at the same time, using the same data points and ideas. For example, if several customers are fans of a particular musician or band (e.g., Maroon 5), when that group releases a new album, you can send it to each of them. Remember, presents don't need to be expensive—they just need to be personalized and thoughtful.

Customer Appreciation Events

As you notice trends within your customer base, you can start to plan customer appreciation events built around their common interests. If 40 percent of your customers love golf, a group golf outing at a hard-to-access golf course could be a great way to build rapport across this particular segment of your customer base.

THIS ONE'S FOR YOU

Now that you've considered how to incorporate more personalization into your customer communications and interactions as part of the Personalize process, you're ready to move on to the final step—Surprise!

SURPRISE—*Going Above and Beyond to Make Your Customers Smile*

The final step in the process is surprise. In the typical business the thought of a surprise usually falls into the category of sending an annual holiday gift, which is often a fruit basket or some other meaningless, non-personalized item that doesn't create a connection with the customer. In recent years, the fruit basket has been replaced by the all-too-popular gift card to a national chain retail establishment.

When was the last time that a gift card made you feel a relationship was meaningful or special?

Imagine if your parents gave you a gift card to a national chain restaurant for your birthday.

I'm guessing that wouldn't qualify as the best gift you ever received.

When we treat our customers in this commoditized way, the message we send is that they don't matter as individuals. We also send the message that the convenience of giving the same gift to every customer outweighs the investment of time it would take to give something personalized or special.

When it comes to presents and gifting, my good friend John Ruhlin of the Ruhlin Group (remember—he's the guy who produced the locker room wood speakers for the Chicago Cubs) is one of the world's top experts. John teaches and speaks on the topic of *strategic appreciation*—a regular practice and policy of gifting a customer in order to show appreciation and to build a foundation for increased business and personal interactions in the future. John's book *Giftology: The Art and Science of Using Gifts to Cut Through the Noise, Increase Referrals, and Strengthen Retention* offers a quick guide to incorporating strategic appreciation into your business.

I first met John when we both attended the same conference. After a few minutes of conversation we agreed to exchange business cards and stay in touch, as John's approach to customer care was in alignment with my philosophy for creating remarkable customer experiences. Arriving home from the event several days later, I was surprised to find a box addressed to me with a return address from John. When I opened the package I found a beautiful chef's knife engraved with a message: *Handcrafted Exclusively for the Joey and Berit Coleman Family.* Nowhere on the knife did it say John Ruhlin's name. Nowhere on the knife did it have any messaging about his business. John's present was a true gift *and* it was personalized to my family.

One of the most interesting things about this gift from John is that it gets two "touches" in our house every night. My wife cooks dinner and I wash the dishes. She reaches for the "John Ruhlin knife" every night when preparing dinner, and I clean it by hand every night after dinner (before returning it to the woodblock John also sent along with his thoughtful gift).

John gets thought of at least twice in our house every single night, despite the *lack of markings of his name or company name* anywhere on the gift he gave us. This is a testament to his belief in creating artifacts and signature pieces that are representative of the relationship you have and desire with your customers.

The other interesting part of this gift is the actual inscription. The inscription is made out to the whole family: me, my wife, and by referencing "family," our children.

When gifting your customers, it's important to recognize that the surprise needs to be a surprise for all of the recipients, not just the primary point of contact. John regularly talks about taking advantage of the opportunity to gift the spouse of your customer or the family of your customer. This creates an even greater impact on the relationship and the various recipients.

As someone who certainly appreciates gifts, I actually find myself more appreciative of a gift directed toward my wife or my two sons. It gives me the opportunity to see the joy in their faces when they open and use the gift and it becomes a more lasting connection to the gift giver. It's meaningful to us, it's an experience we can share, and it's not just something for me.

You also want to consider the quality of the gift. In a separate instance, John also sent me the best scissors I have ever owned—or used for that matter. The Cutco scissors with red handles (my brand color) are also engraved and get regular use in our home. The fact that they sit in the knife block next to the knives John has gifted me over the years (yes—he's added to the collection over time) just adds to the experience.

SURPRISE: A STEP-BY-STEP PROCESS

Now that you know all about your customers and have personalized your interactions and communications, it's time to enhance the experience by surprising them. Most organizations think of surprises and gifts too late and then rush to do something for every customer—the *same* thing for every customer, done at the last minute. To avoid giving gifts that either are a waste of money or, in some circumstances, will actually hurt the relationship, consider these recommended things to do—and not to do—many of which are covered in much greater depth in John Ruhlin's book *Giftology*.

Surprise the Spouse and Family
All too often, organizations overlook the people who have the most influence on customers' decisions and behaviors. If you surprise the customer's spouse and any children they may have with special gifts, you can almost guarantee that the family will sing your praises to your target customer. This type of encouragement coming from your customer's loved ones is some of the best support and promotion money can buy.

Remember the Assistant and Team Members
By delivering moments of surprise and delight to your customer's assistant and/or fellow team members, you can gain an ally in the office. Giving gifts that make your customer look like a hero will certainly win you points with your customer, while broadening your reach and reputation within the organization. Should your customer leave the company for any reason, you will already have a foundation of solid relationships with those who stay behind.

Eliminate Your Logo, Tagline, or Any Other Message or
Image About You
Let's be honest—if you give a customer an item with your logo or name on it, you're not giving a gift. You're giving a marketing tool that you hope the customer will show to their friends, which ideally will lead to more business for you. There is nothing wrong with promotional prod-

ucts or branded items—they just aren't gifts. Don't pat yourself on the back for your gifting acumen if the item in question has any reference to you or your brand (logo, inscription, brand colors, etc.). Instead, strive to give a gift that is so remarkable in its own right that when other people see it, they will immediately ask your customer, "Where did you get that?"

Put the Recipient's Name on It

Where appropriate, personalize the gift with the recipient and/or their family's name. As discussed earlier in this chapter, using a customer's name is one of the most powerful ways for you to build connection and rapport. Giving the customer a quality item that is personalized by name not only guarantees a deeper emotional connection to the item, but it almost guarantees the customer will keep the item for a long time.

Give the Very Best You Can Afford

Make sure any gifts you give are best in class. Nothing ruins a relationship faster than a cheap gift. It sends the very clear message that you see the relationship as being worth very little. Instead, budget for customer surprises as you would for any other business expense. John Ruhlin recommends (and I agree) that you should set aside from 2 to 10 percent of your net profits to use for gifting. This is a necessary relationship investment—as important as the software you use to track your customer interactions. If you're willing to take a customer to a nice dinner or provide tickets to a sporting event or concert, you should be willing to spend the same amount of money on a nice gift.

Experiences Are Great, but Help the Customer Remember
Gifting your customers with remarkable experiences is fantastic, but don't forget to memorialize the experience with a memento. Dinners, concerts, golf outings, and the like tend to be forgotten rather quickly—but not when paired with a cookbook from the restaurant, a framed photo of the band from the concert, or a piece of golf apparel from the pro shop at the golf course you played. These are the types of gifts that keep on giving long after the experience.

Pay Attention to the Calendar
Surprisingly, there is a bad time to surprise your customer with a gift—anytime around a major holiday. This is when everyone sends gifts, and it's easy to get lost in the noise. Instead, give gifts when no one expects it. By making your surprises more random, you make them more memorable.

Be Better Than Average
The average person gives money, or gift cards, or food. Each of these can be problematic. Money can feel transactional, gift cards lack personalization or warmth, and food gets consumed and then forgotten. Instead, seek out "practical luxuries," the types of items that will delight your customer in the days, weeks, and months ahead. You needn't spend a lot of money, but you should spend a lot of time selecting and perfecting the gift for your customer.

Don't Worry About Pleasing Everyone
Have you ever received a gift that missed the mark? We all have. If you incorporate more surprises into your strategic appreciation of customers, you won't please everyone, and that's okay. For every surprise that

doesn't work, many more will. Most organizations try to come up with a single gift to give to every customer that won't offend or stand out too much. Yet these same organizations are surprised when the reactions from their customers are less than positive—or missing altogether. Instead of gifting everyone, start by giving remarkable gifts to two or three customers. You will be amazed at your return on investment.

Don't Forget the Note

If you're going to make the effort to surprise someone, you should be willing to make the effort to write a handwritten note to accompany your gift. If you're not willing to do that, please don't even bother with the gift.

Don't Give to Receive

When I was growing up, my mother used to say, "Never give a gift just to get the thank-you card." What incredible words of wisdom from an equally incredible person. Give presents and surprises because you want to, not because you want to be seen a certain way or you think it will lead to something else in return. No one likes a present that arrives with strings attached. Trust me, the return on your gifting will work its way back to you even faster if you have no expectation for it.

NO SURPRISE HERE—YOU'VE DONE IT!

Congratulations on learning all the tips and tricks of strategic appreciation and giving surprises as outlined in this step-by-step process. You now have everything you need to effectively implement gifting into your customer onboarding processes. You also have a clear, four-step process for positioning your organization to implement the eight phases of a remarkable customer experience journey.

HOW DO I GET MY EMPLOYEES TO FOLLOW THIS PROCESS?

Often the CEO or an executive leader in a company will learn about this process and, while excited about the possibilities, will immediately turn skeptical because of the need to enlist employees in the implementation. Rest assured there are a number of proven ways to get employee buy-in when it comes to adopting a customer experience enhancement program.

Get Employees Involved from the Beginning

All too often, senior management decides to make the customer a priority and then proceeds to find consultants and advisers to develop the strategy and oversee the implementation. Invariably this leads to revised systems and processes, upgraded technology solutions, and restructuring of titles and compensation plans. Needless to say, when these initiatives are finally introduced to the employees at large, they are often met with a lackluster response. Employees view these activities as "flash in the pan/flavor of the month" endeavors that will soon be abandoned or forgotten. As such, they don't buy into the reasons for the shift, nor do they adopt the behaviors necessary for implementing a successful customer experience program. In order for customer experience to get better, the employees must be part of the planning from the outset.

Let Employees Co-create the Experience

By involving employees from the start in the design and structure of all customer experience initiatives, not only do you increase the likelihood that they will embrace these new activities, but you boost the likelihood of success. Employees often know more about how to improve the customer experience than management imagines. Giving employees a voice in the design of the customer journey establishes feelings of significance and value, and instills a sense of ownership in executing on the strategy and plan.

Give Employees Autonomy to Create Their Own Experience
Just because they have offices/cars/clothes that are nicer/bigger/more expensive doesn't mean the management team has a monopoly on good ideas and great experiences. By giving employees the freedom to develop their own approach to customer experience, you will be able to harness their creativity while also encouraging them to be good stewards of organizational resources.

Establish a Customer Experience Budget
While creating remarkable experiences is more often about intention than investment, allocating a budget to enhancement activities increases the likelihood of program success. Assigning a "per customer" budget that must be spent on customer experience in the First 100 Days of the relationship guarantees that actions will be taken early in the customer journey to mark the customer's value and signal appreciation for the business.

Track and Celebrate the Small Wins
All too often, customer experience efforts focus on the large victories instead of the small wins. By paying attention to little improvements and then honoring them with big celebrations, managers can send a clear message to employees that the details matter and that minor improvements in the customer experience have a compounding effect

when collected over time. By praising progress at any scale, organizations can build momentum and enthusiasm for a commitment to customer experience (that by definition is a never-ending effort).

Form a Brand Experience Team

Assembling a group of employees to serve as your "Brand Experience Team" and giving them authority to oversee and operate the customer experience enhancement activities instills a sense of pride and ownership. Establishing a commitment to putting the customer first further strengthens the organizational culture. Consider assigning no more than half of the members of the Brand Experience Team and seek volunteers for the remaining positions. Don't hesitate to look for participants in every department, role, and position within the company. You will often find a commitment to customer experience where you least expect it.

By giving employees a major role in the development, execution, and management of your customer experience initiatives, not only will you see a cultural shift across the organization, but you will ensure customer experience remains a priority in your organization for many years to come.

HOW DO I GET MY EMPLOYER TO MAKE THIS A PRIORITY?

Sometimes management is so focused on the day-to-day activities of the organization that they can miss big-picture problems. Getting senior leaders to realize the importance of prioritizing the customer is often a daunting task that appears to have no upside worth pursuing. Time and time again, however, the individuals who take the lead in customer experience enhancement activities see promotion and advancement that outpace their colleagues—not only because of the increased interactions with senior management, but because of the direct correlation between the employees' activities and new increases in revenue, retention, and profit.

Buy Them This Book!

Sometimes the best way to persuade a member of senior management to pursue an idea is to make sure the idea comes from someone outside of the company and its chain of command. I'm happy to play that role for you! Just purchase a copy of this book for the person you're trying to persuade and ask them to read it. I've worked to make the book applicable at both a strategic and tactical level, so my hope is that it speaks to executives with both dispositions.

Give Them a Copy of the Quick Start Kit

You can download the *Never Lose a Customer Again Quick Start Kit* here: *www.JoeyColeman.com/QuickStart*. It's a fast read that shares an overview of the philosophy and methodology outlined in this book and then augments it with a series of exercises and recommendations designed to get the reader thinking and feeling differently about customer experience. After that, the Quick Start Kit is designed to help garner some initial wins and build momentum for these types of customer experience programs.

Lend Them Your Copy of This Book!

If you've been the diligent reader that I know you to be if you are reading this sentence, you've taken notes and answered the questions at the conclusion of the preceding chapters. By lending your copy of this book to a member of senior management, you show (a) your commitment to growth and learning, (b) your interest in customer experience, and (c) your willingness to "do the homework" for them. Your understanding of the methodologies, philosophies, and systems outlined in this book should give them confidence in the fact that at least one of their employees has bought in and is ready to take action.

Numbers Tell and Sell the Story

There are two statistics that regularly get the attention of the senior management team: First, somewhere between 20 and 70 percent of all new customers, across all industries, leave within the first hundred days of the relationship, never to do business with that organization again. Second, if you can keep just 5 percent of the customers who are leaving, it will *increase profits* by 25 to 100 percent.

These statistics aren't mine. They are combined from dozens of sources across a variety of disciplines. In short, retention is where it's at, and there is no way to grow revenues or profits faster than by keeping your existing customers.

Expose Them to Reality

Most senior management types haven't been in the field or seen the frontline interactions of the business in ages. They have grown distant and are now surrounded by rarefied air. They have forgotten what it's like to speak to an irate customer on the phone. They haven't spoken to an actual customer in days, weeks, months, or even years. By exposing executives to the reality of the current customer experience, you can bring their attention to focus and connect them to the pain and struggle customers experience interacting with your brand.

Improve the Customer Experience Without Asking

I've been a fan of the saying "It's better to beg for forgiveness than to ask for permission" for decades. The applicability to your situation is as follows: Go take the necessary steps to improve the customer experience starting tomorrow. Track and document your efforts and see what happens. I'd be willing to bet that either the customer experience will improve (in which case you can point to your activities as a success) or your efforts will have no appreciable impact on the business (in which case you can refine, hone, and start again). In all my years of working in customer experience, over 90 percent of employees who moved ahead with initiative were rewarded, while the other 10 percent still managed to learn a lot (about themselves and customer experience) in the process.

INVESTIGATE, OBSERVE, PERSONALIZE, AND SURPRISE: IT REALLY IS THAT EASY TO CREATE REMARKABLE CUSTOMER EXPERIENCES

By incorporating the four-step process of Investigate, Observe, Personalize, and Surprise, any business can dramatically enhance customer experiences across all eight phases of the customer life cycle. Using this four-step process allows you to design and deliver remarkable customer experiences throughout your organization.

CHAPTER SEVENTEEN

Conclusion: If Comcast Can Do It, So Can You

As part of my work helping companies enhance their customer experiences (and in the process keep more of their customers), I do workshops around the world where we dive into the specific operations of individual businesses. To start these workshops, I often ask the audience a question:

> *Think of the worst experience you've ever had with a business you*
> *interact with as a customer.*

I then request that they take two minutes to write down the name of the brand and the associated experience. The pens start flying across the page, and it never takes the full two minutes before the audience members have vented their collective frustrations at a variety of brands.

After doing this exercise with tens of thousands of audience members around the world, there is one name that consistently comes up: Comcast.

I've never been shocked by this answer, as I experienced Comcast as a customer years ago.

And it was horrible.

LET'S GET YOU SIGNED UP FOR INTERNET AND CABLE!

My Comcast journey began with my request to start a new account and schedule installation for both Internet access and cable TV service. The representative set me up and then explained that the earliest they could come for my installation was a week later, which was disappointing. The representative asked if I wanted a morning or afternoon appointment, and I told her a morning appointment would work best.

She then said the technician would arrive sometime between 8:00 a.m. and 12:00 p.m.

"That seems like a rather large potential arrival window," I noted. "Can you give me a more specific idea than that?"

"No," she replied without hesitation or recognition that this was a significant inconvenience to me.

Because I wanted Internet and cable service, I agreed to her offer. A week later, having taken the morning off work, I waited in my apartment for the Comcast technician to arrive and complete my installation.

He didn't arrive at 8:00 a.m., or anywhere within the stated window of time. In fact, he didn't arrive at all.

At 12:01 p.m. I called Comcast in frustration, explaining that the technician never arrived.

Without so much as an apology, the call center representative said he could reschedule me for a second visit, *a week later*, with the same four-hour window for the appointment.

I was now two weeks out from when I originally signed up for service, which left me feeling less than appreciated as a new customer. The feelings of buyer's remorse were in full effect. I spent most of the next week wondering whether I was going to be burned again by Comcast.

Seven days later, I found myself once again waiting in my apartment for the Comcast technician to arrive. I needed to take off another half day of work, and I was now eating into my vacation days.

Once again, the four-hour window came and passed without the technician showing up. I called Comcast in frustration and they promised he was en route and would be there directly.

An hour and a half later, the technician finally arrived. He came in and hooked everything up without even acknowledging, let alone apologizing for, his late arrival. I now had cable TV and Internet access, but I also had a bad taste in my mouth from the poor customer experience with Comcast.

MY COMCAST EXPERIENCE WAS NOT UNIQUE

Customer Experience Index 2010, authored by customer experience expert Bruce Temkin and published by Forrester Research Inc., mirrored my personal experience with Comcast.

Forrester conducted a survey by interviewing more than 4,600 U.S. consumers about their interactions with a variety of companies. The survey gauged the usefulness, ease of use, and enjoyability of their experiences with a variety of well-known brands. Based on these consumer responses, Forrester calculated the "Consumer Experience Index" for 133 firms across fourteen different industries.

Comcast placed near the bottom of the survey results for *all* industries.

- For Comcast TV, 48 percent of customers said the experience was *very poor.*

- For Comcast Internet, 47 percent of customers said the experience was *very poor.*

Almost half of the people dealing with Comcast at the time rated their experience as *very poor*—the lowest possible rating they could give.

THEN SOMETHING CHANGED

You can imagine my surprise when my good friend Jay Baer (author of the fantastic book *Hug Your Haters*) contacted me and said, "Joey, you need to check out what Comcast is doing to improve their customer experience."

I was completely caught off guard. . . .

Comcast?!

Jay introduced me to Charlie Herrin, chief customer experience officer at Comcast Cable, and we had a series of conversations about Comcast's customer experiences. I even went on-site to Comcast's headquarters in Philadelphia to learn more about its efforts to improve.

I was absolutely blown away.

REPAIRING A BROKEN CABLE COMPANY EXPERIENCE

For many years, Comcast was well known in the marketplace for having a poor customer experience. To solve this problem, the senior management team knew that continuing to attempt Band-Aid fixes wasn't going to work long-term.

Contrary to the usual practice, Comcast decided not to put a customer experience person in the new role it was developing, but rather to put a technology person in charge of this new initiative. In Comcast's view, customer service people have a tendency to see the world in a reactionary way, whereas technology people usually try to solve problems before they happen.

Charlie believes that "customer service" is what happens when you experience a broken element of the business. He knew Comcast needed to adopt a more active and proactive approach to dealing with customers and to focus on the overall customer experience. At the end of 2014, after serving for years as the senior vice president of product development (where he oversaw the design of Comcast's Xfinity products from conception through consumer testing and deployment), Charlie Herrin was promoted to the position of executive vice president, customer experience (now chief customer experience officer).

In his product role, Charlie was familiar with looking at everything a customer experienced from beginning to end of the customer life cycle. In the product development world, this approach is considered the normal way of doing things.

Charlie quickly realized that within the broader organization of Comcast, this holistic approach to customer experience wasn't the norm. Most of the individuals and departments he explored at Comcast viewed interactions with customers as transactions, not part of a larger, ongoing relationship. The sales team focused on getting the sale in the door but did nothing around the setup, the out-of-the-box experience, or the communications early in the customer relationship—let alone the ongoing interactions as the customer continued to do business with Comcast.

In the early days on the job, Charlie went around to the various departments in Comcast and asked, "Who has the hardest job in this company?"

Almost universally, employees responded that it was the frontline employees who dealt with customers, especially during the early stages of the relationship.

But the more Charlie dug for answers, the more employees started to change their opinion. Fairly quickly, the majority of employees came to the conclusion: The customers actually had it the hardest.

BAD FOR THE CUSTOMER, BAD FOR THE BUSINESS, BAD FOR THE BRAND

Charlie looked at the customers' journeys. He conducted an analysis of the Billing Journey, the Repair Journey, the Perception Journey, and finally the Onboarding Journey. His team defined onboarding as: where a customer needed to go for help, knowing what comes next, and understanding the value of what they purchase.

Charlie and his team realized the very structure of Comcast was causing issues. The business operations were too siloed, with individual departments passing customers back and forth, time and time again. No one took responsibility for the customers' issues and, as a result, they often went unresolved.

There was no formal system in place to educate new customers about the products and services they purchased. Customers were left to fend for themselves as they navigated start-up screens, confusing written documentation, and a complicated website that made finding any answers nearly impossible.

In addition, despite having an interactive voice response (IVR) queue in place (what you or I might refer to as a phone tree), the ability to fully anticipate customer needs was lacking. Calls poured in, day after day, as new customers tried to explain what they needed and, if they were lucky, were able to resolve the issue by speaking with a single representative. However, when a customer moved, they were required to call to set up billing at the new residence, and then needed to call a different number to schedule the installation appointment.

In short, Charlie recognized the entire Comcast onboarding process was a total nightmare for customers *and* employees alike.

The more Charlie researched, the more he found devastating statistics. "We were making things harder by an order of three or four times' magnitude," Charlie observed. "In the first ninety days, we experienced 1.5 times the truck rolls (trucks being dispatched to customer homes or businesses), 2 times the calls, and higher churn than at any other time in the customer life cycle!"

Ironically enough, Charlie's experience with Comcast aligned with a common revelation my clients have when we start working together and they explore their customers' journeys. . . .

How did it ever get this bad?

And what are we supposed to do to fix this?

To say that Charlie was frustrated by his findings is an understatement. "We spend all sorts of money on marketing and building great products here at Comcast," Charlie noted, "and then we let our customers down when we try to get them engaged early in the process."

A MAJOR OVERHAUL OF THE CUSTOMER EXPERIENCE

Charlie knew Comcast needed a significant commitment from management and major changes, and he knew it needed a high level of commitment and buy-in to accomplish these changes.

Charlie was part of the team (along with Tom Karinshak, executive vice president of customer service at Comcast Cable) to spearhead Comcast's initiative to invest more than $1 billion over four years to enhance the customer experience throughout the business. Charlie knew they needed the right team, a commitment to developing new technology to assist both employees and customers, and a series of product enhancements that would serve customers better, particularly in the first few months of their new customer experience.

As Tom observed, "We needed to undergo an evolution from where we were—processing transactions—to a place where we were proactive in building relationships with our customers and personalizing our interactions with them."

This initiative to enhance the overall customer experience focused on a series of key areas, including training, business processes, and product enhancements.

TRAINING: EVERYONE IS RESPONSIBLE FOR THE CUSTOMER EXPERIENCE

As part of the investigations into Comcast operations, Tom realized the employee experience throughout the organization was incredibly disjointed. The typical Comcast employee didn't know customer experience was part of their job responsibility. Most employees fixated on the very narrow responsibilities associated with their job titles, as opposed to the emotional needs and desires of the customers. Most employees assumed that "someone else" in the company was taking care of the customers and that the overall customer experience was monitored by another department.

Realizing that before Comcast could fix the external experience it needed to repair the internal experience, Tom launched a new training initiative to remedy the situation within fifteen months. To support this goal, Comcast did six thousand peer-led training sessions with more than eighty thousand employees, focusing on what they needed to do to deliver a better customer experience.

To make navigating the customer life cycle smoother, Comcast streamlined internal tools that recorded customer information and were used to resolve service and operations issues. In short order, Comcast shifted from using twelve different agent tools in the on-boarding and account management process to using just four. This marked difference in information flow streamlined the operations, placed more data at every employee's fingertips, and reduced the potential for human error across the enterprise.

Finally, to keep the customer "front and center" in every internal discussion, an empty chair was placed in each meeting to represent the customer. This visual reminder made sure the customer's needs were "visible" and considered in every meeting within the organization.

BUSINESS PROCESSES: WE CAUSE MOST OF OUR OWN PROBLEMS

"We create a lot of onboarding situations, purely as the result of our business model," Charlie Herrin observed. "This has nothing to do with the customer and everything to do with how we categorize them for our own internal purposes. As a result, it became clear that major changes in the structure of our business needed to be made if we wanted to create remarkable experiences for our customers."

Comcast was well known for its bad scheduling reputation. To fix this problem, Comcast narrowed the appointment window from four hours to two hours, requiring employees to be more focused in scheduling calls and in making sure technicians arrive on time.

If the technician is late by even one minute, a $20 credit is automatically applied to the customer's bill. The customer doesn't have to request this credit. Instead, Comcast proactively acknowledges that it failed to respect the customer's time and the credit is automatically applied to the customer's first invoice. This improved on-time arrivals dramatically: now 97 percent of scheduled appointments occur on time. The significant increase in on-time scheduled appointments is a huge and visible win for the organization and the customers—especially in light of the fact that customers previously identified this as a major issue.

To ensure that new customers reached a well-prepared agent, Charlie created a series of new onboarding call centers that were specifically designed to handle any inbound call from a customer in the first ninety days of the new customer life cycle. The call center agents were able to handle every question and didn't need to transfer a new customer to another department to resolve the issue. This was revolutionary. Now almost every potential new customer scenario could be handled in a single call.

The early results from these new customer call centers were astounding. There was a whopping 27 percent reduction in call volume in the first nine months after launching the improved call centers.

In addition, Comcast adopted a mantra of "fix it *right* the first time." This effort put a focus on solving the core customer problem during the customer's initial contact. Over the course of the first year, this approach led to a 5 percent improvement in first-time resolution, reducing repeat visits within the first thirty days by 2 percent. While these numbers may seem small, when viewed in the light of Comcast's total new customer base (858,000 new customers in FY 2016), the overall impact is significant, as it improves the experience of almost 43,000 customers.

Finally, as part of the improved business operations, Comcast took a hard look at one of the major causes of customer problems: billing questions. The billing experience at Comcast prior to these initiatives was absolutely horrible. Multiple line items and charges the customer didn't understand complicated bills. Complex listings left customers concerned that they were paying more than they needed to, or being charged for services they didn't have.

Comcast took steps to improve the overall billing experience by simplifying the pricing, making it more consistent across all offerings, and providing digital receipts so customers knew what they were being charged for and why. Comcast also eliminated policies and fees that didn't make sense, most notably recategorizing install fees into a single fee that covered all forms of installation.

Comcast made understanding its invoices easy by creating incredible, personalized "Explain My Bill" videos. A customer receives an email with a personalized video that identifies the customer by name and points out the particulars of the first bill. The customer then receives a new explanation video every time there are significant changes to the account (e.g., new services, additional channels, new equipment, etc.). This effort to enhance customer understanding of other efforts to simplify billing drove a 10 percent reduction in calls—eliminating 6 million "billing matter" phone calls in 2016 alone. These improvements saved Comcast customers an estimated 2.5 million hours of call time and countless amounts of frustration.

PRODUCT ENHANCEMENTS: THE PRODUCT *IS* THE EXPERIENCE

The third experience enhancement stemmed from Charlie's repeated statement to his engineers: "You have to build your product as if a call center doesn't exist."

Prior to this new initiative, Comcast was relying too much on the luxury of multiple call centers to fix a problem after the fact. When developing Comcast X1 customer service, Charlie was taken aback when he noticed that every time there was an error screen on the TV, it prompted the customer to "call Comcast." He realized this wasn't the way it should be. "We should see the error on our end and message the customer proactively, telling them that we're on it, we will fix the problem, and we will text them when the situation has been resolved," he observed. Taking advantage of two-way communications put Comcast in a better position to build and develop relationships with its customers, instead of operating in a one-way environment.

Comcast also recognized the need to develop 100 percent self-healing products that resulted in customers' fixing the majority of problems by themselves, while positioning Comcast to fix any problems that the customer couldn't handle. "We needed to distinguish between what we teach the customer (an active discovery process) and what they learn from using our product (a passive discovery process). We needed to put the customer experience into the product—focusing on ease of use and self-healing."

The results from changing this focus at the product development level were fast and significant. After rolling out the "My Account" app, Comcast saw immediate impact as upward of 73 percent of customers using the app never had to call. The System Refresh Tool resulted in 92 percent of customers refreshing their systems without making a phone call to request it. This is a huge impact for a company that deals with more than ten thousand refresh requests per day.

Comcast's commitment to digital tools and placing power directly in the customers' hands dramatically affected the customer experience and gave customers a sense of ownership and agency. "We eliminated calls from millions of customers who didn't want to call us! Instead, we've enabled them to interact with us the way they want," notes John Williamson, senior vice president and general manager of digital.

This commitment to product enhancement aligned with Charlie's belief that the product *is* the experience, if you do it right.

IF COMCAST CAN DO THIS, ANYONE CAN

Comcast is digging out of a customer experience and reputation hole that, in many ways, is unprecedented in modern business. It has hundreds of thousands of employees operating all over America, it deals with customers ranging from the wealthiest to the poorest in society, and it provides a complex technology product that is not understood by the consumers who purchase it.

And yet Comcast is willing to push forward.

Dana Wilson, vice president of customer experience assurance, explained the scope of this new Comcast commitment and where she sees it going. "The entire company is rallying around the customer—trying to understand the experience. Historically we've operated to the numbers and now we're humanizing our efforts and it's infectious. From our frontline employees to our senior leaders we have more empathy for the customer than in the past. The energy that comes from this is going to empower us to develop the next customer experience."

This newfound enthusiasm and focus on the customer experience is particularly evident in the RealTime Assist product. RealTime Assist is a personalized service messaging platform designed to save customers time and simplify their experience. It provides real-time updates to customers directly via SMS text messages, keeping them in the loop on all aspects of their service. The primary goal of RealTime Assist is to provide customers with the *right information* at exactly the *right time*. Customers receive instructional content and videos to help them in real time.

Piers Lingle, senior vice president on the customer experience team and leader of the CX Solutions team, notes that prior to implementing RealTime Assist, "we used very orchestrated email campaigns and a series of websites—but we weren't reaching customers when they needed us most, using the *customer's* most convenient method of communication. We would get so excited and want to send them one hundred things—when instead we needed to identify the really important points of the journey and just focus on those."

Comcast has committed to enhancing the customer experience—especially in the onboarding process—to make sure their one-time customers become customers for life. Charlie believes that "retention starts at the sale. We need to be crystal clear that we're on the same page as the customer from the outset so we can continue to serve that customer for years to come."

Are you willing to do what Comcast does?

REMEMBER WHY YOU STARTED

I want you to take a moment to think back to when you first got into the business you're in. Whether you started the business, joined it in the early stages, or just joined the team, there is a reason you decided to spend your days in your business.

I'd be willing to bet that one of the biggest reasons you chose this business, career, or position was to help people. Yes, of course you want to make money and you like the benefits, but, for most of you, it was more than that. You had an interest, appreciation, or even a love for the work the organization does and you cared about the people your work affected.

If you're like most people, over time your focus shifted from the customer to the bottom line. You and your organization lost sight of what you came to do in the first place—*serve the needs of your customers.*

Throughout this book, I've encouraged you to bring your focus back to the customer.

The process outlined in the preceding chapters is nothing more than a framework to get you back to where you started. The goal is to do it in a way that reengages you with the meaning you once held so high and, along the way, produce tangible results in your business.

By focusing on the eight phases, you will connect with your customers' wants and needs. My hope is that the examples outlined herein illustrate the importance of going beyond the objective needs your customers have and encourage you to focus on your customers' subjective, emotional needs. By connecting with your customers on a regular basis and guiding them through the phases in the First 100 Days after they start working with you, your morale will go up. You will feel better about what you do for a living and you will be as excited as you were when you first started at your current organization.

When you focus on your customers and fulfill their needs, your needs and emotions will be fulfilled as well, as will the needs and emotions of your entire team. One of the most significant, yet unexpected benefits of incorporating this methodology is the impact on employee morale. Nothing can reinvigorate and excite a team like a newfound purpose and a commitment to achieving it.

A RISING TIDE LIFTS ALL BOATS

Enhancing the experience your customers have creates a ripple effect that goes well beyond the walls of your organization.

One of the additional benefits of focusing on the customer experience is that as one company makes customer experience a priority, it forces all the competitors in the industry to follow suit. When a company gives users an extraordinary experience, it raises the bar for everyone else. Moving slowly at first, but then racing forward with abandon, a shift in customer expectations soon overtakes the entire marketplace.

A major example of this type of shift can be found in the free two-day shipping offered by Amazon. Back in the early days of online e-commerce, if you ordered something, you had to pay to have it shipped to you. As a differentiator, Amazon decided early on to offer free two-day ground shipping on purchases over $25.

This offer eventually evolved to the point where Amazon became known as the company that could get a product to your doorstep, for free, in a very short amount of time. Because Amazon made the decision to offer shipping as a free bonus to the customer, the company distinguished itself from other online retailers that charged exorbitant processing and handling fees to get the product from the warehouse to the end user.

Now when we go online to purchase any product, it's only natural to feel annoyed when we get to the checkout and realize the provider expects us to pay for shipping.

This is a complete change in how humans think about receiving products from retailers, and it happened in under a decade. Prior to Amazon, we would have thought it crazy to expect a company would pay to ship items we wanted delivered directly to our doors.

Now almost everyone who wants to succeed in e-commerce offers free shipping as a standard operating procedure.

This decision by Amazon not only changed the expectations of its other competitors in the online retail space, but it forced anyone who sells anything online to seriously consider, and in most cases embrace, the free shipping model.

But the change doesn't stop there. As the customer experience improves in one industry, it improves in all industries. As customers begin to seek better treatment and more remarkable experiences in one area of their lives, this expectation carries over to all of their interactions.

If an organization doesn't change its behavior to meet this new-found customer expectation and "rise with the tide," the business will sink and go out of business.

Making customers a priority and making their experience a foundational element of your business operations not only sets you apart from the competition, but possibly leads to the adoption of the trend worldwide.

REMARKABLE CUSTOMER EXPERIENCES HAVE THE POTENTIAL TO CREATE A HAPPIER WORLD

I hope I am not sounding naïve; that isn't my intention. My point is simply this: The global economy is a collection of businesses selling goods and services to people. These businesses are run by real people, and they exist to serve the needs of real people.

Everything about our economy and our businesses is ultimately about *people*. Whether they are the people running the businesses or the people buying the products and services—it's all people.

I wrote this book for one reason: to help people serve other people.

When the customer experience becomes the focus of an organization, customers are happy. Happier customers lead to happier employees. When employees live and work with meaning and purpose, and interact with the fellow humans they serve, they feel good about themselves. Employees who feel more connected to the work they're doing boost employee morale and overall engagement rises dramatically across the entire organization.

As employees become more engaged and excited about their work, their emotional state naturally translates into their interactions with customers. The customers respond positively and feed those emotions back to the employees.

The remarkable experiences layer upon one another throughout the interactions and touchpoints, creating an unforgettable experience for both the customers and the employees.

A cycle of happiness is created.

As your customers and your employees become happier, your business becomes more profitable. As your business becomes more profitable, you become happier, and the reach of your business becomes greater.

Happier employees, owners, and customers make for a happier world, a world where the expectation for customer experience shifts and we go from remarkable experience to remarkable experience in our businesses interactions and in our personal lives.

This all combines to create a happier world.

Let's go make it that way—shall we?

With My Sincerest Thanks . . .

While I have the pleasure of being listed as the author of this book, I now fully understand the axiom that no book is written by just one person. A book is the culmination of insights achieved, observations made, and perspectives gained from a multitude of interactions with other people. To that end, I would like to thank the many people (individually and collectively) who played a role in making this book a possibility. I also want to extend my sincere apologies to anyone I inadvertently fail to mention by name in the following acknowledgments. Rest assured I'll remember you in my next book!

No book on customer experience would be complete without customers, and I am eternally indebted to my customers, clients, and friends who graciously allowed me to tell their stories in the form of case studies in this book, including: Dr. Katie McCann (Aurora Modern Dentistry), Garrett Gunderson (Wealth Factory), Mike Dooley (Notes from the Universe), Tony Robbins (Anthony Robbins Companies), Paul LeBlanc (Zogics), Yanik Silver and Sophia Umanski (Maverick1000), Richard

Cooper (Total Debt Freedom), Tucker Max and Zach Obront (Book in a Box), Derek and Melanie Coburn (CADRE), Brad Pedersen (Tech 4 Kids), Jammie Avila (Cornerstone Retirement), Saud Juman and Yusuf Rawji (PolicyMedical), Juliet Starrett (San Francisco CrossFit), Bob Glazer (Acceleration Partners), Kirk Drake (Ongoing Operations), Jon Goodman (Online Trainer Academy), Chris Yoko (Yoko Co), Michel Falcon (Baro), Berit Coleman (dōTERRA), John Ruhlin (Ruhlin Group), Jim and Maggie Umlauf (4Knines), Jayson Gaignard (Mastermind-Talks), and Charlie Herrin, Tom Karinshak, John Williamson, Heather Hollis, Dana Wilson, Patti Loyack, Piers Lingle, Jennifer Sala, and Rachel Zabinski (Comcast). And to Clay's mother, Barb Herbert, for your diligence in reviewing the manuscript in the 11th hour to look for errors and inconsistencies. You're a lifesaver!

To the customer experience professionals and thought leaders who inspire me to create better customer service and better customer experience every day. To quote Sir Isaac Newton, "If I have seen further it is by standing on the shoulders of giants." Some of these giants include: Brent Adamson, Ian Altman, James Altucher, Katya Andresen, Jay Baer, David Bach, Rohit Bhargava, Jeanne Bliss, Dorie Clark, Joel Comm, Keith Cunningham, John R. DiJulius III, Jeremy Epstein, Nir Eyal, Tim Ferriss, Dan Gingiss, Seth Godin, John Hall, Ann Handley, Chip Heath, Dan Heath, Sally Hogshead, Ryan Holiday, Lewis Howes, Jackie Huba, Michael Hyatt, Shep Hyken, AJ Jacobs, John Jantsch, Mitch Joel, Ron Kaufman, Bryan Kramer, Harvey Mackay, Scott McKain, Danny Meyer, Mike Michalowicz, Mary Kunkel Miller, Gary and Blaine Millet, Scott Monty, Tom Peters, Dan Pink, Fred Reichheld, Robbe Richman, Tony Robbins, Kevin Roberts, David Rockwell, John Ruhlin, Ramit Sethi, Colin Shaw, Marcus Sheridan, Steve Sims, Brian Solis, Micah Solomon, Scott Stratten, Vanessa Van Edwards, Gary Vaynerchuk, John Warrillow, Ari Weinzweig, and Jessica Weisz.

To those audiences who've watched me present—live and online—in workshops, keynotes, and courses. You contributed tremendously to the organic growth of the concepts outlined in this book and any clarity of thought or messaging in these frameworks comes directly from your feedback, reactions, and responses.

To those who offered me "shelter" during this book-writing process, most specifically, Rutger von Post and Jennifer Savoie (New York), Joe and Sharon Coleman (Iowa), Kevin and Lezlie Coleman (Massachusetts), Davin and Heidi Seamon (West Virginia), Rick Corrado and Faith Green (Washington, D.C.), Christopher and Lauren Coleman (Illinois), Jim and Maggie Umlauf (Arizona), Ilo and Peggy Leppik (Minnesota), and Delta Airlines (35,000 feet).

To the 5 Minute Journal (created by UJ Ramdas, Alex Ikonn, and Mimi Ikoun), which keeps me focused, grounded, and thankful every day.

To my "brains" behind the scenes who helped research the more nuanced parts of the book, including: Tucker Max, James Tonn, Tom Webster, Callaghan Coleman, and Sara Stibitz.

To my sounding board of family members, friends, advisers, supporters, and confidants who offered guidance, inspiration, promotion, insight, and assistance every step of the way, including: Stephan Aarstol, Sasha Ablitt, Olivia Abtahi, Dr. Matthew Accurso, Kathy Albarado, Frank Albinder, Shari Aldrich, Shari Alexander, Jason Atkins, Zach Axelrod, Firoozeh Azarbaidjani, Chaz Baker, Zvi Band, Dev Basu, Matthew Bertulli, Raj Bhaskar, Eileen Bischoff (Murphy), Jenny Blake, Kevin Bombino, Adam Bornstein, Briana and Peter Borten, John Bowen, Heather Bradley, Chris Brogan, Danielle Brooks, Michael Brubeck, David Burkus, Dmitry and Maia Buterin, Hollis Carter, Tiffany Turner Cavegn, Victor Cheng, Jeremy Choi, Dave Christensen, Tim Christmann, Matt Clark, James Clear, Jason Connell, Tom Cooper, Honoree Corder, Matt and Sarah Cosgrove, Andrew Davis, Mat-

thew De Miglio, Joe DeNoyior, Colin Dombroski, Steve Dorfman,
Sven Drumev, John Du Cane, Craig Dye, Joe and Jenn Dziedzic, Colin
Eagen, Carolyn Ellis, Hal Elrod, Brian Fanzo, Megan Buckley Fass,
Ezra Firestone, Jason Fladlien, Joe Foley, Cody Foster, Shawn Fuller,
Kandis Gaignard, Mike Ganino, Tony and Giuditta Gareri, David Site-
man Garland, Michael and Jess Gebben, Jay and Ruba Georgi, Barry
Glassman, Sonny Goel, Denise Ward Gosnell, Tim Grahl, Rachel
Green, Ben Greenfield, Jay Greenstein, Suzy and Phil Grybas, Marc Gut-
man, John Hall, Derek Halpern, Cheyenne Hamacher, Will Hamilton,
Walt Hampton, Ryan Hanley, Stephen Hanselman, Rikke Hansen, Jor-
dan Harbinger, Marcos Harkness, Samantha Hansler, Ryan Hawk,
Tim Hawkins, Mark Hemingway, Nick and Monica Hemmert, Jeremy
and Louise Hendon, Cameron Herold, Ed Herold, Weaver Hickerson,
Darryl Hicks, Kate Hill, Kenton and Nadine Ho, Charlie Hoehn, Lewis
Howes, Tim Hughes, Scott Hoffman, Alex and Mimi Ikonn, Danny
Iny, Ron Ipach, Tracey Forster Ivanyshyn, Jeff and Tina Jacobs, Neen
James, Brad Johnson, Dr. Isaac Jones, Alex Kane, Jason Katzenback,
Scott Kavanagh, Matt Kazam, Matt Kepnes, Seth and Kerry Kilander,
Neeley Koester, Krista Kotrla, Dmitriy Kozlov, Nicholas Kusmich, Jim
Kwik, Mathieu Lachaîne, Shelby and Kerry Larson, Ryan Levesque,
Jeff Linihan, Ian Lingwood, Bob London, Floyd Marinescu, Dan Mar-
tell and Renée Warren, Yaniv Masjedi, Pauline McKernan, Stu McLaren,
Joe and Erica Mechlinski, Brad Meltzer, Lance Metcalf, Joshua Fields
Millburn, Cynthia Miller, Katie Gutierrez Miller, Taki Moore, Ryan
Moran, Craig Morantz, Nick Morgan, Nicole Mortimer, Sarah Moster,
Phoebe Mroczek, Gabe Muller, Chad Mureta, Shiv Narayanan, Ryan
Nicodemus, Christopher Novais, Ron Novak, Brent Novoselsky, Rob
Nunnery, Jessica Olman, Tyler Orchard, Sol Orwell, Laura Gassner Ot-
ting, Krishna Patel, Re Perez, Tamas and Andrea Perlaky, Matt Phil-
lips, Danielle Pilon, Al Pittampalli, Nicolette Pizzitola, Chris Plough,

Jack Quarles, Dush and Terra Ramachandran, UJ Ramdas, Phil Randazzo, Srinivas Rao, Landon Ray, Tiffany and Eric Reinhardt, Lena Requist, Dr. Tim and Pam Reynolds, Tony Ricciardi, John Romaniello, Ben and Sarah Roy, Frankie Saucier, Harry Schechter, Stephen Shapiro, Jeff Shaw, Jamie Sheils, Todd Sherbacow, Jenny Shtipelman, Niesa Silzer, Michael Simmons, Steve Sims, Paul Sinclair, Molly Singer, Steve Sisler, Pam Slim, Bill Smith, Greg Smith, Meqa Smith, Stephan Spencer, Melanie Spring, Cyrus Stahlberg, Don Stanley, H. David Starr, Michael Stelzner, Mark Stevenson, Jane Hoffman and Jill Strachan, Adam Summers, Joe and Jamika Taijeron, Brent and Sarah Thacker, Laurence Tham, George Thomas, Nate and Heather Thompson, Scott Thompson, Bob Thordarson, Greg and Christina Tindale, Ron Tite, Joey Tominovich, Ryan Twedt, Satya Tweena, Todd Tzeng, Pete Vargas III, Bella Vasta, Maggy Wallace, Andrew Warner, Robert Watson, Brent Weaver, Steve and Katesha Weaver, D'Arcy Webb, Tamsen Webster, Frank Weimann, Jeremy Weise, Jason Weisenthal, Ken Williams, Blackie Wills, KC Baney and Abbey Woodcock, Colin Wright, and Steve Young.

To the supporters, encouragers, and instigators who comprise my network of peers and collection of colleagues: the true mavericks who form the membership of Maverick1000, the rockstars of CADRE, and the big thinkers and doers of MastermindTalks. You collectively motivate me to be the very best I can be and encourage me to never settle for anything less than the best I can offer.

To my mentors, advisers, and coaches on the stage who helped me shape my presentation skills and the First 100 Days story "live" long before it saw the written word, including: the Saint Edmonds High School speech and debate coach, Mike Maffin; the late Gene Fanning at the University of Notre Dame; Dean Alfreda Robinson at The George Washington University School of Law; the incredibly talented Amy and Michael Port; and all of my Speak & Spill colleagues.

To my circle of closest advisers, friends, and confidants, including: Clay Hebert, Philip McKernan, Jim Sheils, James Tonn, Jim Umlauf, and James Wallace. Your wisdom, support, insights, and blind-spot identification help me to keep going and avoid pitfalls along the way.

To Sheryl Netzky—thank you for the cradle of kindness, your skill at zipping time, your help with the book jacket, and all the incredible ways you've brought your teachings, energy, encouragement, and guidance to this endeavor and everything that I do.

To those who supported the book "early and often," as they say in Chicago. You know who you are and I hope this book is commensurate with your early faith in me.

To my siblings—Callaghan, K.C., Chris, Tommy, Dani, Lori, and (almost sibling) Mari—and their spouses/significant others—Annalise, Amy, Lauren, Bridget, and Chad—you each support and encourage me in your own unique way, and for that I am thankful.

To my parents—Sharon and Joe Coleman—for bringing me into the world and then supporting, encouraging, motivating, and inspiring me to be the best version of myself in my eclectic path of careers and identities. You were the first people to believe in me and I am forever grateful.

To Sean Maisch—the master of design and graphics who always brings my visions into reality. Your willingness to burn the midnight oil pushing pixels is appreciated more than you will ever know.

To Chris Guillebeau—who believed in this book even before I did and was always quick to push me to keep going.

To Jay Baer—who inspires me on the stage, encourages me on the air, and opened his personal Rolodex to introduce me to my fantastic agent.

To Elizabeth Marshall—who rode to the rescue as the sun was setting and helped make the launch of this book easier, more organized, more successful, and more fun. I can't thank you enough for your advice, guidance, assistance, enthusiasm, and intuition. You are an absolute joy to work with and immediately fit into the team as if you'd been here all along. I'm lucky to count you among my friends.

To Clay Hebert—my dear friend, thought partner, and overall font of knowledge. Your contributions to this endeavor—especially in the area of marketing and promotion—were instrumental to the success of our launch and the ongoing efforts to make this book a perennial seller.

To Yanik Silver and Jayson Gaignard—two great friends who opened their respective stages to me so I could share the First 100 Days message publicly for the first time. You took a chance on me and will forever be remembered as "Day 1" in the origin story of this work. This book is the direct result of your faith in both me and the importance/timeliness of this message.

To Mark Chait—outliner and editor extraordinaire. You helped bring my ideas from the stage to the page and put together a proposal that took these concepts from speech to book.

To Tucker Max—they broke the mold when they made you, Tucker (thankfully), and (also thankfully) I got the chance to benefit from your insights, encouragement, and support. From kicking my tail/publicly shaming me to get my book proposal done to helping me polish the final manuscript, your efforts were the work of a true mentor and friend.

To my publishing team at Portfolio—including Adrian Zackheim, Will Weisser, Alie Coolidge, Taylor Edwards, Daniel Lagin, and Henry James Nuhn—for helping a kid from rural Iowa navigate the world of New York City publishing. Thank you for your patience, your support, and your promotion of me, this book, and the ideas it strives to bring to the world.

To Helen Healey (editorial assistant at Portfolio), who worked tirelessly to get the images in this book right—as well as all the minutiae and fine details that make the finished copy sparkle. I know I was a challenge to work with at times and your patience was appreciated more than you will ever know.

To my world-class editor, Leah Trouwborst—the best authors I know say that an editor makes or breaks a book, and let there be no doubt about it, Leah, you made this book. Working with you was an absolute delight and I feel so fortunate to have landed in your hands. With respect to everyone else I met during my New York tour of publishers, I walked out of our first meeting and told Jim that I didn't know which publisher we would end up working with, but that I wanted to work with you most of all. You understood this book when it was a twinkle in my eye and your grace and poise in holding my hand as I navigated the book-writing process (the Acclimate phase, as we would call it!) was incredible. Thank you, thank you, thank you. Any success this book ever has is equally your success as well.

To my incredible agent, Jim Levine—How does a guy who represents future NFL Hall of Famers, CEOs of industry-leading companies, and some of the most successful entrepreneurs in the history of business and finance end up as my agent? Pure luck on my part. You understood the book from "Day 1" and your deft hand and gentle guidance made the process of finding a publisher and creating a book a real treat. You won me over with your first question on our very first call, and I look forward to a long and fruitful relationship for many years to come.

To my *anteambulo* (an ancient Roman term for "the person who clears the path") Sara Stibitz—from keeping the trains on schedule, to navigating my schedule, to providing advice, guidance, perspective, and intuition at a moment's notice, you were a true partner in the creation of this book. Make no mistake about it—this book would not exist if not for your research, writing, coordinating, editing, revising, pacifying, and laughing. Are we having fun yet? You bet we are. ;-P

To my sons, Lochlan and Kjellen—thanks for putting up with "Daddy on deadline"—including the long hours, the distracted focus, and the waning presence. You inspire me to lead by example and the litmus test you offer me (to be a man whom my sons are proud of) keeps me going in the late nights and early mornings. I hope you end up being as proud of this book as I am of you.

And last but not least, to the person who makes all of my days remarkable—my incredible wife, Berit. You believed in this book before anyone else. You believe in me before anyone else. The ineffable support you give to all of my endeavors never ceases to amaze me and I hope you know that the greatest successes of my life in the last decade and the potential successes of the years to come are the direct result of your steadfast encouragement, sage advice, and measured counsel. A person is lucky to achieve a standing in life where they have a best friend, a seasoned business mentor, a trusted confidante, and a supportive spouse. How fortunate I am that all four personas come rolled into one incredible person—you. Codfish!

Audience Information Categories

When it comes to tracking details about your customers, it's important to have a clear strategy for why you want to track the information. In addition, you must commit to using it sometime in the not-too-distant future to create personal and emotional connections with your customers—otherwise you might as well not bother. To help you consider what sort of information you want to record about your customers, the following list* should be useful. To be clear, you don't need to track all of this information, nor should you. This list is merely offered to spark your curiosity about what information to research about each of your customers and to give you ideas about the types of information your customers may share with you, either directly or indirectly.

---

*To assess your current customer intelligence findings and plan for future improvements, download a copy of the Audience Information Categories checklist at: *www.JoeyColeman.com/AudienceInfoTracking*.

BASIC INFO	
Date Data Originally Acquired (to determine "freshness" and accuracy of your information)	First Name
Date Data Last Acquired (to make data tracking a regular habit and practice)	Last Name
	Maiden Name
	Nickname

PROFESSIONAL	
Company Name	Other Key Professional Elements
Company Address	Sensitive Professional Elements
Business Phone	Professional Social Media URLs
Business Email	Proudest Professional Achievement
Business Mobile	Long-term Professional Goals
Position/Title	Short-term Professional Goals
Professional/Trade Association Memberships	

WORK HISTORY	
Former Company #1	Former Company #2
Location	Location
Position/Title	Position/Title
Dates of Employment	Dates of Employment
Key Takeaways	Key Takeaways
Attitude Toward Position/Company	Attitude Toward Position/Company

PERSONAL	
Home Address	Other Key Elements
Home Phone	Sensitive Personal Elements
Home Email	Personal Social Media URLs
Home Mobile	Drinker: Y/N
Involvement Within Community	If yes, Favorite Drink
Clubs	Smoker: Y/N

PERSONAL	
Hobbies/Interests	Height (approximate)
Favorite Sports & Teams (spectator)	Weight (approximate)
Favorite Sports & Teams (participant)	Clothing Sizes (T-shirt, shirt, jacket, etc.)
Favorite Vacation Type/Location	Technologies of Choice
Political Affiliation	Car of Choice
*Attitude Toward Political Affiliation	Proudest Personal Achievement
Religious Affiliation	Long-term Personal Goals
*Attitude Toward Religious Affiliation	Short-term Personal Goals

PREFERENCES	
Preferred Name	Preferred Day of Week to Be Contacted
Preferred Mailing Address (business, home, other)	Preferred Format of Communication (mail, email, phone, in person, etc.)
Preferred Email (business, home, other)	Preferred Frequency of Communication (daily, weekly, monthly, quarterly, etc.)
Preferred Phone (business, home, other)	

BACKGROUND	
Date of Birth	College
Place of Birth	Location
Hometown/Home State	Year Graduated (*if)
Siblings (names, ages)	*Attitude Toward Not Graduating from College
Other Key Background Elements	Activities/Clubs
Sensitive Background Elements	Honors
High School Name	Fraternity/Sorority
Location	*Attitude Toward Not Attending College
Year Graduated (*if)	
*Attitude Toward Not Graduating from High School	
Activities/Clubs	
Honors	

FAMILY	
Spouse/Partner/Significant Other (Yes or No)	
Name	Education
Date of Birth	Interests
Occupation	Anniversary
Former Spouse/Partner/Significant Other (Yes or No)	
Name	Education
Date of Birth	Interests
Occupation	*Attitude Toward Former Spouse/Partner/ Significant Other
Child #1	
Name	Education
Date of Birth	Interests (hobbies, activities, etc.)
Age (date)	
Child #2	
Name	Education
Date of Birth	Interests (hobbies, activities, etc.)
Age (date)	
Child #3	
Name	Education
Date of Birth	Interests (hobbies, activities, etc.)
Age (date)	
Pet	
Pet Name	Breed/Type

MILITARY SERVICE	
Branch	Duty Postings/Stations
Discharge Rank	Attitude Toward Being in the Service

CUSTOMER ACTIVITY	
Customer Number	Item/Service Purchased
Closest Customer Persona	Stated Reason for Purchase
Customer Segment(s)	Actual Reason for Purchase
First Customer Purchase Date	Results Achieved

CUSTOMER ACTIVITY (cont.)	
Item/Service Purchased	Overall Disposition
Stated Reason for Purchase	Next Customer Purchase Date
Actual Reason for Purchase	Item/Service Purchased
Results Achieved	Stated Reason for Purchase
Overall Disposition	Actual Reason for Purchase Results Achieved
Next Customer Purchase Date	Overall Disposition

OTHER KEY NOTES/INFORMATION	

For a PDF download of this list, descriptions of why/how this data can be useful, and an exercise to help inspire your team to collect this data, visit: *www.JoeyColeman.com/AudienceInfoTrack.*

You made it to the end of the book! Congratulations—you win some prizes! (At this point, did you expect anything else?!) Go to *www.Joey Coleman.com/BookBonuses* to access the following bonuses that we didn't have room to include in the book.

THE ENDNOTES

As a "recovering" attorney, I did my best to cite my sources throughout the book. The good news? There are endnotes. The bad news? If we included them here the book would have been 7,323 pages long. Okay, that's an exaggeration—but there are a lot! I'm happy to share the references, sources, and other background information I used in writing the book (you might find it useful). Just go to: *www.JoeyColeman.com/Book Bonuses.*

THE SPECIAL BONUSES

While writing the book, I came up with some fun companion pieces that I wanted to include but, alas, space would not allow. What are they? That's a surprise for you to discover! Luckily, you can access them all for FREE. Just go to: *www.JoeyColeman.com/BookBonuses*.

THE COURSE

I have an online course that "brings to life" the strategies and techniques described in the book. Plus—have you ever read a book and wondered what the author sounds like in real life? Wonder no more! You can access a FREE lesson from the course and dive deeper into the methodology and techniques. Just go to: *www.JoeyColeman.com/Book Bonuses*.

THANK YOU

I can't say enough how much I appreciate you investing your time and attention as you read this book. I don't take that gift lightly and I hope the payoff has been worth it—both in the short term and in the years to come. Thanks for coming along on the journey and let me know if I can ever be of assistance or answer any questions you may have. If you're thinking about reaching out to me, just do it! I promise you'll hear back from me and I can always be reached at: *JoeyC@JoeyCole man.com*.

Anderson, Stephen P. *Seductive Interaction Design: Creating Playful, Fun, and Effective User Experiences.* Berkeley, CA: New Riders, 2011.

Baer, Jay. *Hug Your Haters: How to Embrace Complaints and Keep Your Customers.* New York: Portfolio/Penguin, 2016.

Barlow, Janelle, and Paul Stewart. *Branded Customer Service: The New Competitive Edge.* San Francisco: Berrett-Koehler, 2006.

Bell, Chip R. *Sprinkles: Creating Awesome Experiences Through Innovative Service.* Austin, TX: Greenleaf Book Group, 2015.

Bhargava, Rohit. *Non Obvious: How to Think Different, Curate Ideas & Predict the Future.* Oakton, VA: IdeaPress, 2015.

Bliss, Jeanne. *Chief Customer Officer: Getting Past Lip Service to Passionate Action.* San Francisco: Jossey-Bass, 2006.

Buley, Leah. *The User Experience Team of One: A Research and Design Survival Guide.* New York: Rosenfeld Media, 2013.

Cagan, Marty. *Inspired: How to Create Products Customers Love.* Sunnyvale, CA: SVPG, 2008.

Calloway, Joe. *Indispensable: How to Become the Company That Your Customers Can't Live Without.* Hoboken, NJ: John Wiley & Sons, 2005.

Cutting, Donna. *The Celebrity Experience: Insider Secrets to Delivering Red Carpet Customer Service.* Chichester, UK: John Wiley & Sons, 2010.

DiJulius, John R., III. *Secret Service: Hidden Systems That Deliver Unforgettable Customer Service.* New York: AMACOM, 2003.

Diller, Stephen, Nathan Shedroff, and Darrel Rhea. *Making Meaning: How Successful Businesses Deliver Meaningful Customer Experiences.* Berkeley, CA: New Riders, 2008.

Drake, Kirk. *CU 2.0: A Guide for Credit Unions Competing in the Digital Age.* Austin, TX: Lioncrest Publishing, 2017.

Dunn, Elizabeth, and Michael Norton. *Happy Money: The Science of Happier Spending.* New York: Simon & Schuster, 2013.

Eyal, Nir, and Ryan Hoover. *Hooked: How to Build Habit-Forming Products.* London: Portfolio/Penguin, 2014.

Gingiss, Dan. *Winning at Social Customer Care: How Top Brands Create Engaging Experiences on Social Media.* North Charleston, SC: CreateSpace Independent Publishing, 2017.

Giovanni, Katharine C. *Going Above and Beyond: Reach the Pinnacle of Customer Service by Learning How to Think and Act Like a Concierge.* Wake Forest, NC: NewRoad, 2009.

Godin, Seth. *Purple Cow: Transform Your Business by Being Remarkable.* New York: Portfolio, 2009.

Griffin, Jill. *Customer Loyalty: How to Earn It, How to Keep It.* Chichester, UK: John Wiley & Sons, 1995.

Gross, T. Scott, Andrew Szabo, and Michael Hoffman. *Positively Outrageous Service: How to Delight and Astound Your Customers and Win Them for Life.* New York: Allworth, 2016.

Hall, Stacey, and Jan Bragniez. *Attracting Perfect Customers: The Power of Strategic Synchronicity.* N.p.: Readhowyouwant.com, 2011.

Harvard Business Review. *Increasing Customer Loyalty.* Boston: Harvard Business Review, 2011.

Heath, Chip, and Dan Heath. *The Power of Moments: Why Certain Moments Have Extraordinary Impact.* New York: Simon & Schuster, 2017.

Huba, Jackie. *Monster Loyalty: How Lady Gaga Turns Followers into Fanatics.* New York: Portfolio/Penguin, 2013.

Hyken, Shep. *Amaze Every Customer Every Time: 52 Tools for Delivering the Most Amazing Customer Service on the Planet.* Austin, TX: Greenleaf Book Group, 2013.

———. *The Amazement Revolution: Seven Customer Service Strategies to Create an Amazing Customer (and Employee) Experience.* Austin, TX: Greenleaf Book Group, 2012.

———. *Moments of Magic: Be a Star with Your Customers & Keep Them Forever.* Lawrence, KS: The Alan Press, 2012.

Inghilleri, Leonardo, and Micah Solomon. *Exceptional Service, Exceptional Profit: The Secrets of Building a Five-Star Customer Service Organization.* New York: AMACOM, 2010.

Jantsch, John. *Duct Tape Selling: Think Like a Marketer, Sell Like a Superstar.* New York: Portfolio/Penguin, 2014.

———. *The Referral Engine: Teaching Your Business How to Market Itself.* London: Portfolio, 2013.

Kalbach, James. *Mapping Experiences: A Guide to Creating Value Through Journeys, Blueprints, and Diagrams.* Beijing: O'Reilly, 2016.

Kaufman, Ron. *Uplifting Service: The Proven Path to Delighting Your Customers, Colleagues, and Everyone Else You Meet.* New York: Evolve, 2012.

Kinni, Theodore B. *Be Our Guest: Perfecting the Art of Customer Service.* New York: Disney Editions, 2011.

Kolko, Jon. *Well-Designed: How to Use Empathy to Create Products People Love.* Boston: Harvard Business Review, 2014.

Levesque, Ryan. *Ask: The Counterintuitive Online Formula to Discover Exactly What Your Customers Want to Buy ... Create a Mass of Raving Fans ... and Take Any Business to the Next Level.* Nashville, TN: Dunham, 2015.

Lichaw, Donna. *The User's Journey: Storymapping Products That People Love.* Brooklyn, NY: Rosenfeld Media, 2016.

Mack, Benjamin. *Think Two Products Ahead: Secrets the Big Advertising Agencies Don't Want You to Know and How to Use Them for Bigger Profits.* Hoboken, NJ: John Wiley & Sons, 2007.

Mackay, Harvey. *Beware the Naked Man Who Offers You His Shirt: Do What You Love, Love What You Do and Deliver More than You Promise.* New York: Fawcett Columbine, 1990.

———. *Dig Your Well Before You're Thirsty: The Only Networking Book You'll Ever Need.* New York: Random House, 1999.

———. *Pushing the Envelope: All the Way to the Top.* London: Vermilion, 2000.

———. *Use Your Head to Get Your Foot in the Door: Job Search Secrets No One Else Will Tell You.* London: Piatkus, 2011.

McKain, Scott. *ALL Business Is STILL Show Business: Create Distinction and Earn Standing Ovations from Customers in a Hyper-competitive Marketplace.* Louisville, KY: CreateSpace Independent Publishing Platform, 2017.

———. *7 Tenets of Taxi Terry: How Every Employee Can Create and Deliver the Ultimate Customer Experience.* New York: McGraw-Hill, 2014.

———. *What Customers Really Want: Bridging the Gap Between What Your Company Offers and What Your Clients Crave*. Nashville, TN: Thomas Nelson, 2006.

Meyer, Danny. *Setting the Table: Lessons and Inspirations from One of the World's Leading Entrepreneurs*. London: Marshall Cavendish, 2010.

Millet, Gary W., and Blaine W. Millet. *Creating and Delivering Totally Awesome Customer Experiences: The Art and Science of Customer Experience Mapping*. Salt Lake City: Customer Experiences, 2002.

Patnaik, Dev, and Peter Mortensen. *Wired to Care: How Companies Prosper When They Create Widespread Empathy*. Upper Saddle River, NJ: Pearson Education, 2009.

Patton, Jeff, and Peter Economy. *User Story Mapping: Discover the Whole Story, Build the Right Product*. Beijing: O'Reilly, 2014.

Pennington, Alan. *The Customer Experience Book: How to Design, Measure and Improve Customer Experience in Your Business*. Harlow, UK: Pearson Education, 2016.

Rapaille, Clotaire. *The Culture Code: An Ingenious Way to Understand Why People Around the World Live and Buy as They Do*. New York: Crown Business, 2013.

Reichheld, Fred. *The Ultimate Question: Driving Good Profits and True Growth*. Boston: Harvard Business School, 2008.

Reichheld, Frederick F., and Thomas Teal. *The Loyalty Effect: The Hidden Force Behind Growth, Profits, and Lasting Value*. Boston: Harvard Business School, 2008.

Richman, Robert. *The Culture Blueprint: A Guide to Building the High-Performance Workplace*. N.p.: Creative Commons License, n.d.

Roberts, Kevin. *Lovemarks: The Future Beyond Brands*. Brooklyn, NY: powerHouse Books, 2005.

———. *The Lovemarks Effect*. London: British Brands Group, 2006.

Rockwell, David, and Bruce Mau. *Spectacle*. London: Phaidon Press, 2006.

Ruhlin, John. *Giftology: The Art and Science of Using Gifts to Cut Through the Noise, Increase Referrals, and Strengthen Retention*. Austin, TX: Lioncrest, 2016.

Saffer, Dan. *Microinteractions: Designing with Details*. Sebastopol, CA: O'Reilly, 2014.

Shankman, Peter. *Zombie Loyalists: Using Great Service to Create Rabid Fans*. New York: Palgrave Macmillan, 2015.

Shaw, Colin. *DNA of Customer Experience: How Emotions Drive Value*. Basingstoke, UK: Palgrave Macmillan, 2014.

———. *Revolutionize Your Customer Experience*. Basingstoke, UK: Palgrave Macmillan, 2014.

———, and Ryan Hamilton. *The Intuitive Customer: 7 Imperatives for Moving Your Customer Experience to the Next Level*. London: Palgrave Macmillan, 2016.

———, and John Ivens. *Building Great Customer Experiences*. Basingstoke, UK: Palgrave Macmillan, 2008.

Silverstein, Michael, Neil Fiske, and John Butman. *Trading Up: Why Consumers Want New Luxury Goods—and How Companies Create Them*. New York: Portfolio/Penguin, 2008.

Smith, Shaun, and Joe Wheeler. *Managing the Customer Experience: Turning Customers into Advocates*. London: Financial Times Prentice Hall, 2007.

Solis, Brian. *What's the Future of Business? Changing the Way Businesses Create Experiences*. Hoboken, NJ: John Wiley & Sons, 2013.

———. *X: The Experience When Business Meets Design*. Hoboken, NJ: John Wiley & Sons, 2015.

Spector, Robert, and Patrick D. McCarthy. *The Nordstrom Way: An inside Story of America's #1 Customer Service Company*. New York: John Wiley & Sons, 2000.

Stewart, Thomas A., and Patricia O'Connell. *Woo, Wow, and Win: Service Design, Strategy, and the Art of Customer Delight*. New York: HarperBusiness, 2016.

Stickdorn, Marc, and Jakob Schneider. *This Is Service Design Thinking: Basics, Tools, Cases*. Amsterdam: BIS, 2016.

Stratten, Scott. *The Book of Business Awesome: How Engaging Your Customers and Employees Can Make Your Business Thrive; The Book of Business Unawesome: The Cost of Not Listening, Engaging, or Being Great at What You Do*. Hoboken, NJ: John Wiley & Sons, 2012.

Tancer, Bill. *Everyone's a Critic: Winning Customers in a Review-Driven World*. New York: Portfolio/Penguin, 2014.

Vaynerchuk, Gary. *Jab, Jab, Jab, Right Hook: How to Tell Your Story in a Noisy, Social World*. New York: HarperCollins, 2013.

Vitale, Joe. *There's a Customer Born Every Minute: P. T. Barnum's Secrets to Business Success*. New York: AMACOM, 1998.

Warrillow, John. *The Automatic Customer: Creating a Subscription Business in Any Industry*. London: Portfolio/Penguin, 2016.

Watkinson, Matt. *The Ten Principles Behind Great Customer Experiences*. Harlow, UK: Pearson Education Limited, 2013.

Webb, Nicholas J. *What Customers Crave: How to Create Relevant and Memorable Experiences at Every Touchpoint*. New York: AMACOM, 2017.

Weinzweig, Ari. *Zingerman's Guide to Giving Great Service*. New York: Hyperion, 2004.

Wright, Travis, and Chris J. Snook. *Digital Sense: The Common Sense Approach to Effectively Blending Social Business Strategy, Marketing Technology, and Customer Experience*. Hoboken, NJ: John Wiley & Sons, 2017.